REBUILDING TRUST FOR CHRISTIANS

A Couple's Guide to Healing After Betrayal

MATT AND LAURA BURTON

Becoming Well, LLC

REBUILDING TRUST FOR CHRISTIANS

A Couple's Guide to Healing After Betrayal

Copyright © 2023 by Becoming Well, LLC

All rights reserved. No part of this book may be reproduced or transmitted in any form, or by any means, electronic or mechanical, including photocopying, recording, or by information storage or retrieval systems, without permission in writing from the copyright owner.

The views and opinions expressed in this book are those of the author, and do not necessarily reflect the official policy or position of Becoming Well, LLC

Published by Becoming Well, LLC www.MyBecomingWell.com

Library of Congress Control Number

Paperback ISBN: 979-8-3302-8628-7

E-book ISBN: 979-8-3302-8631-7

Cover design by Monira

Printed in the United States of America

Table Of Contents

Acknowledgments IX

Authors' Note XI

Introduction XIII

PART 1
Intimacy Avoidance and Betrayal 1

PART 2
The Rebuilding Trust Pyramid 5

PART 3
Rebuilding Trust Pyramid Layer #1 13
TRUST-BUILDING BEHAVIORS 15

PART 4
Preparing A Disclosure 21

PART 5
Trust-Building Behavior #2 29

PART 6
Trust-Building Behavior #3 37

PART 7
Asking Questions 45

PART 8
Final Thoughts on Trust-Building Behaviors 57

PART 9
Trust-Breaking Behavior #1 65

PART 10
The Role of Boundaries 75

PART 11
Trust-Breaking Behavior #2 85

PART 12
Trust-Building Belief #1 93
Trust-Building Belief #2 96

PART 13
Trust-Breaking Belief #1 101
Trust-Breaking Belief #2 104
Trust-Breaking Belief #3 109
Trust-Breaking Belief #4 111

PART 14
Rebuilding Trust Pyramid Layer #2 115

PART 15
Wounded Partner Pitfalls Pitfall #1 125
Pitfall #2 126
Pitfall #3 128
Pitfall #4 130
Pitfall #5 133

PART 16
Wounding Partner Pitfalls 135

PART 17
Pitfalls As a Couple 145

PART 18
Recovery Plans 155

PART 19
Recovery Plan #4 167

PART 20
Recovery Plan #5 175

PART 21
Recovery Plan #6 185

PART 22
Rebuilding Trust Pyramid Layer #3 191

PART 23
Relationship Consistency 205

PART 24
Rebuilding Trust Pyramid Layer #4 213

PART 25
The Importance of Cultivating Good Intimacy Habits 221

PART 26
What is Forgiveness? 227

PART 27
What Forgiveness Is Not 235

PART 28
Reconciliation 239

PART 29
Wounding Partner: What Are You Really Asking For? 247

PART 30
Self-Pity, Shame, and True Repentance 255
The Path to Forgiveness 257

Conclusion 263

References 265

Glossary 269

About the Authors 273

Acknowledgments

Behind this book stand numerous people who helped, encouraged, and ultimately believed in us and in this work. We want to thank our family, friends, fellow recovery coaches and counselors, as well as the many individuals and couple clients that have trusted us to guide them through some of the hardest times in their lives. It has been the ultimate privilege to witness the transformational breakthroughs that happened when they followed the process and did the work. Thank you all.

Matt and Laura

Authors' Note

Although the publisher and the authors have made every effort to ensure that the information in this book was correct at press time and while this publication is designed to provide accurate information in regard to the subject matter covered, the publisher and the author assume no responsibility for errors, inaccuracies, omissions, or any other inconsistencies herein and hereby disclaim any liability to any party for any loss, damage, or disruption caused by errors or omissions, whether such errors or omissions result from negligence, accident, or any other cause.

This publication is meant as a source of valuable information for the reader, however it is not meant as a substitute for direct expert assistance. If such a level of assistance is required, the services of a competent professional should be sought.

Matt and Laura Burton

www.MyBecomingWell.com

Introduction

Praise for Deliverance from Troubles

Psalm 34 MSG

<u>1</u> I bless God every chance I get; my lungs expand with his praise. <u>2</u> I live and breathe God; if things aren't going well, hear this and be happy: <u>3</u> Join me in spreading the news; together let's get the word out. <u>4</u> God met me more than halfway; he freed me from my anxious fears. <u>5</u> Look at him; give him your warmest smile. Never hide your feelings from him. <u>6</u> When I was desperate, I called out, and God got me out of a tight spot. <u>7</u> God's angel sets up a circle of protection around us while we pray. <u>8</u> Open your mouth and taste, open your eyes and see - how good God is. Blessed are you who run to him. <u>9</u> Worship God if you want the best; worship opens doors to all his goodness. <u>10</u> Young lions on the prowl get hungry, but God-seekers are full of God.

<u>11</u> Come, children, listen closely; I'll give you a lesson in God worship. <u>12</u> Who out there has a lust for life? Can't wait each day to come upon beauty? <u>13</u> Guard your tongue from profanity, and no more lying through your teeth. <u>14</u> Turn your back on sin; do something good. Embrace peace - don't let it get away! <u>15</u> God keeps an eye on his friends, his ears pick up every moan and groan. <u>16</u> God won't put up with rebels; he'll cull them from the pack. <u>17</u> Is anyone crying for help? God is listening, ready to rescue you. <u>18</u> If your heart is broken, you'll find God right there; if you're kicked in the gut, he'll help you catch your breath. <u>19</u> Disciples so often get into trouble; still, God is there every time. <u>20</u> He's your bodyguard, shielding every bone; not even a finger gets broken. <u>21</u> The wicked commit slow suicide; they waste their lives hating the good. <u>22</u> God pays for each slave's freedom; no one who runs to him loses out.

Prayer for the wounding and wounded partner:

Father,

We are crying out for help. We know that You are listening and ready to rescue us. Our hearts are broken, and we've been kicked in the gut. Heal our broken hearts and help us to catch our breath. We have fallen into trouble. Deliver us! We accept the sacrifice that Jesus made to pay for our freedom, and we praise You for it. In Jesus' name, Amen.

Even as we write this book, we realize that no one who doesn't work in the same field that we do truly wants to be in a place where they need to read it. If you are here, and are not a coach or counselor, we assume that you have been affected by infidelity in one way or another and are likely in a great deal of emotional pain. For that, we are truly sorry. Perhaps you are someone who has engaged in infidelity-related behavior and are trying to understand what you can do in order to help your partner heal. Or maybe you are someone who has found out about your partner's betrayal and are trying to find a way to put the pieces of your life back together. Whatever your circumstances, we want to welcome you and to tell you that we are truly sorry for what you are going through. We also want to say that we are happy you picked up this book because we believe that it contains the help that you need in order to begin to rebuild trust in your relationship. Although the tools and advice offered here are in no way meant to replace professional therapy or coaching, the methods we describe have brought success to many couples wishing to rebuild their relationship in the aftermath betrayal. If you are a coach or counselor reading this, we hope that the information contained in these pages will equip you with the knowledge you need to help your clients that are struggling to rebuild trust after betrayal.

We feel that it is important to note that we take a three- part approach when it comes to recovery from betrayal. For many couples, the sole focus after betrayal for one or both partners is on the survival of the relationship. We believe that betrayal recovery happens in three distinct areas: recovery for the wounding partner, recovery for the wounded partner, and recovery for the relationship. When the focus is solely on saving the relationship, partners often miss the individual work that they could be doing to increase their chances of success. A relationship is only strong if both parties in that relationship bring their best efforts to the table. It is not possible to have a healthy relationship if both parties neglect their own personal development. Neither is it possible to have a strong relationship when one partner does the majority of the heavy lifting while the other one neglects their responsibility to show up. The relationship will struggle if both partners are not 100% committed to doing whatever it takes to make it strong.

This book was written as a companion to the group and individual intensives that we offer. These intensives were designed to help couples struggling through the aftermath of betrayal. Our goal in writing this material was to give you a clear path to rebuilding trust. We think it is important to point out that, even though we provide a roadmap to trust in this book, we are not suggesting that trusting again after betrayal is simple in any way. The path to recovery is long and, many times, difficult. It is full of unexpected twists and turns that will need to be navigated successfully over time if trust is to be restored. In our experience, the bulk of the heavy lifting involved in rebuilding trust takes an average of two years. This process can be significantly lengthened by complicating factors such as intimacy avoidance and dribbling disclosure. The reason for this is that those issues, especially when combined with the wounding partner's reluctance to be 100% accountable and transparent moving forward, create an unsafe situation for the wounded partner. Without safety, trust cannot be rebuilt.

As you read through this book, you will likely notice that much of the emphasis is placed on what the wounding partner needs to change in order to facilitate the rebuilding trust process. This is intentional. Although we understand it takes two to make a relationship work, and that no partner in any given relationship is perfect, standard relationship counseling and coaching do not work for couples experiencing difficulties from betrayal. It is our firm belief that, until the actions of the wounding partner have been fully addressed and atoned for, it is inappropriate to address other issues within the relationship. Additionally, any coach or counselor who asks a wounded partner to take even partial ownership of a wounding partner's bad behavior only adds to the immense pain that the wounded partner is already experiencing. A person who coaches or counsels in this way may inadvertently be excusing and/or minimizing the effect that a wounding partner's choices have had on the relationship. This is devastating to the wounded partner. We have worked with countless wounded partners who have not only been damaged by this type of coaching and counseling but have actually experienced it as a secondary form of abuse.

Infidelity is a major problem in relationships today. A study conducted by MSNBC of 70,000 people found that 28% of male participants and 18% of female participants admitted to cheating on their spouses. (Weaver, 2007) Although this percentage may not seem large, if it is at all representative of the country's population, we can assume that, in any one given population, over 45 million men and almost 30 million women have cheated on their spouses in the United States alone—and that only accounts for the married ones. One study through the American Psychological Association showed that 20-40% of divorces in the U.S. can be attributed to infidelity and that 42% of these divorced individuals reported having more than one affair. (Christiansen, Marin, Atkins, 2014) Furthermore, studies have shown positive correlations between infidelity and marital stress, conflict, depression, and anxiety.

(Gordon, Baucom, 1999) Research shows that emotional affairs are far more common than sexual ones. A study of over 94,000 participants showed that 90% of female participants and 77% of male participants admitted to having an emotional affair at some point during their relationship. (Truth About Deception, 2022) Sexual and emotional infidelity are not the only issues when it comes to divorce and emotional pain. A study published in the *Journal of Sex Research* found that *the probability of divorce roughly doubled for married Americans who* used pornography. (Perry, Schleifer, 2017) An additional study found that pornography use can diminish the effects of connection and intimacy by taking the brain's natural chemical process and "supercharging" it—making the natural release of bonding chemicals in a relationship seem underwhelming. (Voon, et.al, 2014) Whatever the statistic, it is apparent that betrayal from infidelity, in any form, can greatly damage a relationship and can have negative impacts on the mental health of both parties involved.

Terms Used in This Book

Throughout this book, we use several terms that require some definition. These have been included in the Glossary section at the back of the book. We encourage you to take a few momentsand go through them in order to prevent confusion as you read along.

PART 1

Intimacy Avoidance and Betrayal

In Laura's classes and groups for partners, she outlines the different types of betrayal we encounter regularly in our practice. These are sexual infidelity (a.k.a. "cheating"), emotional infidelity (a.k.a. "emotional affair"), and infidelity through pornography. In the first section of the class, she cites intimacy avoidance as a complicating factor to the issue of infidelity in a relationship. We see intimacy avoidance as a unique type of betrayal because the intimacy avoidant person is so concerned with protecting themselves that they betray their partner by withholding themselves on multiple levels. Terms often used to describe the phenomenon of intimacy avoidance are intimacy anorexia®, a term coined by Dr. Doug Weiss, narcissism or narcissistic relationship (not to be confused with Narcissistic Personality Disorder), sexual anorexia, and sexless marriage. If you are unsure whether or not intimacy avoidance is complicating your situation, here are some common symptoms of this issue:

- Can't seem to commit fully to the relationship
- Often holds the partner to impossible, unattainable standards
- Is perfectionistic and/or feels unlovable when they themselves aren't perfect
- Stays so busy with work and projects that they have little time to spend with their partner
- Has little to no trust for their partner, even if they have earned it
- When issues/arguments arise, the person's first response is to put the blame back on their partner
- Has little to no empathy
- Plays the victim, especially after being confronted with wrongdoing on their part
- Seems distant during sex or regularly avoids sex
- Makes sexual performance a condition of staying in the relationship
- Acts like listening to their partner's feelings is a huge imposition and/or extremely taxing
- Seems overly sensitive to criticism (real or perceived)
- Dismisses their partner's valid issues and emotions with a "just get over it" attitude

- Refrains from showing love to their partner in ways they know the partner needs or appreciates
- Refuses to praise or compliment their partner
- Is unwilling or unable to share true feelings with their partner
- Uses anger, disapproval, and/or silence as a means to control or punish their partner
- Has ongoing or ungrounded criticism of their partner and verbalizes it, or frequently seems silently judgmental
- Gets overly angry and/or defensive when challenged

The reason we feel that it is important to bring up intimacy avoidance right after the introduction section is that, if this is an issue, rebuilding trust in the relationship becomes significantly more complicated. In relationships struggling with intimacy avoidance, intimacy and trust have been absent for most of the relationship's duration. Ongoing gaslighting, devaluation, and minimization are typically present, which means that trust needs to be rebuilt, or built for the first time, on multiple levels because it has been broken down by these things in addition to the other types of betrayal. As outlined in the definitions section, the term "gaslighting" describes a subtle or overt form of manipulation in which the gaslighter attempts to sow seeds of doubt in their partner's mind about the validity of their emotions and reality. This is done in an attempt to shirk responsibility for bad behavior and is always at the expense of the person being gaslighted. Some examples of gaslighting can include saying something wasn't said when it was, presenting an image of being a caring person in public while acting uncaring and unempathetic at home, and telling a person that they are exaggerating when their feelings have been hurt—effectively invalidating that person's experience.

Partners of intimacy avoidants often blame themselves for the problems in their relationship. This is because the gaslighting and minimization they have experienced is a form of emotional and mental abuse that erodes a person's trust in their own perceptions. They tend to take on too much responsibility in response to their partner's lack of accountability. Oftentimes, their thinking has become muddied from years, and sometimes decades, of gaslighting. This can lead the wounded partner to take on responsibility that isn't theirs when it comes to rebuilding trust—and the intimacy avoidant is often happy to let them do it. When a person struggling with intimacy avoidance is caught in infidelity-related behavior, it is not at all uncommon for them to blame their partner in an attempt to avoid taking personal responsibility for their actions. As a result of years of systematic emotional abuse in the form of gaslighting, devaluation, and undermining, it is common for a partner of an intimacy avoidant to accept, at least in part, the responsibility for their partner's behavior.

It is important that we point out that, no matter what the circumstances, our stance is that the partner who engages in infidelity-related behavior is 100% responsible for their choice to be unfaithful. Although all relationships have issues and no one is perfect, the idea that anyone is forced into acting unfaithfully is ludicrous. Infidelity is never a viable option for dealing with problems, either real or perceived. There are many choices that the wounding partner could have made besides engaging in infidelity-related behavior. With the intimacy avoidant, blame shifting, for infidelity or for other bad behavior, is par for the course. This is extremely damaging and can even be dangerous for a wounded partner who believes that all they need to do is to work harder at forgiveness and/or on themselves in order to "save" the relationship. Meanwhile, the intimacy avoidant, who is the source of the issue, escapes accountability.

We have worked successfully with many couples dealing with betrayal when intimacy avoidance is a complicating factor. That being said, we feel it is important to point out that the intimacy avoidant's behavior must be dealt with as urgently as any issues arising from betrayal if trust is ever to be rebuilt. In relationships where intimacy avoidance is present, infidelity is only *one* of the serious problems that a couple faces. These relationships are commonly riddled with issues such as lying, undermining, gaslighting, demeaning, and invalidation that must be dealt with along with the damage done from the betrayal itself. It is imperative that the intimacy avoidant both face and change these bad behaviors along with their infidelity-related behaviors if the relationship is to be considered a healthy one. It is also important to note that ongoing accountability is important before the partner of an intimacy avoidant can determine if trust should be extended. Unfortunately, many intimacy avoidants are especially adept at doing and saying the right things, at least in the beginning, in order to avoid the consequences of their behavior. Only time will tell if they are truly remorseful for what they have done and are willing to do the recovery work necessary to change their ways. This includes building empathy, which intimacy avoidants typically lack, in order to see things from the wounded partner's perspective.

The Bible proves that the research is accurate. Let's look at what Jesus says:

Mark 7: 20-23 KJV:
[20] And he said, "That which cometh out of the man, that defiles the man.
[21] For from within, out of the heart of men, proceed evil thoughts, adulteries, fornications, murders,
[22] Thefts, covetousness, wickedness, deceit, lasciviousness, an evil eye, blasphemy, pride, foolishness:
[23] All these evil things come from within and defile the man."

This verse supports and contains all of the attributes of someone with intimacy avoidance.

But we are in the business of rebuilding trust. Just as David so grievously sinned against the Almighty, and sought His mercy and forgiveness, God extends His mercy and forgiveness towards us.

Psalm 51: 1-2 KJV states:

51 Have mercy upon me, O God, according to thy lovingkindness: according unto the multitude of thy tender mercies blot out my transgressions.

² Wash me thoroughly from mine iniquity and cleanse me from my sin.

Prayer for the wounding partner:

Father, have mercy on me. I repent and turn away from ALL sin. I seek your lovingkindness and tender mercies. Please blot out my sins, my transgressions and wash me thoroughly from all stain of sin. In Jesus' name. Amen.

PART 2

The Rebuilding Trust Pyramid

There is a lot of information out there when it comes to rebuilding trust in relationships. Our challenge was how to break it down into a simple form so that our clients could understand the overall process. In the end, we created the Rebuilding Trust Pyramid. The four layers of this structure include honesty, safety, consistency, and intimacy. While this book is specific to rebuilding trust after betrayal, we feel that the pyramid can be applied to most romantic relationships, friendships, and even family relationships where a breach of trust has taken place. Let's take a look at each of these layers in detail:

Figure 1: The Rebuilding Trust Pyramid

Honesty

Honesty is the foundation of trust in all healthy relationships. Without honesty, relationships fail to thrive. When we work with wounded partners, they often tell us that the lies they were told by the wounding partner are just as hard, if not harder, to move past than the infidelity-related behavior. Lying, for most wounded partners, represents multiple betrayals. These betrayals often make them feel disrespected and foolish. Not only did the wounding partner break the agreement that was between the couple when they engaged in the infidelity-related behavior, but they lied about it. In many cases, the wounding partner has been lying for quite some time. This causes the wounded partner to call into question everything that happened before and after the lies were told. They now question who their partner is as a person because lies demonstrate selfishness, a major character defect, on the wounding partner's part. The fact that the wounded partner may not have realized the depth of this character defect often causes them to conclude that they don't know the wounding partner at all. Additionally, the wounded partner also questions whether the wounding partner ever really loved them. This creates an excruciatingly painful situation that is difficult for the wounded partner to wrap their head around.

Lying also creates an imbalance in the relationship. The wounded partner assumed that their partner was as committed to the relationship as they were. However, the betrayal and the lying causes them to question whether or not their partner ever truly gave their heart to them at all. Every word, every action, every holiday, every meaningful event, every sexual encounter now all seem suspect. The question in the wounded partner's mind becomes, "If you could do this and lie about it, is everything else also a lie?"

Finally, lies punctuate the intentionality of infidelity. Much of the wounding partner's infidelity-related behavior can be at least partially explained by things like addiction, self-centeredness, immaturity, etc. However, the fact that the behavior was intentionally covered up by the wounding partner's lies is something that can't be explained other than to say that the wounding partner knew, on some level, that what they were doing was wrong. The calculated nature of lying highlights the fact that, to some extent, the actions engaged in by the wounding partner were deliberate. This feels highly personal to the wounded partner. In our work, we are often told by wounded partners that they don't feel like they know their partner anymore, and that maybe they never did. This indicates a profound loss of trust—not only in the wounding partner, but in the soundness of the relationship and even in life as they knew it to be.

If a couple is to have a chance at rebuilding their relationship after betrayal, it must be built on a foundation of honesty and transparency. Ongoing lying and dishonesty will send the wounded partner the message that the wounding partner is primarily concerned with their own comfort, even if it is at the expense of the wounded partner's heart. This is seen as, and is in fact, another betrayal. If honesty cannot be established, what remains is a relationship devoid of trust and intimacy.

Lying is a characteristic of the devil.
John 8:44 NIV.
[44] You belong to your father, the devil, and you want to carry out your father's desires. He was a murderer from the beginning, not holding to the truth, for there is no truth in him. When he lies, he speaks his native language, for he is a liar and the father of lies.

Paul writes to the Colossians admonishing them to give up their wicked ways. He stressed the importance of honesty.

Colossians 3:9-10 KJV

⁹ Lie not one to another, seeing that ye have put off the old man with his deeds,

¹⁰ And have put on the new man, which is renewed in knowledge after the image of him that created him:

We are to imitate the image of Christ in God. Honesty rebuilds trust.

Safety

Although honesty can help build safety in a relationship, in the case of betrayal, more needs to be done in order to achieve this. When we speak with wounded partners who have been hurt by their partner's infidelity-related behavior, they almost always describe feeling unsafe. First and foremost, this is because the predictability of the relationship is now gone. This typically initiates a fight or flight response from the wounded partner because the wounding partner's actions have caused betrayal trauma. Unfortunately, it can take the wounded partner weeks and months (in some cases longer) before their body and mind stop reacting to the trauma. Safety in the relationship must be reestablished if the wounded partner is ever to get out of a hyper vigilant mode of operation. In the case of relationships where intimacy avoidance is present, safety may never have been properly established in the first place. This is because partners of intimacy avoidants often feel an overall lack of acceptance from their partner and, therefore, never felt safe to begin with.

When betrayal occurs, it can cause a lack of safety in several areas. The types of safety that are most often violated are physical/ sexual, emotional, and commitment. Other types of safety that may be affected can include community standing (when the discovery of infidelity-related behavior causes a loss of status or friends), financial (when the wounding partner spends money on their infidelity-related behavior), and even personal (when the wounding partner shares details of the relationship or the family with an affair partner). An area where safety can be damaged *after* infidelity has been disclosed or discovered is in the area of communication. This typically happens through inappropriate displays of emotions (such as name calling or shaming), stonewalling, defending, and threatening. During group and individual intensives, we work with couples at length to establish plans to address the different areas where safety has been violated and needs to be restored.

God's word teaches that integrity produces security.

Proverbs 10:9 NIV

Whoever walks in integrity walks securely, but whoever takes crooked paths will be found out.

Proverbs 3:21-26 NIV

States that wisdom, understanding, sound judgment and discretion provides safety and security.

My son, do not let wisdom and understanding out of your sight, preserve sound judgment and discretion; 22 they will be life for you, an ornament to grace your neck. 23 Then you will go on your way in safety, and your foot will not stumble. 24 When you lie down, you will not be afraid; when you lie down, your sleep will be sweet. 25 Have no fear of sudden disaster or of the ruin that overtakes the wicked, 26 for the Lord will be at your side and will keep your foot from being snared.

Safety is a byproduct of integrity, wisdom, understanding, sound judgement and discretion.

Consistency

Considered to be the "meat and potatoes" of recovery from betrayal, consistency is key if trust is truly to be rebuilt. Consistency is an important ingredient to trust because it shows the wounded partner that they can depend on the wounding partner to follow through. When we work with couples to develop plans to create safety, we always explain that, without consistency, those plans are basically useless. When the wounding partner engages in infidelity-related behavior, they send a message to the wounded partner that they can't be trusted to uphold the promises and agreements that are important to the health of the relationship. If the wounding partner wants their partner to accept that they can change this, they must be consistent. Anyone can profess remorse and make promises, actions speak louder than words. If the day-to-day actions of the wounding partner include defensiveness, a lack of accountability, ongoing lying (even about seemingly small things), playing the victim, and criticism, the wounded partner receives the message loud and clear that their partner lacks the commitment necessary to rebuild trust. The result is that the chance of rebuilding trust diminishes. The proof of the wounding partner's commitment to do whatever it takes to restore the relationship lies in their day-to-day behavior. The consistency phase of rebuilding trust is ongoing and takes the longest time to establish.

God has a lot to say about consistency.

Galatians 6:9 NIV

⁹ Let us not become weary in doing good, for at the proper time we will reap a harvest if we do not give up. ¹⁰ Therefore, as we have opportunity, let us do good to all people, especially to those who belong to the family of believers.

1 Corinthians 15:58 NIV

⁵⁸ Therefore, my dear brothers and sisters, stand firm. Let nothing move you. Always give yourselves fully to the work of the Lord, because you know that your labor in the Lord is not in vain.

We are to be consistent in doing good to the family of believers. How much more consistent are we to sow good things in our relationship with our partners? Marriage is the work of the Lord, and we are expected to give fully of ourselves in this sacred endeavor! Can you imagine the harvest of consistently sowing good deeds and walking in love?

Intimacy

When we think of intimacy, people tend to jump straight to sex. Although this is one type of intimacy and is often an expression of other types, it is not the only one. Some common areas of intimacy that a couple can share are created by sharing emotions, resolving conflict successfully, sharing goals and dreams, sharing and respecting each other's thoughts and opinions, connecting around religion and spiritual ideas and beliefs, and sharing hobbies and interests.

The feelings of devastation, betrayal, loneliness, ambivalence, and confusion caused by betrayal cause a breakdown in intimacy between partners. One of the reasons for this is because these feelings can cause one or both parties in the relationship to withdraw. Although this is common for a period of time when infidelity is discovered or disclosed, both partners will need to recommit to the relationship if trust is to be restored. In the case of relationships where intimacy avoidance is present, little to no intimacy was present in the relationship prior to the discovery or disclosure of a betrayal. When we test couples for the strength of their relationship structures (more on this later in the book), we typically find that most of these are completely missing. The issues caused by intimacy avoidance, intimacy anorexia®, and generally self-centered behavior leave the relationship weak. Adding betrayal to this already weak structure makes it extremely difficult for couples dealing with these issues to survive unless the intimacy avoidant is willing to admit to the totality of their bad behavior and begin recovery right away.

The fact that intimacy is at the top of the Rebuilding Trust Pyramid is a bit deceptive as it implies that intimacy will not be developed until honesty, safety, and consistency are completely in place. The truth is that intimacy will be built all along the recovery journey, and that the "ingredients" of honesty, safety, and consistency are what produce intimacy. When we think of it this way, the diagram looks like this:

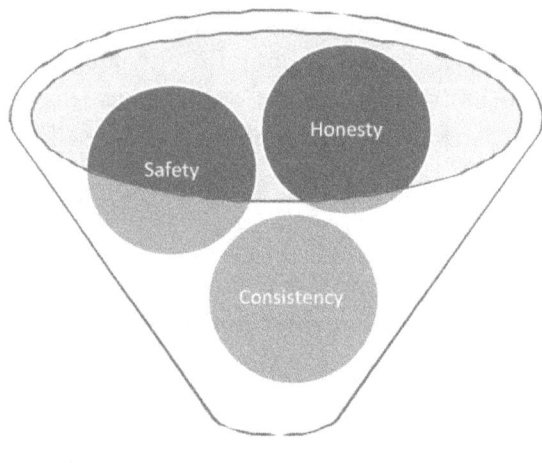

Intimacy
Figure 2: Ingredients of Intimacy

The building of intimacy in a relationship is an ongoing process. Intimacy is like a plant that grows over time as each person in the relationship gives it what it needs in order to thrive. It is not a destination that, once reached, can be checked off the list and ignored. When any of the ingredients to intimacy are missing in a relationship, it fails to thrive and, ultimately, dies on the vine. It must be constantly watered and nurtured if it is to remain. This is the work of commitment within a relationship. For the purposes of this book, however, we will be addressing intimacy as a separate element in order to give you ways in which you can actively nurture it.

Listen to how the woman in Song of Solomon describes her beloved:

Song of Solomon 5:16 NIV

This is my beloved, this is my friend, daughters of Jerusalem.

Friend is translated as companion, or intimate (1).

She shared her heart and her desires with him, she shared secrets with him. She shared life goals with him. It wasn't all about sex, but sex was the deep expression of intimacy.

Listen to how the man describes his beloved.

Song of Solomon 4:9

You have stolen my heart, my sister, my bride; you have stolen my heart.

Stolen is translated as become intelligent, to get a mind (2).

He shared his mind with her and his intelligence with her. He shared his purpose in life with her. It wasn't all about sex, she wasn't to be used.

Intimacy between man and woman was created by God and He said it was good.

Prayer for the wounding partner:

Father, give me the grace to be consistent and steadfast in character. I choose to fear You. I choose not to lie and will never let wisdom and understanding get out of my sight. Help me to preserve sound judgment and discretion. They will be life for me, an ornament to grace my neck. Then I will be safe, and my foot will not stumble. When I lie down, I will not be afraid. When I lie down, my sleep will be sweet. Then I will have no fear of sudden disaster or of the ruin that overtakes the wicked. You will be at my side and will keep my foot from being snared. In Jesus' name. Amen.

Prayer for the wounded partner:

Father, give me the grace not to be weary and give up in doing good. At the proper time I will reap a harvest. With every opportunity that presents itself, I will do good for my partner. I will not let anything move or discourage me. My work in the Lord is not in vain but will reap a mighty harvest! In Jesus' name. Amen.

References:

1). Strong's Concordance H7453
2). Strong's Concordance H269

PART 3

Rebuilding Trust Pyramid Layer #1

Honesty

"I'm not upset that you lied to me, I'm upset from now on I can't believe you."—Nietzsche

We would like to preface this section on honesty by stating that much of the information contained here will be directed at the wounding partner. Although both parties play an active role in rebuilding trust, it falls to the wounding partner to do much of the work in the beginning stages because they are the one who broke the trust by engaging in infidelity- related behavior. In our experience, if a wounding partner is granted a chance to regain trust from the wounded partner, how they respond to that chance is crucial to trust being rebuilt. If the wounding partner doesn't take this responsibility seriously and put all of their effort toward doing whatever it takes, the relationship can be further damaged. If this goes on for too long, the relationship stands little chance of ever being a healthy one and is more likely than not to end completely.

As we stated in the Introduction section, honesty is the foundation of trust in relationships. Lies and trust can't coexist in a healthy relationship over the long term. When we lie to our partner, we disrespect them by leaving them in the dark and refusing to take responsibility for our actions. We essentially tell them that we consider our own self-interest to be more important than theirs. This leads our partner to feel unloved and uncared for. Lies indicate that we don't put much value on the relationship and, therefore, can't be trusted to take care of it—or of them.

To punctuate the seriousness of lying, let's look at one of the many instances when God, the Faithful Holy One of Israel, addressed deception. His covenant people, the remnant especially chosen from all the peoples of the earth, flippantly traded His magnificent glory and majesty that surrounded and preserved them, for the worship of idols. Highly offended and deeply wounded, God calls them out over the sin of deception in the Book of Hosea.

Hosea 11:12 NIV

Ephraim has surrounded me with lies, Israel with deceit. And Judah is unruly against God, even against the faithful Holy One.

When infidelity is discovered or disclosed, the wounded partner is sent reeling. This is because betrayal injures attachment. It causes intense trauma to a wounded partner because the violation of trust suddenly calls everything—the past, present, and future of the relationship—into question. The bond between the couple, known as a pair bond, is ruptured. (Johnson, 2004) Studies have shown that pair bonds play an essential role in human health because they act as buffers against stress, depression, and anxiety. (Young, 2003) When these bonds are broken, the trauma caused by the break engages the limbic system, which results in a fight or flight response. It is not uncommon for wounded partners to become disoriented and alternate between anxious-preoccupied responses and fearful-avoidant responses. (Cluff-Schade, Sandberg, 2012) Since there are so many systems and hormones involved with bonding, the wounded partner's entire equilibrium is thrown off when infidelity is discovered or disclosed.

Empowered with this modern-day research, we better comprehend the significance and profoundness of this much quoted verse:

Genesis 2:24 NIV
That is why a man leaves his father and mother and is united to his wife, and they become one flesh.

Our purpose in telling you this is not to discourage you. Instead, it is to impress upon you the seriousness of the situation. It is our hope that, if you understand what has happened, then the issue of betrayal and the resulting turmoil in your relationship will be given the attention it deserves. Rebuilding trust after betrayal is a long and difficult process that cannot be rushed. Given the information that you just read, we hope you can see why. Trust must be rebuilt brick by brick with intentional effort, and this starts with honesty and transparency moving forward. There are several ways that we work with couples trying to establish honesty as a foundation for rebuilding trust. In order to address the main ones, we have broken them into four categories: trust-building behaviors, trust-breaking behaviors, trust-building beliefs, and trust-breaking beliefs.

TRUST-BUILDING BEHAVIORS

Trust-Building Behavior #1: Complete Disclosure

The first trust-building behavior is complete disclosure. Other than the wounding partner ceasing to engage in infidelity-related behavior, how disclosure is handled is the most crucial part of rebuilding trust. In order to start rebuilding trust, the wounding partner must first trust the wounded partner with the information regarding their infidelity-related behavior. Without complete disclosure, it is very difficult (if not impossible) for couples to make progress in the rebuilding trust process.

Although we highly recommend that disclosure be done in a therapeutic setting with a trained coach or counselor, we do get a number of couples who have attempted disclosure or plan to attempt disclosure on their own. Due to the serious nature of disclosure and the potential damage that it can do to one or both parties in the relationship, **we do not recommend that you attempt disclosure on your own.** The information contained here on the most common mistakes made during disclosure and the guides to what should be included in disclosure and what questions to ask should be used for informational purposes only. **This information is not designed as a do-it-yourself tool.**

Some of you may already be through the disclosure process. For you, we would suggest still reading this section because you may learn something new that could be helpful to you. If you are currently engaged in some of these common mistakes, consider this a chance to correct those. For those of you who have not made it through the process, please read through this section carefully so that you can avoid the most common mistakes made during disclosure.

In order to better prepare you for the therapeutic disclosure process, we would like to highlight the top 3 mistakes that couples make when attempting a disclosure conversation. It may seem counterintuitive, but research shows that the wounding partner's willingness to completely disclose infidelity-related behaviors and answer the wounded partner's questions without defense facilitates healthy recovery. One of the biggest barriers to complete disclosure is the need for the wounding partner to control the flow of information.

Common Mistake #1: Dribble Disclosure

The term "dribble disclosure" is used to describe a situation in which the truth about infidelity-related behavior is "dribbled" out over time. This is usually because the wounding partner fears the wounded partner's reaction to the information. Therefore, the temptation is for the wounding partner to withhold information and release it in smaller chunks. Many times, this is a misguided attempt to make it somehow easier for the wounded partner to handle. Also, if the wounding partner is being honest with themselves, they are often doing it in an attempt to lessen their own consequences. Many wounding partners realize that what they have done is a mistake and have an intense fear that disclosing information will lose them the relationship. The problem with this is that it sends the message to the wounded partner that the wounding partner's primary focus is still on themselves and their own discomfort, instead of on the relationship. Although the wounding partner's fears are understandable, attempts to control the flow of information are misguided.

A research study done by well-known author and infidelity expert Peggy Vaughn found that 72% of betrayed women and 70% of betrayed men actually found the deception harder to get over than the infidelity itself. (Vaughn, 2010) The implications of this study are that, even though details of the infidelity will be hurtful to the wounded partner, the deception around infidelity and disclosure is far more damaging to the rebuilding of trust. This is why dribble disclosure is so harmful to the recovery process. Each time the wounding partner holds back critical information, they are deceiving the wounded partner yet again. When this is done, it lessens the chances that the wounded partner will recover in time to be able to participate in the process of rebuilding trust. Each experience amounts to a new deception and betrayal to them. This essentially cuts their legs out from under them in terms of their journey toward recovery.

The other issue with dribble disclosure is that it communicates the message that the wounding partner is still disloyal. When information is withheld, it is usually because the wounding partner is being more loyal to themselves and/or their infidelity partner(s) than they are to their wounded partner. This is like pouring salt into a cut. The truth can serve to realign loyalty in the relationship. Dribble disclosure undermines this.

Proverbs 28:13 NIV

Whoever conceals their sins does not prosper but the one who confesses and renounces them finds mercy.

Proverbs 28:13 (paraphrased)

Whoever covers their sins to protect themselves will not advance in a situation or have it concluded successfully. In order to be successful, one must confess in a way that is precise as if shooting an arrow towards a determined target. Along with confession, one must depart, forsake and abandon their self-centered ways in order for God to impart mercy and compassion towards that individual.

Common Mistake #2: Believing that disclosure willmake things worse

Although it may seem futile to disclose information and answer questions because it will likely end up in a fight, anger, or tears, nothing could be further from the truth. Withholding information from the wounded partner regarding something that has deeply affected their life is not only controlling, but also unfair and even cruel. Without the necessary information, the wounded partner will likely deal with one or more of the following:

- An inability to trust again because they can't make sense of the information in order to help them recover
- Constant triggers from unresolved trauma
- A feeling that the entire history of the relationship has been tainted because they don't understand the extent of the betrayal
- An inability to trust their own judgement because they don't know how they have been deceived
- Hyper-arousal from constant worry and fear of danger
- A feeling of being robbed of having an authentic relationship
- A feeling of foolishness for staying with the wounding partner
- A feeling of being doubly wounded. First, by the betrayal and second, by the withholding of information
- A feeling of needing to protect themselves, ensuring that the wounded and wounding partners will never be on the same page in the relationship.

Additionally, the wounding partner is likely to experience one or more of the following:

- A sense that their partner would never love them if they really knew what they have done
- Repeated infidelity-related behavior because the first behavior was kept in the dark and never dealt with
- Anxiety over the wounded partner finding out what has happened

Failure to completely disclose infidelity-related behavior will also likely result in one or more of the following consequences to the relationship and/or family:

- A marked increase in recovery time
- Prolonged emotional instability
- Additional trauma
- A feeling of chaos due to a failure to create safety
- The possible destruction of the parts of the relationship that are good
- Decreased possibility of relationship recovery
- Increased fighting
- Increased potential of children being hurt in the process

Common Mistake #3: Giving too many or too few details

It is important to note that the disclosure process **should be driven by what the wounded partner needs to know**. The wounding partner must be willing to submit to this idea if rebuilding trust is going to be possible. Answering the wounded partner's questions plays a vital role in the recovery process. Without answers, the wounded partner is likely to think on the subject night and day. Their mind is likely to run wild with possible scenarios that never happened.

It is not uncommon for wounded partners to ask an extraordinary amount of questions. For most, asking more and more details is their way of trying to get a handle on the situation. With patience and honesty on the wounding partner's part, the intensity of question-asking should lessen over time.

That being said, it is important for the wounded partner to carefully consider what they truly need to know. A detail, once known, cannot be unknown. Two common ways in which the wounded partner can be further wounded while asking questions is if 1) they ask questions that may cause them to compare themselves with others or 2) too many "why" questions that prolong the disclosure process. Although it is important to understand why the betrayal happened, too many "why" questions early on can lead to frustration because the wounding partner is often not self-reflective enough to understand the "why" themselves. We do, however, recommend that the wounded partner ask at least some "why" questions early on to give the wounding partner the opportunity to answer them. Though, the wounded partner should not be surprised if the answers change over time as the wounding partner gets more recovery and is able to reflect on their motives in a deeper manner.

The following is a list of detailed information that we recommend **should not be included in the disclosure process**:

- Graphic or explicit details regarding specific sexual behavior
- Names of affair partner(s), unless they are known to the wounded partner
- Specific locations where the wounding partner engaged in infidelity-related behavior, unless the locations are within the circle of safety (see Glossary definition) of the wounded partner
- Specific fantasies (it is okay to disclose that the wounding partner fantasizes during sex, but it is not recommended to get into specifics)

We want to make it clear that the disclosure process should be driven by what the wounded partner feels they need to know in order to make decisions about how to proceed in the relationship. We can't stress the fact enough that **it isn't up to the wounding partner to decide how much the wounded partner gets to know**. That being said, the list above was put together based on our experience as to the types of information that are typically the most damaging. As stated above, once a detail is known, it cannot be unknown. Explicit, graphic, and/or unnecessary details will only serve to create more triggers for the wounded partner and will almost certainly prolong the recovery process. We have had experience helping multiple couples where the wounded partner's knowledge of explicit details was the nail that sealed the coffin of the relationship because they could not move past it.

As a general rule, it is not a good idea for the wounded partner to ask questions in the heat of the moment. We advocate at least a 24-hour evaluation period prior to asking questions. Our advice is for the wounded partner to write down any questions they may have and commit to not asking them for a minimum of 24 hours. Additionally, we advise that the wounded partner ask themselves the following questions about each question to determine whether or not they truly need to be asked:

1. Why do I want to know the answer to this question?
2. Will the answer to this question help me recover? (yes or no)
3. If yes, how will the answer to this question help me recover?

If the answer to a particular question will not aid in the recovery process in any significant way, we advise that the wounded partner strike it from the list of questions.

For many wounded partners, asking more and more details is their way of trying to get a handle on their situation. They mistakenly believe that if they just find out one more detail, they will finally make sense out of what has happened to them. Sadly, the truth is that there will be a portion of the betrayal that they may never make sense of. For most wounded partners, this inability to make sense of the wounding partner's behavior stems from the fact that they could never fathom doing what their partner has done themselves. Most wounded partners that we work with would never betray their partner in the way that they have been betrayed. The fact that the wounding partner could set them and the relationship aside in order to engage in infidelity- related behavior is unfathomable. Asking more questions will do very little to explain the disparity between how the wounding partner thinks and how the wounded partner thinks. It is a sad fact that the wounding partner's behavior was selfishly motivated, and this will never make sense to someone who's primary loyalty is to their partner and the relationship.

Unfortunately, this is a necessary suffering, like childbirth or surgery, for both the wounding partner and the wounded partner. The wounded partner will feel indescribable pain. But know that the God of all comfort will be there offer aid.

Jeremiah 15:18 NIV

Why is my pain unending and my wound grievous and incurable?

2 Corinthians 1:3-5 ESV

God of All Comfort

³ Blessed be the God and Father of our Lord Jesus Christ, the Father of mercies and God of all comfort, ⁴ who comforts us in all our affliction, so that we may be able to comfort those who are in any affliction, with the comfort with which we ourselves are comforted by God. ⁵ For as we share abundantly in Christ's sufferings, so through Christ we share abundantly in comfort too.[a]

1 Peter 5:10 NIV

And the God of all grace, who called you to his eternal glory in Christ, after you have suffered a little while, will himself restore you and make you strong, firm and steadfast.

As the wounding partner, it is best to confess in deep remorse and with the understanding that God will meet them where they are at and pull them out of the muck and the mire.

Psalm 32:1-5 NIV

Blessed is the one whose transgressions are forgiven, whose sins are covered. Blessed is the one whose sin the Lord does not count against them and in whose spirit is no deceit. When I kept silent, my bones wasted away through my groaning all day long. For day and night your hand was heavy on me; my strength was sapped as in the heat of summer. Then I acknowledged my sin to you and did not cover up my iniquity. I said, "I will confess my transgression to the Lord." And you forgave the guilt of my sin.

However painful this first step may be, it is a giant leap forward towards the healing process and in rebuilding trust.

Prayer for the wounding partner

Father, thank You for the sacrifice that Jesus made for me. Cover all of my sins. Cause me not to have any lies or deceit within myself in any way, shape or form. Thank you for removing all of my guilt and for giving me the grace to walk in honesty and integrity all the days of my life. In Jesus' name. Amen.

Prayer for the wounded partner

Father, heal my broken heart. I feel like my bones are wasting within me. Strengthen me by Your Holy Spirit and cause me to experience the joy of my salvation. In Jesus' name. Amen.

PART 4

Preparing A Disclosure

As we stated above, we recommend that disclosure be made in the presence of a trained coach or counselor and the information detailed here should not be used as a do- it-yourself guide. That being said, we would like to offer you some guidance as to what information should be included in a disclosure as well as what types of questions we recommend for the wounded partner to ask.

In an effort for the wounding partner to get honest with the wounded partner, if they haven't already, the following can be used as a guideline to prepare a document containing the facts of the infidelity-related behavior. Typically, the information contained in a disclosure consists of any infidelity-related or addictive behavior that the wounding partner engaged in after having entered into a committed relationship with the wounded partner. However, in many cases, it is important that details of certain behavior that was engaged in prior to the commencement of the relationship be included as well. This holds especially true if the wounding partner has an addiction to sex or pornography and/or if they misrepresented themselves to their partner at all during the relationship. Some examples of this include when the wounding partner has a history of cheating or pornography use that wasn't disclosed, was lied about, or was minimized. This also holds true if the number of sexual partners the wounding partner had prior to meeting the wounded partner was lied about. Since the wounded partner likely engaged in the relationship based on the information provided to them by the wounding partner, the lies (either blatant or by omission) represent a significant betrayal of trust.

Although the disclosure process should be driven by what the wounded partner needs to know in order to heal, here is a rough outline as well as some examples of information typically included. For your reference, we have included a disclosure guide that outlines behavior engaged in prior to the wounding partner's relationship with the wounded partner as well as one that does not include that information. It is important to note that, when working on disclosure with a trained counselor or coach, they will likely have their own format for you to use.

Sample #1

Nature of the Betrayal

- Type of betrayal
- Frequency of contact
- Types of contact
- Approximate money spent
- Lies or gaslighting involved

Timeline

- From__to_____, I engaged in _____ approximately_____perweek/month

- From__to_____, I engaged in _____ approximately_____per week/month

- From__to_____, I engaged in _____ approximately_____per week/month

Examples:

From January – April of 2021, I engaged in a texting relationship with a co-worker. We texted approximately four times per day during this time. We discussed our relationships with our spouses.

From April of 2021 to December of 2021, I engaged in a sexual relationship with a coworker. We met twice per week at their house and had sex.

From December of 2017 to January of 2020, I engaged in a sexual relationship with an escort that I found online. We met once per month at a hotel. The approximate money I spent on this was____.

Clarifications

Please also make a list of what your harmful behavior did/ did not involve:

- Involve unprotected sexual intercourse
- Impact our family's safety (e.g., texting while driving, giving out personal identifying information, having people in our home)
- Occur in our home

- Involve individuals that you know
- Risk a loss of job or legal consequences
- Exposure of the infidelity to our children

Devices, apps, and websites used

To pave the way for future accountability, the wounding partner should make a list of the following:

- Website name
- App name
- Laptop
- Cell phone
- Work computer

Sample #2

Masturbation

Started age:

Ended age or last time:

Places (types of place not names of places): Frequency:___per week

Most common associated co addictions:

Pornography/Sexually Stimulating Images

Started age:

Ended age or last time:

Places (types of places not names of places): Frequency:___per week

Most common associated co addictions: Forms used (videos, etc.):

Sites used:

Strip Clubs

Started age:

Ended age or last time:

Places (types of places not names of places): Frequency:

Money spent:

Drugs

Started age:

Ended age or last time:

Types of drugs Frequency:

Money spent:

Phone Sex

Started age:

Ended age or last time:

Types of Places/Locations (not names): Frequency:

Money spent:

Online Chat Rooms

Started age:

Ended age or last time:

Types of Places/Locations (not names):

Frequency:

Money spent:

After Relationship Affairs

Started age:

Ended age or last time:

Number of different people

Of those, how many were 1 time with same person Of those, how many were 2-6 times with same person

Of those, how many were over 6 times with same person

Types of Places/Locations (not names):

Anyone your partner knew

Ever in home, their/your vehicle etc. Protected or unprotected sex

Are you currently in contact with any Last time you were in contact with any How you met them

Money spent:

After Relationship/Commitment Paid Sex

Started age:

Ended age or last time:

Number of different people

Of those, how many were 1 time with same person

Of those, how many were 2-6 times with same person Of those, how many were over 6 times with same person Types of Places/Locations (not names):

Anyone your wife knew

Ever in home, her/your vehicle etc. Protected or unprotected sex

Are you currently in contact with any Last time you were in contact with any How met them

Money spent:

After Relationship/Commitment Emotional Attachments/Affairs

Started age:

Ended age or last time:

Number of different people

Of those, how many were 1 time with same person Of those, how many were 2-6 times with same person

Of those, how many were over 6 times with same person

Types of Places/Locations (not names):

Anyone your partner knew

Ever in home, their/your vehicle etc. Protected or unprotected sex

Are you currently in contact with any Last time you were in contact with any How met them

Money spent:

Pre-Relationship Sexual Relationships Misrepresented/Not Disclosed

Started age:

Ended age or last time:

Number of different people

Things not involved (Answer yes or no)

None of our Children involved or know Friends or family members

No STD symptoms

Was never in love or fantasy of love No underage contact or fantasy No homosexual contact or fantasy No animal contact or fantasy

Secret devices, bank accounts

In order to pave the way for accountability moving forward, the wounding partner should disclose any devices they have kept hidden from the wounded partner as well as any hidden bank accounts.

If the wounding partner used other means to engage in infidelity-related behavior, they should include it. Just because the option doesn't appear in this document doesn't mean it should be left off. Remember, a lie by omission is still a lie. We would like to stress that the wounding partner should never leave something off the disclosure with the assumption that it isn't going to be a big deal. We guarantee that it will be a big deal. An example of this is when a wounding partner leaves pornography use off of their disclosure assuming it won't be a big deal in comparison to 3 sexual affairs that were previously disclosed. **All relevant information to addiction and infidelity-related behavior must be disclosed.** When it comes to relevancy, the wounded partner should be the one to decide what is relevant and what is not.

Admitting to Manipulation, Lying, and Gaslighting

To assure that the disclosure process is truly complete, the wounding partner will need to take full ownership for the unfair and painful ways they have tried to manipulate the situation so that their infidelity-related behavior would not be discovered or called into question. For many wounded partners, the lies told by the wounding partner are even more painful than the betrayal itself because it made them doubt their ability to read the situation correctly. This often leads to an erosion of confidence as well as a diminished capacity for trusting themselves.

These include:

- Outright lying
- Becoming defensive and angry when questioned
- Playing the victim and acting like the wounded partner had done the wrong thing by asking questions or being suspicious
- Acting hurt by the questions that were being asked
- Omitting crucial information and details about whereabouts and activities

- Acting like the wounded partner was crazy or was imagining things that were actually true
- Initiating fights or arguments to avoid having to talk about it
- Deleting browser histories, using separate devices, and the like to cover the wounding partner's tracks
- Blaming the relationship or the wounded partner for the wounding partner's distance from them and/or the family
- Blaming the wounded partner for the wounding partner's infidelity-related behavior
- Fault finding as a way to detract from the issues

In order to help the wounded partner heal, the wounding partner not only needs to own up to the above-listed behaviors, but will also need to commit to eliminating lying, blaming, shaming, rage, and manipulation from the relationship in the future. This is especially true of relationships complicated by the factor of intimacy avoidance. Trust cannot be rebuilt if these behaviors are not eliminated because they cause a lack of safety in the relationship.

God's word tells us how He feels about His child who is hard hearted and stubborn, not willing to humble themselves and confess their sins.

Psalm 32:8-9 NIV

I will instruct you and teach you the way you should go; I will counsel you with my loving eye on you. Do not be like the horse or the mule, which have no understanding but must be controlled by bit and bridle or they will not come to you.

But God gives the wounding partner a way out of their mess.

Proverbs 11:3 NIV

The integrity of the upright guides them, but the unfaithful are destroyed by their duplicity.

When a sin is wholly confessed, and the individual is truly repentant (defined as totally turning around and choosing to do the opposite of the practiced wicked behavior in every form, a total 180-degree change) then God will consider them upright and He will provide them with guidance and counsel.

1 Peter 3:12 NIV

For "Whoever would love life and see good days must keep their tongue from evil and their lips from deceitful speech they must turn from evil and do good; they must seek peace and pursue it. For the eyes of the Lord are on the righteous and his ears are attentive to their prayer, but the face of the Lord is against those who do evil."

When you turn from evil, do good and speak truth, God will consider you righteous! When you are righteous, He will give you peace, the pursuit of discipline to think and act according to God's statutes.

1 John 3:18 NIV

Dear children, let us not love with words or speech but with actions and in truth.

Pursuing peace requires you to think and to do what is right in His sight. And then God will hear and answer your prayer (1 Peter 3:12).

When the wounding partner is postured in this position, then they are qualified and capable of praying for the wounded partner in order to soften the impact of this deeply emotional blow.

The wounding partner needs to ask God for forgiveness for their transgressions and for breaking their covenant.

Ephesians 5:25-28 NIV

Husbands, love your wives, just as Christ loved the church and gave Himself up for her to make her holy, cleansing her by the washing with water through the word, and to present her to Himself as a radiant church, without stain or wrinkle or other blemish, but holy and blameless. In this same way, husbands ought to love their wives as their own bodies. He who loves his wife loves himself.

This is a suggested prayer for the wounding partner to pray *before* disclosure takes place:

Father, I have not loved my spouse as Christ loves the Church and gave Himself up for it. I have not made my wounded partner holy. I have not cleansed my partner by the washing of with the water of Your word; not in my thought life, not by example, not by protection from wickedness, not through keeping my body exclusively for my partner and not by praying for my partner. I have not kept my partner holy and blameless by preventing any stain or wrinkle from entering our covenant. I have not loved my partner or treated my wounded partner the way I expect to be loved and treated. Please forgive me and cleanse me of all unrighteousness.

Father, I pray for my wounded partner and for what they are about to hear in this disclosure. I ask that You give them Your supernatural grace to endure this tremendous hardship. Multiply Your comfort and peace to my wounded partner in this unbearable season they are about to enter. Be close to my wounded partner, heal their broken hearts and bind up their jagged wounds. Give my wounded partner grace to forgive me for splitting our Soul into two, violating my covenant with them and breaking their trust. I implore Your help for my wounded partner to arise victoriously from this evil battle that I selfishly enlisted them to fight. Do miracles on their behalf. I praise You because You are a God of miracles. In Jesus' name, Amen.

PART 5

Trust-Building Behavior #2

Polygraph

The second trust-building behavior is the wounding partner's willingness to take a polygraph examination. In our experience, the polygraph is a powerful instrument that can help pave the way to rebuilding trust in a relationship because it can provide a couple with a baseline of truth when there has been deception involved. Polygraphs are helpful to the wounded partner because they address the issue of ongoing lying on the part of the wounding partner. Unfortunately, due to the deception involved with betrayal of any kind, the wounded partner is often at a loss as to what to believe moving forward. Since the wounding partner has proven that their words cannot be trusted, the polygraph provides a powerful, objective tool by which the wounded partner can measure the wounding partner's statements and, hopefully, move forward toward reconciliation.

God keeps records and demands an account of both righteous and unrighteous actions.

Hebrews 4:13

Nothing in all creation is hidden from God's sight. Everything is uncovered and laid bare before the eyes of him to whom we must give account.

God's word also demands that we have accountability to one another and that can only happen as we live in truth and light.

1 John 1: 6-7 NIV

If we say we have fellowship with him while we walk in darkness, we lie and do not practice the truth. But if we walk in the light, as he is in the light, we have fellowship with one another, and the blood of Jesus his Son cleanses us from all sin.

This verse makes 3 points very clear.

> **Point 1** - To be restored into fellowship with God, we cannot continue to lie.
>
> **Point 2** - When we are truthful, we are imitating Jesus, because He is light, and we are walking in the light.
>
> **Point 3** - In order to have fellowship/relationship with one another, we must walk in light and tell the truth.

Truth is the prerequisite for restoration. For one to be forgiven for the debt they have incurred, they must be truthful. There is no other way to restore our relationship with God and there is no other way to restore our relationship with our wounded partner. We must tell the truth. Only then will we be forgiven and cleansed by the blood of Jesus and considered righteous.

Polygraph examinations can also be a useful therapeutic tool for the wounding partner because, when used on an ongoing basis, the examination can help deter relapse. We have talked with countless wounding partners that have told us that the polygraph helped keep them honest in the beginning stages of recovery in a way that neither we nor the wounding partner could. Infidelity-related behavior, especially when combined with addiction, is not an easy thing to overcome. Ongoing polygraph examinations can help with this because, sometimes, the fear of getting caught is the only thing that keeps certain people honest in the beginning. The polygraph can be the tool these people need to gain recovery until they develop the discipline and emotional capacity to deal with life in a way other than engaging in infidelity-related behavior. For ongoing accountability, our recommendation is that the wounding partner take a minimum of two polygraph examinations in the first year, two the second year, and one per year thereafter or until the couple decides polygraphs are no longer needed. Please be aware that we recommend that polygraphs be done at least once per year indefinitely when sex addiction and/or pornography addiction are present.

Luke 5:18-20 NIV

Four men arrived carrying a paralyzed man on a mat. They couldn't bring him to Jesus because of the crowd, so they dug a hole through the roof above his head. Then they lowered the man on his mat, right down in front of Jesus. Seeing their faith, Jesus said to the paralyzed man, "My child, your sins are forgiven."

This man was not only paralyzed physically, but he was also paralyzed in his mind, will and emotions. Jesus healed the paralyzed man based on *their* faith, the faith of his friends! The man didn't have the faith to be healed. But, his friends trusted in Jesus' willingness and ability to heal, and they did everything in their power to make him well again! They carried his dead weight up a rooftop, dug a hole in the roof and boldly lowered him right in front of Jesus!

Like the paralyzed man who was totally dependent upon his friends to transport him to the only person in the world who could heal him, we have brothers and sisters that need others to stand in faith for them and give them all the help and assistance they need to overcome their addiction.

With a team of people who trusted Jesus, and with tools to hoist the man and tear off a portion of roof, and pulleys to lower him down to where he can get the help he so desperately needed, this paralyzed man was made whole. This is a lesson we can all learn.

Infidelity is traumatizing and the effect on both the wounding partner and the wounded partner is paralysis, the inability to function and think linearly and logically because their souls have been split apart and inundated with a flood of visceral emotions.

The wounding partner doesn't have the ability to overcome this addiction by themselves. In a very real sense they are paralyzed, disabled, unable to function and reason rationally. Polygraphs are a modern-day tool, similar to the tools used by the friends of the paralyzed man, that provide the wounding partner access to expertise that can bring deliverance from their involvement with darkness and transfer them into the Kingdom of Light.

The wounded partner doesn't have the ability to overcome this adversity by themselves. They have been run over by an emotional freight train and they are also in dire need of support.

John 16:13 NIV

But when he, the Spirit of truth, comes, he will guide you into all the truth. He will not speak on his own; he will speak only what he hears, and he will tell you what is yet to come.

Polygraphs provide honest answers for the wounded partner. With knowledge of the truth, comes enlightenment and guidance. As painful as truth can be, it will produce freedom for both the wounding partner and the wounded partner.

John 8:32 NIV

Then you will know the truth, and the truth will set you free.

It is important to note that we always consider the use of polygraph examinations to be at the discretion of the client. That being said, we highly recommend them for couples struggling to rebuild trust because lying is such a difficult thing to detect. Although we consider ourselves competent in the areas of infidelity, addiction, and intimacy avoidance, we can never be 100% sure whether someone is lying or not. We have had discussions with many of our colleagues around this, and they feel the same way. Even though polygraphs have their limitations, they are still valuable as a therapeutic tool to address honesty in the disclosure process and ongoing accountability for the wounding partner. Additionally, sometimes even the mention of a polygraph can serve as a tool to help wounding partners get honest and/or help the wounded partner gauge the willingness for their partner to do whatever it takes to help rebuild trust.

Galatians 6:1-2 NIV

Brothers and sisters, if someone is caught in a sin, you who live by the Spirit should restore that person gently. But watch yourselves, or you also may be tempted. Carry each other's burdens, and in this way you will fulfill the law of Christ.

God is all about restoration. He wants us to lift up the weaker party and put them back on their feet again! Jesus restored people everywhere he went, and He expects us to follow His lead. Polygraphs are a great tool to help the weak to become strong. Jesus always makes a way of escape for us.

1 Corinthians 10:13 NIV

No temptation has overtaken you except what is common to mankind. And God is faithful; he will not let you be tempted beyond what you can bear. But when you are tempted, he will also provide a way out so that you can endure it.

A common question that we get asked by the wounding partner is, "If I don't remember everything, will it show that I am lying?" It is important to remember that a polygraph doesn't test memory. It only tests whether or not the wounding partner is being deceptive about not remembering. If the wounding partner truly doesn't remember certain things because their memory is fuzzy from the passage of time, addiction, or substance use, the polygraph will not typically show deception.

We want to stress that the polygraph should never be used by the wounded partner as a means of punishment for the wounding partner's actions. Polygraph examinations are most useful in rebuilding trust when both partners agree to use them for the good of the relationship. It is important to note that polygraphs, especially the initial one, can be extremely anxiety provoking for the wounding partner. Therefore, it is important that they engage in the polygraph process willingly for the benefit of the relationship. It is also important to note that polygraphs are not a replacement for empathy and compassion on the wounding partner's part. Although polygraph examinations are a useful tool in helping a couple rebuild trust after betrayal, they are not the most important. Empathy, compassion, a lack of defensiveness, expressions of remorse, and a willingness to be self-reflective are all critical if the relationship is to be restored. If the wounding partner goes into the polygraph process kicking and screaming and continues to be angry that they had to take one, the polygraph loses a lot of its benefit. This is because, even if they pass the test, the wounding partner's attitude is direct evidence that they are still primarily concerned with their feelings and comfort, instead of with their partner's. Conversely, if the wounded partner refuses to accept the results of the polygraph as valid, the test loses its value as well. We have seen this a handful of times with clients that choose to believe their own version of the truth instead of being open to the fact that what they believe may be based more in emotion than in fact.

Hebrews 13:17 NIV

Have confidence in your leaders and submit to their authority, because they keep watch over you as those who must give an account. Do this so that their work will be a joy, not a burden, for that would be of no benefit to you.

Ephesians 4:29 NIV

Do not let any unwholesome talk come out of your mouths, but only what is helpful for building others up according to their needs, that it may benefit those who listen.

Wounding partner—do not allow lies and false stories to come out of your mouth but tell the truth in love so you can begin to build up the wounded partner and meet their needs. This is not only beneficial to yourself and to your partner, it is also beneficial to your counselors or coaches, so they are empowered to give the greatest amount of help possible to everyone.

The polygraph examination itself consists of three parts: the pre-test, the polygraph examination, and the interpretation of the results. The cost varies between polygraph examiners but usually ranges between $300 to $700. Currently, most polygraph examiners use computerized polygraph instruments, although there are a few out there that may still use the old fashioned analog devices. The computerized polygraph systems can score tests better and more consistently than humans and are, therefore, considered to be superior to analog instruments. When conducted properly, the American Polygraph Association (APA) states that polygraph tests are approximately 90% accurate, although critics claim this percentage is more like 75%. (Iacono, Ben-Shakar, 2019) There is also a new credibility assessment tool called EyeDetect that has been used in the market since 2013. It uses an infrared camera to measure pupil dilation, blink rate, and other eye movements. This system is automated, fast, and gives results (after a 30-minute test) in about 5 minutes. (Converus website) The makers of EyeDetect claim that it can provide up to 90% accuracy, although the APA states that the accuracy is approximately 83%. For therapeutic purposes, we prefer to use live polygraph examiners because we feel that the human touch gives better overall results in the case of fidelity testing.

Most people experience at least some stress and discomfort when lying. The amygdala, which is part of the limbic system and responsible for processing strong emotions, picks up on the fear associated with lying and with getting caught. Once it senses stress, the amygdala sends a distress signal to the hypothalamus. The hypothalamus then activates the sympathetic nervous system by sending signals through the autonomic nerves to other parts of the body. (Harvard Health, 2020) The autonomic nervous system controls involuntary actions such as heart rate, blood pressure, and pupil dilation. The polygraph was designed to detect some of these physiological changes that happen when a person is lying.

The pre-test is the longest portion of the polygraph examination. Although all polygraph examiners use their own method when conducting the pre-test, most will get at least some background information on the wounding partner. Typically, the polygraph examiner asks the wounding partner if and how they prepared for the test (to check for knowledge of countermeasures) and gets a history of addiction and/or infidelity-related behavior. They also go over terminology used in the questions in order to make sure the wounding partner is comfortable with how they are phrased and/or understands the questions' meanings. It is also not uncommon for the polygraph examiner to have a conversation with the wounded partner in order to understand what they are most concerned with knowing or what they are particularly nervous about.

After the pre-test, the examiner places sensors on the wounding partner's fingers, arm, chest, and abdomen in order to measure physiological changes in blood pressure, pulse, and rate of perspiration. Some polygraph examiners will also use sensor pads that they place on the floor. These are used to measure movement in the feet and legs, which can also be associated with lying. Once the equipment has been set up and the sensors put in place, the polygraph examiner will then ask the wounding partner a series of control questions. The testing period will also include questions that the subject will be asked to answer with a false statement in order to gauge how their body reacts when they are lying. Once the control questions have been asked, the polygraph examiner will then ask the questions relevant to the test. The number of questions asked should be no more than four. Asking more than four questions typically decreases the accuracy of a polygraph, according to the APA.

It is highly recommended that you work with a trained professional who understands the therapeutic polygraph process when you are trying to decide which questions should be asked. When we work with couples, we help them draft four relevant questions that adhere to the following guidelines:

- **Time Bound**: When polygraph questions are time bound, they leave far less room for error. An example of a time- bound question is, "Since August 2, 2012, have you engaged in a sex act outside of your marriage?"

- **Yes or No**: Polygraph questions should be designed in such a way that they can be answered with yes or no. Asking questions that require any other type of answer will turn up an inconclusive result.

- **Behaviorally Focused**: Questions around motives and/or emotions are not appropriate for a polygraph. For example, the answer to a question like, "Do you love me?" will likely turn up an inconclusive result. A question like the example above is more appropriate for a polygraph because it focuses on a specific behavior—in this case a "sex act".

We understand that the wounded partner will likely have a lot more than four questions that they need answers to. However, the polygraph examination is not the time to get those answers. When we work with couples, we encourage the wounded partner to prepare questions that they want answered ahead of time. The wounding partner then answers these questions during the disclosure process, and the polygraph is then used to verify whether or not the wounding partner told the truth during the disclosure.

Once the polygraph examination has been completed, the examiner will typically inform the subject as to whether they passed or failed. If one or more of the wounding partner's answers show deception, the polygraph examiner will inform the subject of the issue(s) and dig deeper into why a particular answer might have been deceptive. If the wounding partner gives the polygraph examiner new information to help explain discrepancies, the polygraph examiner will then conduct a confirmation test in order to determine whether or not the new information supplied by the wounding partner explains, in full, the deception. If working directly with our office, the polygraph examiner will then discuss the results with us as well as with the wounded partner. For this to happen, the wounding partner will need to sign a release of information prior to the commencement of the polygraph examination. The polygraph examiner will require the wounding partner to sign other types of paperwork as well.

At Becoming Well, we work closely with the American Polygraph Association to vet any and all polygraph examiners that we send our clients to. In addition, we perform an interview with potential partners in order to determine if they are a good fit for the therapeutic polygraph process. Part of what we are looking for is an examiner who understands the difference between therapeutic polygraphs and criminal ones. Criminal polygraphs are designed to catch those who have committed criminal acts and often involve a stressful atmosphere in which the subject doesn't know which questions they are going to be asked. In the therapeutic polygraph process, wounding partners are fully aware of what questions they are going to be asked ahead of time. If the couple is working directly with us, these questions will have been decided on in a process that includes the couple and ourselves. We find that polygraph examiners that have a gruff exterior and/or act like everyone is guilty until proven innocent add unnecessary stress to the process, and we tend to weed them out. We also ask questions to determine if the potential examiner understands the polygraph guidelines and laws in their state as well as if they run a 2-chart minimum. We currently work with verified polygraph examiners in major cities all over the U.S.

When we work with couples who are considering polygraph examinations as a way to start to rebuild trust, the most common objection we hear is that couples don't want to base their relationship on the results of a polygraph. Our answer to this is that no one should ever base their relationship on the results of a polygraph. Other behaviors such as a willingness to be accountable, empathy, and compassion are even more important than taking a polygraph. Without these, the wounding partner passing a polygraph test will do very little to aid in the rebuilding of trust. As we stated earlier in this section, polygraph examinations are always used at the discretion of the client. The choice of whether or not to use one in your recovery journey is a highly personal one that can only be made by you. That being said, we feel that an unwillingness to take one on the wounding partner's part, especially if the wounded partner has requested it, is quite telling. Although it doesn't necessarily indicate that they are still lying (although in many cases it does), it shows a lack of willingness to do whatever it takes to mend the relationship.

Suggested prayer for the wounding partner before taking the polygraph:

Father, I have been caught in my sin. I want to restore fellowship with You. I no longer want to walk in darkness, but I want to practice truth. Help me to speak the truth in love. I want to walk in the kingdom of light and have fellowship with Your Son, Jesus, with my wounded partner, and with my counselors or coaches. Thank You for cleansing me from all of my sins.

Father, I ask that the Spirit of Truth guide me and my wounded partner into all truth. I know that if I obey Him, He will tell us what we need to do. Thank You for our counselors, for their advice, care and their expertise they so selflessly share with us so we can dig out of this unholy mess and serve You with all of our being. In Jesus' name, Amen.

PART 6

Trust-Building Behavior #3

Expressing Remorse

The third trust-building behavior is the wounding partner's ability to express remorse for what they have done. The words "I'm sorry" are a good start but do very little to help the wounded partner if they are not accompanied by action. In their book *The 5 Apology Languages: The Secret to Healthy Relationships*, authors Gary Chapman and Jennifer Thomas define the 5 apology languages as:

- Expressing regret (saying I'm sorry)
- Accepting responsibility
- Making restitution
- Genuinely repenting (changing behavior)
- Requesting forgiveness

When we work with couples, we work with the wounding partner to help them understand the apology language of the wounded partner. This is because apologies mean very little when the person apologizing is not speaking the language of the person being apologized to. Although every person has their preference as to the way they like to receive an apology, in the case of betrayal, we find that the wounding partner's apology needs to encompass all 5 of the apology languages plus statements that indicate self-reflection as well as the expression of empathy for the wounded partner.

First of all, God sees every act of unfaithfulness as a transgression against Himself. He makes it clear in His word that apology and restitution are key to compensating for the betrayal of the covenant made between Him and you and your partner in order to restore trust back to its original status before the transgression occurred.

Numbers 5:6-7 NIV

6 "Say to the Israelites: 'Any man or woman who wrongs another in any way[a] and so is unfaithful to the Lord is guilty

7 and must confess the sin they have committed. They must make full restitution for the wrong they have done, add a fifth of the value to it and give it all to the person they have wronged.

So what do we mean by remorse? We define remorse as a strong feeling of regret, grief, or sadness when contemplating one's past actions that compels one to admit to their guilt and to change behavior moving forward. The fact that true remorse involves action separates it from the feelings of guilt and shame. It is particularly important to point out that the self-pity that often accompanies guilt and shame are usually not received well by the wounded partner and do nothing to heal the relationship. This is because self-pity keeps the focus on the wounding partner instead of on the wounded partner and comes off as self-serving and defensive.

Matthew 27:3-5 NIV

3 When Judas, who had betrayed him, saw that Jesus was condemned, he was seized with remorse and returned the thirty pieces of silver to the chief priests and the elders. 4 "I have sinned," he said, "for I have betrayed innocent blood." "What is that to us?" they replied. "That's your responsibility." 5 So Judas threw the money into the temple and left. Then he went away and hanged himself.

Here, the verse states that Judas was seized with remorse. However, if you look at Judas' actions, they don't indicate true remorse. In the Greek, the closer meaning is "having regretted it". Regret is different than remorse because it is mainly focused on personal loss or missed opportunities. Remorse, on the other hand, is focused on the harm one's actions have caused to others. In this case, Judas' regret likely led to self-contempt, which then led to self-harm.

Judas could have run to the Roman governors and turned himself in. He could have exposed the liaison made between him and the priests and elders and dismantled an entire system of corruption. Instead, he focused on his own feelings of guilt and shame and decided how he needed to cleanse himself of his wrongdoing. So, returning the thirty pieces of silver in his mind was restitution of his position as Jesus' friend before his act of betrayal. But his focus was on his own guilt. True remorse would have produced actions that restored Jesus' position of innocence and allowed him to continue to live His life.

Remorse, as opposed to guilt and shame, requires action in order to communicate it. Here is a formula that the wounding partner can use for expressing remorse:

1. Start off with an apology, stating the specific action(s) that you are apologizing for (expressing regret)

2. Express understanding for at least some of the attitudes that led to these actions (expressing self-reflection, accepting responsibility)

3. Express understanding for how your actions have affected your partner (expressing empathy, taking responsibility)

4. Ask your partner for forgiveness (requesting forgiveness)

5. Explain that you understand why it is important that you change your behavior moving forward (expressing self-reflection, taking responsibility)

6. Ask your partner what you can do to show them that you are truly sorry (making restitution)

7. Do what your partner asks you (expressing genuine repentance, taking responsibility)

8. Commit to making changes (accepting responsibility)

9. Follow through with your commitment to change (expressing genuine repentance)

A true expression of remorse requires that the wounding partner take 100% responsibility for their infidelity-related behavior without asking the wounded partner to accept any of the responsibility for it. As demonstrated in the formula above, it also requires that the wounding partner express at least some understanding of the mindset, attitudes, and entitlement that led to the infidelity-related behavior. As the wounding partner's recovery deepens, deeper awareness will develop over time. It is important to note that the presence of addiction will often hamper the wounding partner's ability to conduct the self-evaluation necessary to express true remorse, which can make the overall process slower. This is because, in order to engage in actions associated with addiction, the wounding partner had to justify those actions in their own mind first. This led to several layers of denial that will need to be addressed if true recovery is to take place. A lack of remorse often indicates the emotional immaturity that typically accompanies addiction. When an addict uses substances, sex, pornography, etc. to deal with their emotions, this stunts emotional growth. This lack of emotional maturity can make it difficult for them to see things from another person's point of view. A lack of remorse is also common in situations where the infidelity-related behavior was not disclosed by the wounding partner but was, instead, discovered by the wounded partner. This is because the wounding partner may not have been ready or willing to own up to their bad behavior prior to getting caught.

Genesis 4:2-12 NIV

Now Abel kept flocks, and Cain worked the soil. 3 In the course of time Cain brought some of the fruits of the soil as an offering to the Lord. 4 And Abel also brought an offering—fat portions from some of the firstborn of his flock. The Lord looked with favor on Abel and his offering, 5 but on Cain and his offering he did not look with favor. So, Cain was very angry, and his face was downcast. 6 Then the Lord said to Cain, "Why are you angry? Why is your face downcast? 7 If you do what is right, will you not be accepted? But if you do not do what is right, sin is crouching at your door; it desires to have you, but you must rule over it." 8 Now Cain said to his brother Abel, "Let's go out to the field."[d] While they were in the field, Cain attacked his brother Abel and killed him. 9 Then the Lord said to Cain, "Where is your brother Abel?" "" I don't know," he replied. "Am I my brother's keeper?" 10 The Lord said, "What have you done? Listen! Your brother's blood cries out to me from the ground. 11 Now you are under a curse and driven from the ground, which opened its mouth to receive your brother's blood from your hand. 12 When you work the ground, it will no longer yield its crops for you. You will be a restless wanderer on the earth."

God caught Cain meditating about betraying his brother Abel and reasoned with him as he contemplated doing harm because of his jealousy. In fact, God gave Cain directions on how to gain His favor and warned him of the danger that lay ahead. However, showing no true remorse, Cain ignored his instructions, murdered his brother and hid his transgression. Again, presenting Cain with another opportunity to disclose his criminal act, He asked Cain about his brother's wellbeing. Cain's response was hostile, defensive and disrespectful! Finally, God called Cain out because he was not willing to own up to his behavior and the consequences were dire. God is long suffering, but He requires absolute true repentance and remorse.

If either of these scenarios describes your situation, it is important that you work with a trained coach or counselor that can help the wounding partner work on developing empathy in order to gain a new perspective.

We are all aware of how Peter betrayed Jesus. Let's deconstruct this event.

Matthew 26:33 NIV 33 Peter replied, "Even if all fall away on account of you, I never will."

Peter had bragged that he loved the Lord more than the rest of the disciples, and then… Peter denied Jesus three times (Luke 22:55–62; Matthew 26:69–75; Mark 14:66–72).

This conversation in Matthew 26 is the baseline from which Jesus addressed Peter's mindset, his attitude and his position of entitlement that led to his betrayal. He claimed that he loved Jesus' more than any other person on the earth. In fact, he announced that he would never deny Him under any circumstance. Peter was filled with self-importance, inflated his character and considered himself as better than anyone else.

John 21:15-25

When they had finished eating, Jesus said to Simon Peter, "Simon son of John, do you love me more than these?" "Yes, Lord," he said, "you know that I love you." Jesus said, "Feed my lambs." 16 Again Jesus said, "Simon son of John, do you love me?" He answered, "Yes, Lord, you know that I love you." Jesus said, "Take care of my sheep." 17 The third time he said to him, "Simon son of John, do you love me?" Peter was hurt because Jesus asked him the third time, "Do you love me?" He said, "Lord, you know all things; you know that I love you." Jesus said, "Feed my sheep. 18 Very truly I tell you, when you were younger you dressed yourself and went where you wanted; but when you are old you will stretch out your hands, and someone else will dress you and lead you where you do not want to go." 19 Jesus said this to indicate the kind of death by which Peter would glorify God. Then he said to him, "Follow me!"-

At this point, Peter didn't argue with Jesus about backing him against a wall or that he had to save himself and the disciples in case something happened to Jesus or that he panicked so of course he kept himself at a distance. No. There was no argument. Peter accepted responsibility for his own actions.

Jesus outlines Peter's future before him. Peter's self-importance will be a lifelong lesson in humility as Jesus explains all the levels of responsibilities that will be required of him. He will feed lambs (new converts), tend sheep (mature Christians) and feed sheep (Christian leaders). He also addressed his inflated character by informing him of the levels of emotional growth he will eventually achieve. Peter will grow from phileo love (deep affection) to agape love (selfless love that will do anything for another). When he is fully grown in his love walk, Peter will not consider himself better than his peers, and will love (agape) Jesus so much that he will be martyred for His sake. Jesus outlined the payment of Peter's compensation for his betrayal by his future actions. History confirms that what Jesus prophesied about Peter came to pass. Peter's life proved that he continually made full restitution of his betrayal culminating in the offering of his own life.

2 Corinthians 7:10 NIV
Godly sorrow brings repentance that leads to salvation and leaves no regret, but worldly sorrow brings death.

If the wounded partner does not see improvement in the expression of remorse as time passes, this should be considered a red flag. When we work with couples, we advise that the wounded partner give the wounding partner a window of time in order to observe their behavior for signs of remorse if they do not see it up front. Of course, the length of the window is a personal decision that a wounded partner must make for themselves. However, our recommendation is about six months. Here are some of the positive changes a wounded partner should see in a wounding partner that is remorseful for their actions:

- A willingness to earn trust slowly
- Increased awareness of motives and attitudes that drove the infidelity-related behavior
- A willingness to accommodate requests from the wounded partner regarding accountability and actions
- A willingness to embrace the consequences of their actions
- An attitude of humility
- An attitude of patience toward the wounded partner when they are expressing their feelings and/or asking questions

The development of discipline/self-control Conversely, here are some of the attitudes of a wounding partner that wounded partners should consider to be red flags:

- Displays of anger and resentment when actions are called into question
- Defensiveness in the form of stonewalling, blame, or excuses
- Displays of entitlement, such as complaining about the consequences of their actions or demanding forgiveness
- Displays of self-pity, such as moping or the silent treatment
- Deflecting the need to be accountable by acting like they are the victim or wallowing in self-pity
- Making excuses for their behavior, blaming the wounded partner, or blaming other people

As stated previously, many of these behaviors may be present when the wounding partner is caught in their infidelity-related behavior and/or addiction is present. However, if the wounding partner is serious about saving the relationship, these should dissipate within the six-month window of recommended time. If a wounding partner is truly interested in reconciliation, they will need to accept the consequences of their actions without blaming the wounded partner or demanding that they "just get over it" and trust them. Trust has to be earned. Demanding trust comes from a place of dishonesty and deception. It indicates that the wounding partner is still in denial of how much their actions have hurt their partner and has, therefore, deceived themselves. This self-deception is indicative of an attitude of entitlement and, often, of active addiction and/or narcissistic attitudes. Entitlement, defensiveness, and a lack of remorse do not support reconciliation.

Trust-Building Behavior #4: Answering Repeated Questions with Empathy

The fourth trust-building behavior is a willingness on the wounding partner's part to answer the wounded partner's repeated questions with patience, empathy, and compassion. When the wounded partner finds out about the wounding partner's infidelity-related behavior, life shatters into a million pieces. Everything they have built their life on up to this point feels like a lie and they are left scrambling to put the pieces back together in a way that makes sense to them. The problem is that making sense of the wounding partner's behavior takes time and some aspects of what happened never end up making sense at all. Repeated questioning is the process by which a wounded partner begins to piece their life back together. For the most part, the urge to find out more and more information is driven by the wounded partner's desire to heal. The problem is that, as much as repeated questioning is a normal and necessary part of the rebuilding trust process, it can lead to anger and exasperation on the wounding partner's part for several reasons:

- It reminds them of what they have done. Many times the wounding partner feels a great deal of shame and regret for their infidelity-related behavior. Questioning by the wounded partner provides a constant, unpleasant reminder of how they have failed.

A wounding partner who responds in anger to their partner's questions is usually struggling with shame.

- They want to escape accountability. This one, like the first one, is often driven by shame. It can also be driven by feelings of entitlement. In order to escape feelings of shame that might be brought on by accountability, the wounding partner chooses to deflect these feelings by acting angry or exasperated. If entitled, the wounding partner may resent facing the consequences of their actions.

- They don't want to self-reflect. Some wounding partners get very comfortable in their denial because it keeps them from acknowledging how they have hurt someone they love and, as a result, feeling bad. An angry response can be used as a smokescreen in order to avoid self-reflection.

- They have resentments. It is not uncommon for wounding partners to build up resentments against the wounded partner for real or perceived wrongdoing. If this is the case, the wounding partner will need to engage in coaching or counseling with a trained professional in order to work through their feelings.

- They are still engaged in infidelity-related behavior. Angry responses don't always signify guilt but, when accompanied by other behaviors, they can indicate ongoing behavior that the wounding partner feels guilty about.

- Their answers make no difference. Unfortunately, sometimes wounded partners ask questions and then don't accept the answers. This is understandable when the wounding partner is stonewalling or trying to avoid accountability. However, when the wounding partner is honestly trying to answer questions to the best of their ability, an unwillingness to listen on the wounded partner's part can be extremely frustrating and discouraging.

Ephesians 4:2-3 NIV

2 Be completely humble and gentle; be patient, bearing with one another in love. 3 Make every effort to keep the unity of the Spirit through the bond of peace.

Patience is also a fruit of the Spirit. It is limitless and cannot be overdosed on.

Galatians 5:22-23 NIV

22 But the fruit of the Spirit is love, joy, peace, forbearance (patience), kindness, goodness, faithfulness, 23 gentleness and self-control. Against such things there is no law.

Patience proves that you are a child of God.

Colossians 3:12

"Therefore, as God's chosen people, holy and dearly loved, clothe yourselves with compassion, kindness, humility, gentleness and patience."

Patience is a sign of self-discipline and great understanding.

Proverbs 14:29

"Whoever is slow to anger has great understanding, but he who has a hasty temper exalts folly."

Prayer for wounding partner:

Father, unfaithfulness is an act of betrayal against You and against my wounded partner. Help me not to wallow in self-pity or defend myself and deepen the wounds I have already inflicted. I apologize to You and to my wounded partner. As a demonstration of my deep remorse, I give You the rest of my life so that I may live in a way that makes full compensation for the betrayal I have committed against You and my wounded partner. Give me the grace to show empathy and be patient with my partner and do all I can to bring comfort and relief. I ask you to heal my wounded partner and help me to assist You in the healing process. In Jesus' name, Amen.

PART 7

Asking Questions

While on the subject of answering repeated questions with empathy, we want to take a moment to address the wounded partner's need to ask questions. When there has been betrayal of any type in a relationship, the questions that need answers are many. Regardless of type, questions center around who the behavior was with (in the case of emotional and sexual affairs), how and when the infidelity-related behavior began, details surrounding the behavior, if the behavior has ended or is ongoing, what the wounding partner is willing to do to make sure it doesn't happen again, and the "why" questions. Let's take a closer look at the 6 categories of questions we just described:

1. Who Was it With?

It is only natural for the wounded partner to want to want to know who their partner has been unfaithful with in the case of either sexual or emotional infidelity. However, we urge the wounded partner to use caution here. Asking questions pertaining to "who" are only useful when it comes to what has happened within the wounded partner's circle of safety. Asking these questions about someone they don't know can cause more harm than good. The reason for this is that asking questions about someone not known to the wounded partner often causes natural curiosity to kick in. We have seen partners get stuck for months looking up pictures of people they don't know. This often leads to unfair comparisons and using their energy to beat themselves up about perceived shortcomings compared to the other person(s). Additionally, partners often waste precious emotional energy seeking after information about total strangers that would be better spent on themselves and/or on their relationship. Finding out what an affair partner looks like, what their hobbies are, etc., while tempting, is unproductive. We recommend that the wounded partner ask themselves what they can possibly know about this person that would make any difference to the situation with their partner.

A better question for the wounded partner to ask the wounding partner up front would be, "Do I know this person?" If the answer is yes, then we recommend following up with a question around who the person is. Knowing who the person is makes a lot more sense if it has been established that the wounded partner knows them first. It is important for the wounded partner to understand if they know those involved because people within the circle of safety present a more complex issue for them. This is because more than one betrayal has taken place: betrayal from their partner as well as betrayal from someone close to them. Additionally, a lack of knowledge as to who this person is can cause a situation in which the wounded partner inadvertently has ongoing contact with someone who has had an inappropriate relationship with their partner. This can be an extremely unsafe and violating experience.

2. How and When Did It Begin?

In order to begin to comprehend what has happened, it is important that the wounded partner understand the circumstances surrounding their partner's infidelity-related behavior. The answers can vary depending on the nature of the infidelity. Typically, infidelity through pornography or betrayal through intimacy avoidance is something that wounding partners carried into the relationship themselves. In our experience, most of these behaviors started long before the wounded partner ever entered the picture.

Here are some examples of appropriate questions to ask:

- When did the infidelity-related behavior start?
- How did the behavior start?
- Who initiated it? (if an affair)
- How long have you been viewing pornography and/or sexually stimulating images?
- How did you start viewing pornography and/or sexually stimulating images?
- How long have you been masturbating to pornography and/or sexually stimulating images?
- How long have you been aware that you've been withholding love from me?
- Were you aware that you had an issue with this prior to our relationship beginning?
- How long have you been gaslighting me? Were you aware that you were doing it?

These are only some examples of the many questions that could be asked in this category. We recommend that the wounded partner write any questions pertaining to "how and when" down and then wait at least 24 hours before asking them.

These examples give an idea of the formula of how sin begins.

2 Samuel 11:1 NIV

In the spring, at the time when kings go off to war, David sent Joab out with the king's men and the whole Israelite army. They destroyed the Ammonites and besieged Rabbah. But David remained in Jerusalem.

1). David was in a place he wasn't supposed to be.

2). David was not performing his kingly responsibilities.

3). David did not surround himself with the men given to him to complete his God given assignment.

That's how every wounding partner becomes a wounding partner! They were in a place they weren't supposed to be, not performing their duties for those individuals they are responsible for and not surrounding themselves with the people that were designated to help them complete their God given assignment.

When did it begin? It always begins with entertaining an evil thought…

2 Samuel 11:2-4 NIV

2 One evening David got up from his bed and walked around on the roof of the palace. From the roof he saw a woman bathing. The woman was very beautiful, 3 and David sent someone to find out about her. The man said, "She is Bathsheba, the daughter of Eliam and the wife of Uriah the Hittite." 4 Then David sent messengers to get her. She came to him, and he slept with her.

David thought it was a good idea not to perform his kingly duties. His condition was one of restlessness during the evening hours. It happened to be spring, so the weather was conducive to walking around outdoors on his rooftop terrace.

1) State of mind: It began when David got out of his bed and his mental state was one of restlessness due to HALT- Hungry, angry, lonely and/or tired. I will add guilt to this mind frame since it is possible, he may have regretted not leading his men into battle.

2) Positioning: David was enjoying mild weather (v 1. springtime) and perched himself on his rooftop where he had visibility to all that was going on around him. Again, a juxtaposition of a leader leading his troops to battle by scoping the land. Let's put this in a present-day allegory: being perched in a dark isolated corner, seated in a comfortable chair and browsing on the computer.

3) Observation: David SAW or perceived a woman bathing. His mind processed that the figure was that of a woman and that she was bathing. It's the same word used describing Eve when she saw the fruit of the tree in Genesis 3:6.

Genesis 3:6 NIV.

6 When the woman saw that the fruit of the tree was good for food and pleasing to the eye, and also desirable for gaining wisdom…

4) Identify: Once David's mind processed that he was looking at a woman, he intensely studied her form and determined that she was extraordinarily beautiful. Being in a HALT frame of mind, he allowed his thoughts to run wild over this moonlight scenario. As a warrior king whose mind was on besieging his enemies, his battle mentality switched over to besieging a naked woman bathing on a rooftop.

5) Gathering Info: In battle, David would scope out the land, pinpoint his enemies and get inside information about them. Bathsheba was his prey, and he sent his spies to get intel about her. He found out her name and who she belonged to.

6) Capture: He sent messengers to bring her to his palace.

7) Intimidate: She entered his space with interpretation and fear, he was her superior. 'She came to him' in the Hebrew is defined as enumeration, in other words she made a list of reasons why what he demanded of her was not ok. He did not concede to her reasoning, and she feared that harm could come to her or her loved ones if she did not submit. Both her husband and her father were soldiers in David's army.

8) Conquer: Then he slept with her, meaning he took possession of someone of great worth, made in the image of God and degraded her status into an item to use for his own pleasure. He dominated what did not belong to him and conquered her.

God gives everyone a way out of trouble! We are required to be good stewards of the responsibilities assigned to us in this life. We are assigned to people connected with us to fulfill our destiny. All our daily steps are planned and ordered by the Lord (Psalm 37:23). When something or someone appears that detours our steps outside of our God given mission, our conscience will warn us that there is a trap ahead. It is our duty to be circumspect and avoid it. If we take these first steps, then no one would ever be in a position to cause harm or wound another.

3. Details of the Infidelity-Related Behavior

This category can be tricky. The wounded partner will want to keep in mind that, while it is important to understand the basic outline of the infidelity-related behavior, too many details will create unnecessary triggers that they don't need.

Examples of good questions to ask are:

- How often did you meet this person?
- How often did you have sex?
- Was protection used?
- How often are you viewingpornography/sexually stimulating images and masturbating?
- Why do you feel that it's acceptable to withhold from me?
- Did it ever occur to you that I was suffering from your withholding?
- Did you ever reveal details about me or our family?
- Where are you accessing pornography and/or sexually stimulating images?
- Where did you find people to have an affair with?
- How much money have you spent on these activities?

- How much time do you spend on this weekly?
- Are you keeping any mementos?
- How did you contact this person/these people?

The list of questions in this category is endless. It is important for the wounded partner to realize that they will never likely understand everything about the wounding partner's activities. The goal is for them to understand enough of the basic idea of what went on to make informed decisions regarding the future.

We would also like to give you an idea of the types of questions that are what we refer to as "Danger Zone" questions. These questions, when asked and answered, can re-traumatize an already-wounded partner as well as lead to an increase in intrusive thoughts and triggers.

- Questions pertaining to specific sex acts, positions, etc.
- Questions pertaining to certain locations that might create a trigger for the wounded partner later on (i.e. specific hotels, cities, etc.)
- Questions regarding details such as hair color, body part sizes, etc.
- Questions pertaining to "dirty talk"
- Questions about lingerie, sex toys, etc.
- Questions pertaining to whether they preferred the affair partner's sexual performance to yours
- Questions like, "What do they have that I don't have?"

It is important for the wounded partner to remember that this is not about them. This is about the wounding partner and their poor choices. The wounded partner did nothing to deserve this. Asking questions that might lead them to feel bad about themselves or blame themselves somehow won't help. The wounding partner could have chosen other ways to behave and, instead, chose to act unfaithfully. It is important that the wounded partner put the blame where it belongs.

When hard information needs to be disclosed, the Bible gives us an excellent example of how much to divulge. Wounded partner, ask the Lord to reveal to you the information that you need to know. Wounding partner, ask the Lord how to give this information in the kindest way possible. It is important that you give your partner information kindly, but not use your "kindness" as an excuse to withhold information from them.

Matthew 36:31-32 NIV

31 Then Jesus told them, "This very night you will all fall away on account of me, for it is written: "'I will strike the shepherd, and the sheep of the flock will be scattered. 32 But after I have risen, I will go ahead of you into Galilee."

Jesus fed the disciples some very hard information about what was going to happen, and what will happen after his death so they can meet again. He told them exactly what they needed to know so they wouldn't misunderstand what needed to be done when the time came.

Wounded partner, when you feel that the information that you are about to hear is more than you can bear, don't ask. Jesus knew how much information the disciples could accept and withheld the rest because it would damage them. The Holy Spirit understands how much hard information you can absorb. He will reveal to you what needs to be known and He will do it in a way that won't be totally devastating.

John 16:12-13 NIV

12 "I have much more to say to you, more than you can now bear. 13 But when he, the Spirit of truth, comes, he will guide you into all the truth.

4. Is the Behavior Ongoing?

In the work we do, we have found that whether the wounding partner is willing to end the infidelity-related behavior is the number one determining factor as to whether a couple will reconcile or not. Relationships fail when the wounding partner isn't able or willing to change their ways

In our experience, most wounded partners want to know if there is any infidelity-related behavior that is ongoing. Here are some helpful questions to ask:

- Has the affair ended? If so, when did it end? Who ended it?
- Are you still in contact with the infidelity partner? If so, how do you communicate?
- Do you love this person?
- Do you still look at pornography and/or sexually stimulating images? When was the last time you looked at pornography/sexually stimulating images?
- Do you intend to end the infidelity-related behavior?
- If you haven't ended the behavior, why not?

These are just a few of the questions that the wounded partner might have regarding the wounding partner's intentions and activity.

God's viewpoint concerning the wounding partner is for them to take sin seriously before it completely destroys them, the wounded partner, the children and all associated with the wounding partner. The devil has a "scorched earth policy" and it is his desire for the wounding partner to cooperate with him. His goal is to annihilate as many of the people associated with the wounding partner as possible.

Hebrews 10:26 NIV

26 If we deliberately keep on sinning after we have received the knowledge of the truth, no sacrifice for sins is left,

John 8:34 NIV 34

Jesus replied, "Very truly I tell you, everyone who sins is a slave to sin.

Prov 28:14 NIV

Blessed is the one who always trembles before God, but whoever hardens their heart falls into trouble.

5. Future Intentions

When considering reconciliation with an wounding partner, it is important for the wounded partner to understand what safeguards their partner has put in place to help ensure that the behavior won't happen again. If the wounded partner discovered their partner's infidelity-related behavior, then the wounding partner won't likely have had time to think about what they should do to get and stay in recovery. In this case, the wounded partner can ask questions about what the wounding partner is willing to do instead. Here are some good questions to ask:

- Have you been STD tested? If not, are you willing to do so?
- Do you still want to be with the other person?
- Have you blocked your access to pornography/sexually stimulating images?
- Do you still want to withhold yourself from me?
- What are your reasons for telling me?
- Do you hope we can reconcile?
- Are you being completely honest?
- Is there anything I haven't asked that you should tell me? (This is a particularly great question because it highlights the fact that information, when withheld, is dishonesty and should be considered another form of betrayal)
- What steps have you taken to block your access to this person, to the porn, etc.?
- Are you willing to join a recovery group?
- Are you willing to do an intensive?
- Are you willing to take a polygraph test?
- Do you feel guilty?

The Lord is Judge of all and he expects the wounding partner to restore relationship with Him and to make reparation for violating the wounded partner.

James 4:17 NIV

If anyone, then, knows the good they ought to do and doesn't do it, it is sin for them.

Ephesians 4:17,18 NIV

17 So I tell you this, and insist on it in the Lord, that you must no longer live as the Gentiles do, in the futility of their thinking. 18 They are darkened in their understanding and separated from the life of God because of the ignorance that is in them due to the hardening of their hearts.

God requires the wounding partner to allow Him to remove their hard stony heart. He did not create us to behave like animals unrestrained from any societal or moral boundaries but to mirror and be a reflection of Him because we are created in His image.

Ephesians 5:15-17 NIV

15 Be very careful, then, how you live—not as unwise but as wise, 16 making the most of every opportunity, because the days are evil. 17 Therefore do not be foolish but understand what the Lord's will is.

What is the Lord's will?

1 Corinthians 15:34 NIV

Come back to your senses as you ought and stop sinning; for there are some who are ignorant of God—I say this to your shame.

Matthew 7:12 NIV

12 So in everything, do to others what you would have them do to you, for this sums up the Law and the Prophets.

Deuteronomy 6:25 NIV

And if we are careful to obey all this law before the Lord our God, as he has commanded us, that will be our righteousness."

6. The "WHY" Questions

The answers to this category of questions are often the most disappointing and frustrating for wounded partners. This is why we recommend that you limit the number of questions you ask in this category. Understanding why seems so key to putting their life back together, yet many of the answers to "why" elude them.

One of the primary reasons for this is that the wounding partner rarely knows why themselves, at least in the beginning stages of recovery. This is especially true in the case of sex/pornography addiction as well as intimacy avoidance.

Early on, wounding partners typically have very little insight into their own behavior. One of the main reasons for this is because, in order to commit betrayal, they had to justify their behavior in their own minds first. This typically leads to several layers of denial that will have to be worked through during recovery. Additionally, someone who has been unfaithful may not feel great about themselves. Poor self-image can lead a person to become defensive when questioned because they're afraid of what the answers might say about them.

Denial and justifications are especially prevalent where addiction is concerned. In order to support the addiction, the wounding partner had to compromise themselves and others around them. Many addicts feel intense shame about their behavior and acknowledging that behavior, especially in the beginning, can be extremely difficult for them. IAs and pornography/sex addicts, in particular, tend to have a marked lack of empathy as well. This is especially hard for a wounded partner who needs to know that their partner understands how they have been hurt and cares about it.

Lack of empathy is a sign of emotional immaturity, and addicts and intimacy avoidants are typically less mature than they should be. Emotional maturity develops, in large part, when we must find healthy ways to deal with intense and/or unpleasant emotions. People emotionally mature when they have to struggle to find a resolution within themselves or when they seek trained professionals to help them grow. When someone has an addiction to sex or pornography or even to withholding themselves from their partner, they go to the addiction time and time again to soothe themselves. In many instances this addictive behavior becomes their primary coping mechanism for all of life's ups and downs. They don't have to deal with life on life's terms and overcome problems because the addiction masks the feelings and gives them an alternative. This leaves them emotionally immature and unable to handle things such as conflict, criticism, and changes they have no control over. It also leaves them with a lack of self-reflection because of the layers of denial it takes to stay in addiction. The very nature of addiction is to "numb out" or escape emotions. As addiction progresses, it muddies the addict's thinking and makes it difficult to evaluate or control their own behavior. Asking someone with little to no self-awareness to explain to you why they did something will often lead to frustration.

Let's look at what the Lord says about someone involved with adultery and how helpful a wounding partner can be to the wounded partner.

Proverbs 6:32 NIV

But a man who commits adultery has no sense; whoever does so destroys himself.

Let's deconstruct this verse:

NO SENSE = the inner man, mind, will, heart, understanding, the soul of man, the mind, knowledge, thinking, reflection, memory, inclination, resolution, will of determination, conscience, moral character, the seat of the appetites, emotions, passions and courage is (1).

DESTROYS = destroyed, corrupt, ruined and decayed (2).

HIMSELF = the activity of mind, the activity of his will and the activity of his character, is dubious (unsettled, unsafe, unreliable) (3).

Paraphrase:

The person who commits adultery puts their entire being into a state of moral, spiritual and emotional corruption and is ruined in every area of life. This person's logic, rationality, reasoning and activity is unsafe to all those around them.

The research backs up the Word of God and they are severely impaired people with no self-awareness who leave a path of destruction behind them.

References:

1. Strong's Concordance H3820
2. Strong's Concordance H7843
3. Strong's Concordance H5315

If this describes your current situation, as a wounded partner, we want to tell you that we completely understand the pain that you are in. We also want to give you hope that, as the wounding partner moves through recovery, they will likely emotionally mature and gain empathy in the process. The work done in recovery is all about self-reflection, which can develop relatively quickly once addiction and numbing-out behavior is removed. Our best advice to you as the wounded partner is that you join a support group and/or see a trained professional that can help you work through some of the "why" questions that the wounding partner isn't currently able to answer.

We most often see wounded partners get stuck in the questioning stage of discovery around the "why" questions. Although it can be helpful to understand why someone did something, it can be highly frustrating when they say that they don't know why or when their answers don't seem to make much sense. Many times, wounded partners simply must come to the realization that they may never fully understand their partner's reasons for doing what they did. In order to move forward, the wounded partner might have to accept the fact that they may never be fully satisfied as to why something happened the way it did and that their partner's confounding behavior will remain, to a point, somewhat of a mystery.

Prov 25:19 NIV

Like a broken tooth or a lame foot is reliance on the unfaithful in a time of trouble.

Isaiah 49: 24-26 NIV

Then you will know that I am the LORD; those who hope in me will not be disappointed." 24 Can plunder be taken from warriors, or captives be rescued from the fierce? 25 But this is what the LORD says, "Yes, captives will be taken from warriors, and plunder retrieved from the fierce; I will contend with those who contend with you…

The wounding partner often is not capable of fully and honestly answering "why" until they are set free by God's grace. Once the brain fog has cleared and the toxins are flushed out, they will come to their senses and ask themselves "why"? Only then will they come to the shocking realization of what they have done and conclude that they were out of their minds. They allowed the enemy of their soul to take them captive. But God will deal with the warriors (demons of addictions) who ravaged our lives. He will judge the fierce (those forces that stole what belonged to God's children by violence and destruction) and were foolish enough to contend with God's children.

God makes it possible to rebuild trust!

Prayer for both the wounding partner and the wounded partner.

Father, we thank You for the power of Your word that answers our innermost questions and teaches us how to be wise and safe. Thank You for the truth that sets us both free. Thank You for healing our hearts and our minds. We understand that You hate what happened to us more than we do. We thank You for dealing with the enemy of our souls that has taken us captive. We thank You for judging those forces that stole what belonged to us. We are Your children, and we can depend on You to restore us. You will never disappoint us. You are our great salvation! In Jesus' name, Amen.

PART 8

Final Thoughts on Trust-Building Behaviors

Something that we would like to mention before closing this section on trust-building behaviors is that there is a big difference between the wounding partners who truly don't understand their own behavior and, therefore, give mediocre answers as to "why" and those who are using the answer "I don't know" as a way to get the conversation over with quicker. If you are reading this book as a wounding partner and you are doing the latter, we want to impress upon you that stonewalling your partner in this way will lead to a further lack of trust in the relationship and will, more likely than not, ultimately contribute to the relationship's demise.

As we explained previously, repeated questioning by the wounded partner is a normal part of the rebuilding trust process. We find that these questions often fall into one of five categories:

- Shock: Questions like, "how could you do this?" and "do you have any idea of how much you have hurt me?" are indications that a wounded partner is struggling to comprehend the situation. When infidelity-related behavior is discovered or disclosed, the losses associated with that knowledge initiate the grieving cycle. A wounded partner asking these types of questions is struggling with the first stage, shock.

- Putting the facts together. This is the most common category of questioning. As we explained previously, when betrayal is discovered or disclosed, it shatters the wounded partner's world. Asking questions about who, what, where, when, and why and getting the answers are a crucial part of the recovery process.

- Testing motives and mindset. Questions that fall into this category sound like, "do you love them more than me?" and "do you wish you could still be with them?" Although these are a normal part of the questioning process, we don't recommend these types of questions because they can lead to additional triggers and unfair comparisons.

- Rapid fire. There are times when the wounded partner asks a series of questions and doesn't seem to wait for the answers and/or doesn't seem to care about the answers given. In our experience working with wounded partners, this category of questions is more about expressing hurt and anger than it is about getting answers. Instead of engaging in this type of questioning, we recommend that wounded partner get in touch with what they are feeling and work that through with their partner or with a trained coach or counselor.

- Reflective. These are the most vulnerable types of questions and usually don't come until late in the recovery process. Although the wounding partner is 100% responsible for engaging in infidelity-related behavior, the wounded partner is likely aware that they aren't perfect. They may start asking questions in order to ascertain what might have gone wrong in the relationship. Although this can lead to deep and productive conversations between partners, it isn't likely to happen until the wounding partner accepts full responsibility for their actions without blaming the wounded partner.

It can be helpful for the wounding partner to understand the motives behind the different types of questions so that they can answer in a way that helps the wounded partner heal.

When David was a young man, he slaughtered Goliath, the giant Philistine warrior who mocked all of Israel and the God of heaven and earth. King Saul noted the anointing of God that was on David's life and filed that piece of information, seeing him as a person of interest. When the women of Israel sang David's praises, Saul's emotional insecurities dominated over him and from that moment on, Saul conspired against David and attempted to kill him. David was the most loyal subject in Israel, but it didn't matter how much good he did for Saul and the Kingdom of Israel. Saul would never bless David with favor and would continue to hunt him down until the day one of them died.

David spares Saul's life twice. TWICE! Both times, David asks Saul why he was being pursued.

1 Samuel 24: 1-15 NIV

24 After Saul returned from pursuing the Philistines, he was told, "David is in the Desert of En Gedi." 2 So Saul took three thousand able young men from all Israel and set out to look for David and his men near the Crags of the Wild Goats.

3 He came to the sheep pens along the way; a cave was there, and Saul went in to relieve himself. David and his men were far back in the cave. 4 The men said, "This is the day the Lord spoke of when he said[b] to you, 'I will give your enemy into your hands for you to deal with as you wish.'" Then David crept up unnoticed and cut off a corner of Saul's robe. 5 Afterward, David was conscience-stricken for having cut off a corner of his robe. 6 He said to his men, "The Lord forbid that I should do such a thing to my master, the Lord's anointed, or lay my hand on him; for he is the anointed of the Lord." 7 With these words David sharply rebuked his men and did not allow them to attack Saul. And Saul left the cave and went his way.

1) David was in shock: Saul carried out an evil plan to march 3000 men to find David and destroy him. David and his men were hidden in the safest place in that region and, in these verses, stumbles in Saul relieving himself. On top of that, his men told David that God allowed Saul to enter their innermost chamber so he could kill him! David was in such a state of distress and shock, he listened to the directions that his men gave him to a point, but only clipped a corner of Saul's robe.

8 Then David went out of the cave and called out to Saul, "My lord the king!" When Saul looked behind him, David bowed down and prostrated himself with his face to the ground. 9 He said to Saul, "Why do you listen when men say, 'David is bent on harming you'? 10 This day you have seen with your own eyes how the Lord delivered you into my hands in the cave. Some urged me to kill you, but I spared you; I said, 'I will not lay my hand on my lord, because he is the Lord's anointed.'

2) David put the facts together: He reasoned with Saul that the information he gathered on David was false. David proved to Saul that he had motive and opportunity to kill him, but he restrained himself because of God's anointing on Saul's life.

11 See, my father, look at this piece of your robe in my hand! I cut off the corner of your robe but did not kill you. See that there is nothing in my hand to indicate that I am guilty of wrongdoing or rebellion. I have not wronged you, but you are hunting me down to take my life. 12 May the Lord judge between you and me. And may the Lord avenge the wrongs you have done to me, but my hand will not touch you.

3) David tested Saul's motive and mindset: David wanted Saul's reason why he believed David was guilty of wrongdoing or rebellion. Then he rightly accused Saul of wrongdoing and rebellion against him.

13 As the old saying goes, 'From evildoers come evil deeds,' so my hand will not touch you. 14 "Against whom has the king of Israel come out? Who are you pursuing? A dead dog? A flea? 15 May the Lord be our judge and decide between us. May he consider my cause and uphold it; may he vindicate me by delivering me from your hand."

4) David asked his questions in rapid fire succession: He asks Saul five questions in this very short discourse.

Verse 9- Why do you listen when men say, "David is bent on harming you?"

Verse 14 - Against whom has the king of Israel come out?

Verse 14 - Who are you pursuing?

Verse 14 - A dead dog?

Verse 14 - A flea?

5) David was reflective: Verse 15 - "May the Lord be our judge and decide who is in the right and who is in the wrong." God understood David's case and judged him as righteous. In fact, David was confident that God would keep him alive and safe from Saul's murderous schemes.

Did Saul ever repent? No. He pursued David until the day he died. The relationship never healed.

How the wounding partner responds to their partner's questions is key to the rebuilding trust process. If the wounding partner engages in any of the following behaviors, they will likely further damage their partner and the relationship:

- Stonewalling by giving the silent treatment or refusing to answer.
- Raging and acting indignant.
- Minimizing the wounded partner's emotional pain.
- Playing the victim and acting hurt or going into shame by saying they are a terrible person.
- Blame-shifting by claiming that the wounded partner wasn't meeting their needs or by pointing out the wounded partner's imperfections.
- Justifying by using addiction as an excuse or saying that stress caused the infidelity-related behavior.
- Prolonged ambivalence. This is expressed when the wounding partner doesn't know what they want. If the relationship is to stand a chance of recovery, both partners must fully commit to working on the rebuilding of trust.

The ability for the wounding partner to respond to the wounded partner's questions with empathy, patience, and compassion is key to the rebuilding trust process. Aside from full disclosure and honesty moving forward, this element is probably the most important determining factor as to whether or not trust will ultimately be rebuilt. One of the main reasons for this is that, when the wounding partner does not show empathy, compassion, and patience to the wounded partner, fighting tends to escalate and those fights tend to remain unresolved. Prolonged, unresolved conflict will tear at the fabric of an already-fragile relationship and eventually destroy whatever hope there is left of saving it.

When the wounded partner asks repeated questions, they are likely trying to resolve the immense pain that they are in. It can be hard for some wounding partners to grasp the extent of their partner's emotional pain, and this can, unfortunately, lead them to minimize it. Studies suggest that when we experience rejection, our brains react similarly to when we experience physical pain. Scientists hypothesize that this is because a human being's best chance for survival is within a group. Therefore, rejection is a very bad thing. (Whitcomb, 2021) A 2003 study done through UCLA monitored participants' brains by fMRI while they played video games with peers. When participants were excluded from the game, the scans showed that the brain experienced distress and, as a result, blood flow to the anterior cingulate and insular cortices was increased. (University of California, 2003). This is the same blood flow pattern that occurs when people feel physical pain. As human beings, we feel intense pain when we are rejected—and there is possibly no worse rejection than being set aside while our partner gives their heart and/or body to someone else or chooses to withhold love from us. If you are a wounding partner who is wondering whether your partner's pain is real, let us assure you that it is.

1) Stonewalling, giving the silent treatment, refusing a request:

1 Samuel 18:17-19 NIV

17 Saul said to David, "Here is my older daughter Merab. I will give her to you in marriage; only serve me bravely and fight the battles of the Lord." For Saul said to himself, "I will not raise a hand against him. Let the Philistines do that!"

18 But David said to Saul, "Who am I, and what is my family or my clan in Israel, that I should become the king's son-in-law?" 19 So when the time came for Merab, Saul's daughter, to be given to David, she was given in marriage to Adriel of Meholah.

Saul never gave his daughter, Merab, to David and he never told him why, even though David met all the requirements to become his faithful son-in-law. Saul stonewalled David.

2) Raging and acting indignant:

1 Samuel 18: 10-11 NIV

10 The next day an evil[a] spirit from God came forcefully on Saul. He was prophesying in his house, while David was playing the lyre, as he usually did. Saul had a spear in his hand 11 and he hurled it, saying to himself, "I'll pin David to the wall." But David eluded him twice.

This is one of many incidents where Saul raged against David with the intent to murder him.

3). Minimizing emotional pain:

1 Samuel 20: 24-28 NIV

24 So David hid in the field, and when the New Moon feast came, the king sat down to eat. 25 He sat in his customary place by the wall, opposite Jonathan,[a] and Abner sat next to Saul, but David's place was empty. 26 Saul said nothing that day, for he thought, "Something must have happened to David to make him ceremonially unclean—surely he is unclean." 27 But the next day, the second day of the month, David's place was empty again. Then Saul said to his son Jonathan, "Why hasn't the son of Jesse come to the meal, either yesterday or today?"

28 Jonathan answered, "David earnestly asked me for permission to go to Bethlehem. 29 He said, 'Let me go, because our family is observing a sacrifice in the town and my brother has ordered me to be there. If I have found favor in your eyes, let me get away to see my brothers.' That is why he has not come to the king's table."

Saul attempted to kill David several times at this point, but expected David to come eat his meal at the table like nothing was wrong. He minimized David's emotional pain.

4). Playing the victim:

1 Samuel 20:30-31 NIV

30 Saul's anger flared up at Jonathan and he said to him, "You son of a perverse and rebellious woman! Don't I know that you have sided with the son of Jesse to your own shame and to the shame of the mother who bore you? 31 As long as the son of Jesse lives on this earth, neither you nor your kingdom will be established. Now send someone to bring him to me, for he must die!"

Saul let Jonathan know that he would never become king as long as David was alive. He reasoned that they were victims of David's popularity and, in order to remain on the throne, David had to die.

5). Blame shifting:

1 Samuel 22: 6-8 NIV

6 Now Saul heard that David and his men had been discovered. And Saul was seated, spear in hand, under the tamarisk tree on the hill at Gibeah, with all his officials standing at his side. 7 He said to them, "Listen, men of Benjamin! Will the son of Jesse give all of you fields and vineyards? Will he make all of you commanders of thousands and commanders of hundreds? 8 Is that why you have all conspired against me? No one tells me when my son makes a covenant with the son of Jesse. None of you is concerned about me or tells me that my son has incited my servant to lie in wait for me, as he does today."

Commentators say that Saul was holding a governmental meeting under the tamarisk tree, and the spear would have been used as his scepter. Evidently, the men in attendance were displeased and made complaints about the condition of their country. Saul shifts the blame of unmet expectations over to David to avoid his responsibility to his countrymen.

6). Justifying saying stress caused the behavior:

1 Samuel 23:19-23 NIV

19 The Ziphites went up to Saul at Gibeah and said, "Is not David hiding among us in the strongholds at Horesh, on the hill of Hakilah, south of Jeshimon? 20 Now, Your Majesty, come down whenever it pleases you to do so, and we will be responsible for giving him into your hands." 21 Saul replied, "The Lord bless you for your concern for me. 22 Go and get more information. Find out where David usually goes and who has seen him there. They tell me he is very crafty. 23 Find out about all the hiding places he uses and come back to me with definite information. Then I will go with you; if he is in the area, I will track him down among all the clans of Judah."

Verse 21 is so revealing. Evidently, the men of Gibeah heard that Saul was losing his mind over David. In order for Saul to relieve his stress induced behavior, it was necessary for David to be captured and placed under Saul's control.

7). Prolonged ambivalence wounding partner doesn't know what they want:

1 Samuel 24:16-21 NIV

16 When David finished saying this, Saul asked, "Is that your voice, David my son?" And he wept aloud. 17 "You are more righteous than I," he said. "You have treated me well, but I have treated you badly. 18 You have just now told me about the good you did to me; the Lord delivered me into your hands, but you did not kill me. 19 When a man finds his enemy, does he let him get away unharmed? May the Lord reward you well for the way you treated me today. 20 I know that you will surely be king and that the kingdom of Israel will be established in your hands. 21 Now swear to me by the Lord that you will not kill off my descendants or wipe out my name from my father's family."

Saul makes a promise that he never keeps. In fact, in 1 Samuel 26, David spares Saul's life again! Saul never resolves his jealousy with David and commits suicide leaving behind a horrible legacy of insanity.

So, how can a wounding partner show empathy to the wounded partner? If you are a wounding partner reading this, here are some ways that a person can convey empathy and concern:

1. Own and lead the recovery process. It is important that you own your recovery and that you take responsibility for it. Reading articles and sharing them with your partner, making a coaching or counseling appointment on your own, and sharing insights about what you are learning are all things that will help the wounded partner know that you are taking your recovery work seriously.

2. Take ownership of your infidelity-related behavior. This doesn't mean that you have to take responsibility for every problem in the relationship but taking responsibility for your infidelity-related behavior without defending yourself or blaming your partner is key to showing that you understand and care about your partner's feelings.

3. Ask the wounded partner to write you a letter. If you are having a hard time being empathetic, ask your partner to write you a 2-3-page letter explaining their feelings. After reading it and processing the information, come back to them and validate their emotions.

4. Deliberately engage in conversations. A common mistake made by wounding partners is that they often avoid conversations that the wounded partner wants to have about the pain they are experiencing. This can happen through refusing to answer questions, saying "I don't know" without attempting to answer to the best of their ability, or physically leaving and/or staying away. Instead, hang in there with your partner and listen to what they have to say. Better yet, commit to starting some of the conversations by asking how they are doing.

1 Peter 3:8-12 MSG

"Summing up: Be agreeable, be sympathetic, be loving, be compassionate, be humble. That goes for all of you, no exceptions. No retaliation. No sharp-tongued sarcasm. Instead, bless—that's your job, to bless. You'll be a blessing and also get a blessing. Whoever wants to embrace life and see the day fill up with good, here's what you do: Say nothing evil or hurtful; Snub evil and cultivate good; run after peace for all you're worth. God looks on all this with approval, listening and responding well to what he's asked; But he turns his back on those who do evil things."

Suggested prayer for the wounding and the wounded partner:

Father, give us the grace to be agreeable, sympathetic, loving, compassionate and humble. Give us the grace not to retaliate. Give us the grace not to be sharp tongued. Give us the grace to bless each other so we can receive Your blessing. Give us the grace to embrace life and cultivate good. Give us the grace not to say anything evil or hurtful. Give us the grace to snub evil and cultivate good. Give us the grace to run after peace with all our hearts. We want Your favor, Your approval in all we listen to and in all our responses. Give us the grace to turn our backs on evil. In Jesus' name, Amen

PART 9

Now that we've wrapped up trust-building behaviors, we would like to discuss the most common trust-breaking behaviors we see in our office.

Trust-Breaking Behavior #1

Failure to End Infidelity-Related Behavior

Whether it be a sexual affair, emotional affair, looking at pornography, or intimacy avoidance, the wounding partner's lack of willingness to end the infidelity-related behavior is the number one reason why couples are unable to reconcile after betrayal has been discovered or disclosed. We would like to preface this section by stating that we understand that ending infidelity-related behavior is not always an easy thing to do. That being said, it is the wounding partner's responsibility to show a commitment to recovery by getting help to end whatever they have gotten caught up in. In our experience, it is not possible to effectively work on a relationship in the long-term if the wounding partner continues to engage in infidelity-related behavior.

The "grass is always greener" mentality is a common issue when it comes to infidelity, especially in the case of sexual and emotional affairs. It is not uncommon for us to hear from a wounding partner that they feel justified with continuing their behavior because their partner is the source of their problems, and that their affair partner meets their needs in a way that their current partner cannot. The idea that engaging in infidelity-related behavior will do anything to resolve issues for the wounding partner, whether real or perceived, is a fallacy. Infidelity does not cure problems. Instead, it creates them. We hear from wounding partners on a regular basis about how they thought that engaging in infidelity-related behavior would help ease their relational and/or personal problems but, instead, are now left with new problems on top of the old ones. Although infidelity in the form of affairs, pornography, and withholding can offer temporary fixes for unpleasant experiences and emotions, they are not a solution to them. The problems of life must be dealt with head-on if they are truly to be resolved. If the wounding partner continues to act out with infidelity-related behavior, they are only temporarily drawing attention away from their issues. The wounded partner is not the source of their problems. In committed relationships, our partner only highlights the problems that are already within ourselves. Therefore, we must each take responsibility for addressing our own issues and reach out for expert help when we need it. Otherwise, we fall into the victim mentality which says that we don't have to be responsible for fixing our issues because other people are responsible for causing them and, therefore, for fixing them.

Infidelity provides a fantasy land for the wounding partner. It offers a temporary fix for the emotional impact of life's problems.

Prov 6: 16-35 MSG

Seven Things God Hates

Here are six things God hates, and one more that He loathes with a passion:

- eyes that are arrogant,
- a tongue that lies,
- hands that murder the innocent,
- a heart that hatches evil plots,
- feet that race down a wicked track,
- a mouth that lies under oath,
- a troublemaker in the family.
- **Warning on Adultery**

Good friend, follow your father's good advice; don't wander off from your mother's teachings. Wrap yourself in them from head to foot; wear them like a scarf around your neck. Wherever you walk, they'll guide you; whenever you rest, they'll guard you.

When you wake up, they'll tell you what's next. For sound advice is a beacon, good teaching is a light, moral discipline is a life path. They'll protect you from promiscuous women, from the seductive talk of some temptress.

Don't lustfully fantasize on her beauty, nor be taken in by her bedroom eyes. You can buy an hour with a prostitute for a loaf of bread, but a promiscuous woman may well eat you alive. Can you build a fire in your lap and not burn your pants? Can you walk barefoot on hot coals and not get blisters?

It's the same when you have sex with your neighbor's wife: Touch her and you'll pay for it. No excuses. Hunger is no excuse for a thief to steal; When he's caught he has to pay it back, even if he has to put his whole house in hock.

Adultery is a brainless act, soul-destroying, self-destructive; Expect a bloody nose, a black eye, and a reputation ruined for good. For jealousy detonates rage in a cheated husband; wild for revenge, he won't make allowances. Nothing you say or pay will make it alright; neither bribes nor reason will satisfy him.

In the case of emotional and sexual affairs, a powerful concoction of neurochemicals are stimulated when limerence or infatuation are present. These are often mistaken for true feelings, or even love. The neurotransmitters involved in infatuation and limerence are part of the brain's reward system. The release of these chemicals causes an intense reaction in the brain that feels like true love but is only the biological reaction that we get during the infatuation stage of love. As most of us know, the infatuation stage is only temporary. However, in the case of affairs, this stage can be prolonged because of the adrenaline involved in the excitement and stress of sneaking around. Let's take a closer look at the main chemicals involved with infatuation and limerence:

- Epinephrine: Also known as adrenaline. Epinephrine makes your heart beat faster, blood pressure rise, and your breathing quicken. Epinephrine is associated with effects onthe heart.
- Norepinephrine: Associated with the fight or flight response. Norepinephrine is similar to epinephrine and is also closely related to dopamine. Norepinephrine is associated with effects on the blood vessels.
- Dopamine: Associated with the reward system of the brain. Known as the "feel good" hormone, dopamine is associatedwith pleasure and libido. It also motivates focus and action.
- Serotonin: Levels of serotonin drop during infatuation, leading to obsessive-type thinking about the other person when we first feel infatuated with someone.
- PEA: Phenylethylamine, or PEA, is known as the "love molecule". It is associated with the flood of chemicals that enter our brain during infatuation and acts as a natural amphetamine that causes us to focus intently on our feelings. (Savulescu, Sandberg, 2008)

The presence of this powerful cocktail of chemicals helps explain why the emotions experienced during affairs can feel so real. This can make them difficult to end. Another reason why affairs are often difficult to end is that the wounding partner tends to perceive the affair partner as kinder, more affectionate, more supportive, and more attentive than the wounded partner. The problem is that these perceptions come about because of the wounding partner's fantasy, which is based on an artificial situation. The pressures of a mortgage, children, illnesses, in- laws, and the tough things that come with life's struggles over time are all absent in the fantasy land of an affair. Research shows that affairs typically don't last and, if they do somehow end up in marriage, the divorce rate is approximately 75%. (Pittman, 1990)

Hebrews 10: 26-31 MSG

If we give up and turn our backs on all we've learned, all we've been given, all the truth we now know, we repudiate Christ's sacrifice and are left on our own to face the Judgment—and a mighty fierce judgment it will be! If the penalty for breaking the law of Moses is physical death, what do you think will happen if you turn on God's Son, spit on the sacrifice that made you whole, and insult this most gracious Spirit? This is no light matter. God has warned us that he'll hold us to account and make us pay. He was quite explicit: "Vengeance is mine, and I won't overlook a thing" and "God will judge his people." Nobody's getting by with anything, believe me.

A word about limerence

We would like to preface this section by explaining our use of the term "limerent object" to describe an affair partner and/ or someone who the wounding partner is infatuated with. This term is not meant to devalue this person in any way. Instead, the word "object" is applied to the subject of the wounding partner's limerence to explain how they are being viewed by the wounding partner. In limerence, the limerent object is being objectified by the other person. As opposed to being viewed in their totality and being loved warts and all, the limerent object has become a subject of a person's fantasy. As a result, they are being idealized in an unrealistic way which is based on the need of the wounding partner to escape reality.

According to the Glossary found in this book, we define limerence as "a strong state of emotional infatuation, longing, and even obsession that lasts as little as 6 months and as long as 3 years." In her book *Love and Limerence: The Experience of Being in Love,* author Dorothy Tennov observed the following features about limerence:

- Frequent intrusive thoughts about the limerent object who is a potential sexual partner
- Increased time spent with or ruminating on the limerent object
- An intense need for feelings to be reciprocated
- Exaggerated mood dependent upon the limerent object's actions (despair when rejected, elated when feelings are reciprocated)
- Temporary relief from unrequited feelings through fantasy about the limerent object
- A desire for exclusivity with the limerent object
- The ability to downplay the limerent object's faults while emphasizing their positive features
- Feelings for the limerent object are intensified through adversity

What makes limerence especially powerful is the fact that the wounding partner's attraction is often based on things or traits that they perceive they lack for themselves. The subject of the limerence is idealized as having the exact attributes that the wounding partner feels that they are lacking in themselves and/ or in their relationship. Limerence is very self-focused in the way that it is about getting something rather than giving something. Wounding partners who are experiencing limerence will need attention, sex, and validation from the limerent object because it fulfills their fantasy. The behaviors of a person in a state of limerence are similar to those of an addict. In the case of limerence, the wounding partner becomes intoxicated with another person in a similar way that alcoholics become intoxicated by using alcohol. In order to punctuate the similarity, here is a list of characteristics commonly associated with those engaging in substance abuse:

- An inability to give up a substance
- Keeping a steady supply of the substance
- Withdrawing from important relationships
- Spending a large amount of time pursuing the substance
- Constantly thinking about the substance
- Engaging in risky behavior
- Not being deterred by negative consequences of substance use
- Engaging in secrecy and deception in order to hide the substance use
- Neglecting responsibilities of work, home, etc.
- Experiencing withdrawal symptoms when the substance is absent

Do these things sound familiar? They should if the wounding partner is engaged in an affair that involves limerence. Since limerence is basically "person addiction", it is a very serious issue that is not easily dealt with. The feelings associated with it feel like real love when, in fact, they are something entirely different. If you or your partner are engaged in an affair where limerence is present, we urge you to seek professional coaching or counseling in order to help break the cycle.

That being said, here are some strategies you can use in order to break the grip of limerence:

1. Cut off all contact. Any engagement with the object of your limerence will only serve to exacerbate the problem. Avoid any situation or person that is associated with the limerent object. Avoid texting, calling, engaging social media, and any other form of contact with this person.

2. Engage with someone who is objective that can help you see the situation for what it is. If you are in a state of limerence, you will not see things clearly. It is important that you engage the help of a trained coach or counselor, trusted friend, spiritual leader, or mentor who you trust have your best interest at heart and to give you sound advice.

3. Replace the behaviors. As with addiction, it is important that you replace the behaviors associated with limerence with new, healthy behaviors. This can be something like exercise but can also be something like making a list of the wounded partner's strengths and positive attributes.

4. Concentrate on the flaws. This isn't meant to be mean. However, much of the problem associated with limerence is that you are likely idealizing this person while simultaneously minimizing their flaws. Make a list of flaws (even if it's just one) and pick one to concentrate on instead of indulging your fantasies about this person.

5. Be accountable. Since the hold of limerence is exceptionally strong, you will need

to enlist outside help in order to stay accountable. We recommend that you engage someone other than your partner who will call you on it when you are not taking recovery seriously and/or are making excuses or indulging addictive behavior.

Limerence is dangerous! It destroys lives and it obliterates families. This case of limerence is recorded in the Bible.

2 Samuel 13 MSG

13 1-4 Some time later, this happened: Absalom, David's son, had a sister who was very attractive. Her name was Tamar. Amnon, also David's son, was in love with her. Amnon was obsessed with his sister Tamar to the point of making himself sick over her. She was a virgin, so he couldn't see how he could get his hands on her. Amnon had a good friend, Jonadab, the son of David's brother Shimeah. Jonadab was exceptionally streetwise. He said to Amnon, "Why are you moping around like this, day after day—you, the son of the king! Tell me what's eating at you."

"In a word, Tamar," said Amnon. "My brother Absalom's sister. I'm in love with her."

5 "Here's what you do," said Jonadab. "Go to bed and pretend you're sick. When your father comes to visit you, say, 'Have my sister Tamar come and prepare some supper for me here where I can watch her and she can feed me.'"

6 So Amnon took to his bed and acted sick. When the king came to visit, Amnon said, "Would you do me a favor? Have my sister Tamar come and make some nourishing dumplings here where I can watch her and be fed by her."

7 David sent word to Tamar who was home at the time: "Go to the house of your brother Amnon and prepare a meal for him."

8-9 So Tamar went to her brother Amnon's house. She took dough, kneaded it, formed it into dumplings, and cooked them while he watched from his bed. But when she took the cooking pot and served him, he wouldn't eat.

9-11 Amnon said, "Clear everyone out of the house," and they all cleared out. Then he said to Tamar, "Bring the food into my bedroom, where we can eat in privacy." She took the nourishing dumplings she had prepared and brought them to her brother Amnon in his bedroom. But when she got ready to feed him, he grabbed her and said, "Come to bed with me, sister!"

12-13 "No, brother!" she said, "Don't hurt me! This kind of thing isn't done in Israel! Don't do this terrible thing! Where could I ever show my face? And you—you'll be out on the street in disgrace. Oh, please! Speak to the king—he'll let you marry me."

14 But he wouldn't listen. Being much stronger than she, he raped her.

15 No sooner had Amnon raped her that he hated her—an immense hatred. The hatred that he felt for her was greater than the love he'd had for her. "Get up," he said, "and get out!"

16-18 "Oh no, brother," she said. "Please! This is an even worse evil than what you just did to me!"

But he wouldn't listen to her. He called for his valet. "Get rid of this woman. Get her out of my sight! And lock the door after her." *The valet threw her out and locked the door behind her.*

18-19 *She was wearing a long-sleeved gown. (That's how virgin princesses used to dress from early adolescence on.) Tamar poured ashes on her head, then she ripped the long-sleeved gown, held her head in her hands, and walked away, sobbing as she went.*

20 *Her brother Absalom said to her,* "Has your brother Amnon had his way with you? Now, my dear sister, let's keep it quiet—a family matter. He is, after all, your brother. Don't take this so hard." *Tamar lived in her brother Absalom's home, bitter and desolate.*

21-22 *King David heard the whole story and was enraged, but he didn't discipline Amnon. David doted on him because he was his firstborn. Absalom quit speaking to Amnon—not a word, whether good or bad—because he hated him for violating his sister Tamar.*

23-24 *Two years went by. One day Absalom threw a sheep-shearing party in Baal Hazor in the vicinity of Ephraim and invited all the king's sons. He also went to the king and invited him.* "Look, I'm throwing a sheep-shearing party. Come, and bring your servants."

25 *But the king said,* "No, son—not this time, and not the whole household. We'd just be a burden to you." *Absalom pushed, but David wouldn't budge. But he did give him his blessing.*

26-27 *Then Absalom said,* "Well, if you won't come, at least let my brother Amnon come."

"And why," *said the king,* "should he go with you?" *But Absalom was so insistent that he gave in and let Amnon and all the rest of the king's sons go.*

28 *Absalom prepared a banquet fit for a king. Then he instructed his servants,* "Look sharp, now. When Amnon is well into the sauce and feeling no pain, and I give the order 'Strike Amnon,' kill him. And don't be afraid—I'm the one giving the command. Courage! You can do it!"

29-31 *Absalom's servants did to Amnon exactly what their master ordered. All the king's sons got out as fast as they could, jumped on their mules, and rode off. While they were still on the road, a rumor came to the king:* "Absalom just killed all the king's sons—not one is left!" *The king stood up, ripped his clothes to shreds, and threw himself on the floor. All his servants who were standing around at the time did the same.*

32-33 *Just then, Jonadab, his brother Shimeah's son, stepped up.* "My master must not think that all the young men, the king's sons, are dead. Only Amnon is dead. This happened because of Absalom's outrage since the day that Amnon violated his sister Tamar. So my master, the king, mustn't make things worse than they are, thinking that all your sons are dead. Only Amnon is dead."

34 Absalom fled.

Just then the sentry on duty looked up and saw a cloud of dust on the road from Horonaim alongside the mountain. He came and told the king, "I've just seen a bunch of men on the Horonaim road, coming around the mountain."

35-37 Then Jonadab exclaimed to the king, "See! It's the king's sons coming, just as I said!" He had no sooner said the words than the king's sons burst in—loud laments and weeping! The king joined in, along with all the servants—loud weeping, many tears. David mourned the death of his son for a long time.

37-39 When Absalom fled, he went to Talmai, son of Ammihud, king of Geshur. He was there for three years. The king finally gave up trying to get back at Absalom. He had come to terms with Amnon's death.

Similar to emotional and sexual affairs, pornography use also creates a type of fantasy land for the user. In this fantasy, the person using porn gets all their sexual needs met without having to give anything in return. The object of their pornographic lust and fantasy is always interested, ready, and able to fulfill all their sexual desires and curiosities. Their sole purpose is to please them sexually and, when that particular fantasy no longer meets their needs, another fantasy is just a mouse click away.

The use of pornography for sexual purposes usually involves masturbation and a resulting orgasm. This is problematic not only in the relationship, but for the person using pornography as well. During sex, orgasm, and even afterwards, three extremely powerful, mood-boosting chemicals are released – dopamine, endorphins, and oxytocin. Dopamine plays a major role in reward-motivated behavior. Pornographic scenes are hyper-stimulating triggers, which ultimately lead to unnaturally high levels of dopamine that can't typically be reproduced in a long-term, committed relationship. As a result, satisfaction during a normal, healthy sexual encounter can be viewed as failing to meet expectations. Additionally, this constant release of powerful chemicals during viewing and, ultimately, orgasm leads to the wounding partner bonding with the process of porn usage instead of with the partner.

Matthew 5:27-30 MSG

27-28 "You know the next commandment pretty well, too: 'Don't go to bed with another's spouse.' But don't think you've preserved your virtue simply by staying out of bed. Your heart can be corrupted by lust even quicker than your body. Those ogling looks you think nobody notices—they also corrupt.

29-30 "Let's not pretend this is easier than it really is. If you want to live a morally pure life, here's what you have to do: You have to blind your right eye the moment you catch it in a lustful leer. You have to choose to live one-eyed or else be dumped on a moral trash pile. And you have to chop off your right hand the moment you notice it raised threateningly. Better a bloody stump than your entire being discarded for good in the dump.

Obviously, we add these verses not to advocate for people to start cutting off body parts, but to emphasize how seriously God takes lusting for someone other than your partner.

We often see intimacy avoidance (IA) in combination with pornography. The escapism offered by pornography is particularly attractive to the IA wounding partner because the need to escape is amplified in someone dealing with this issue. This can be confusing to the wounded partner, especially if the IA is sexually anorexic within the relationship. However, if you remember that the primary motivation of the IA is to keep distance from their partner in order to avoid potential pain, it makes sense. Pornography and masturbation allow the IA to have their sexual needs met without any risk of connection to another human being. We see other forms of infidelity in combination with IA as well, but they are not as common as porn usage. For the IA, everything is about driving enough distance between themselves and their partner that they no longer feel in "danger" of getting hurt. If intimacy avoidance is an issue in your relationship, it is important that this aspect is dealt with properly because the presence of intimacy avoidance typically drives infidelity-related behavior. Additionally, even if the IA stops the porn usage, affair, etc., they are likely to treat the wounded partner exactly the same as when they were engaging in the infidelity-related behavior if this root issue is not dealt with.

God is very clear how He views infidelity-related behavior, fantasizing, limerence, emotional and sexual affairs, pornography, masturbating and intimacy avoidance. If you are a child of God, you have been translated out of the kingdom of darkness into the Kingdom of God's dear Son!

Romans 6 MSG

When Death Becomes Life

1-3 So what do we do? Keep on sinning so God can keep on forgiving? I should hope not! If we've left the country where sin is sovereign, how can we still live in our old house there? Or didn't you realize we packed up and left there for good? That is what happened in baptism. When we went under the water, we left the old country of sin behind; when we came up out of the water, we entered into the new country of grace—a new life in a new land!

3-5 That's what baptism into the life of Jesus means. When we are lowered into the water, it is like the burial of Jesus; when we are raised up out of the water, it is like the resurrection of Jesus. Each of us is raised into a light-filled world by our Father so that we can see where we're going in our new grace-sovereign country.

6-11 Could it be any clearer? Our old way of life was nailed to the cross with Christ, a decisive end to that sin-miserable life—no longer captive to sin's demands! What we believe is this: If we get included in Christ's sin-conquering death, we also get included in his life-saving resurrection. We know that when Jesus was raised from the dead it was a signal of the end of death-as-the-end. Never again will death have the last word. When Jesus died, he took sin down with him, but alive he brings God down to us. From now on, think of it this way: Sin speaks a dead language that means nothing to you; God speaks your mother tongue, and you hang on every word. You are dead to sin and alive to God. That's what Jesus did.

12-14 That means you must not give sin a vote in the way you conduct your lives. Don't give it the time of day. Don't even run little errands that are connected with that old way of life. Throw yourselves wholeheartedly and full-time—remember, you've been raised from the dead!—into God's way of doing things. Sin can't tell you how to live. After all, you're not living under that old tyranny any longer. You're living in the freedom of God.

What Is True Freedom?

15-18 So, since we're out from under the old tyranny, does that mean we can live any old way we want? Since we're free in the freedom of God, can we do anything that comes to mind? Hardly. You know well enough from your own experience that there are some acts of so-called freedom that destroy freedom. Offer yourselves to sin, for instance, and it's your last free act. But offer yourselves to the ways of God and the freedom never quits. All your lives you've let sin tell you what to do. But thank God you've started listening to a new master, one whose commands set you free to live openly in his freedom!

19 I'm using this freedom language because it's easy to picture. You can readily recall, can't you, how at one time the more you did just what you felt like doing—not caring about others, not caring about God—the worse your life became and the less freedom you had? And how much different is it now as you live in God's freedom, your lives healed and expansive in holiness?

20-21 As long as you did what you felt like doing, ignoring God, you didn't have to bother with right thinking or right living, or right anything for that matter. But do you call that a free life? What did you get out of it? Nothing you're proud of now. Where did it get you? A dead end.

22-23 But now that you've found you don't have to listen to sin tell you what to do, and have discovered the delight of listening to God telling you, what a surprise! A whole, healed, put-together life right now, with more and more of life on the way! Work hard for sin your whole life and your pension is death. But God's gift is real life, eternal life, delivered by Jesus, our Master.

Prayer for the wounding partner:

Father, I leave behind my sinful life. My old miserable way of living has been nailed to the cross with Jesus and is buried forever. I am no longer captive to sin and its deadly commands. Sin no longer has a vote on the way I conduct my life. I have been baptized and resurrected into the life of Christ. I am raised to live in a world filled with light. I throw myself wholeheartedly and full time into God's way of living, conduct, and expectations of me. I am discovering the delight of listening to God's word and obeying His precepts. I am fully opening the door of my heart and allowing God to heal my life and the life of my wounded partner. In Jesus' name, Amen.

PART 10

The Role of Boundaries

In a situation where the wounding partner is unwilling to end an affair or give up other infidelity-related behavior, boundaries on the wounded partner's part are of utmost importance. When the wounded partner fails to set boundaries appropriate for the situation, they are unwittingly empowering the wounding partner to keep engaging in the infidelity. Unfortunately, when wounding partners act this way, they are showing a profound lack of empathy that keeps them from seeing the wounded partner's pain. While they may observe the pain that their partner is in, they continue to minimize it to justify their actions. The wounded partner's lack of boundaries continues the wounding partner's self-delusion that everything is all about them. This unhealthy situation is highly unlikely to change until the wounding partner starts to experience the pain of loss because of their actions.

Sometimes, wounded partners mistakenly engage in pursuing a remorseless wounding partner, believing that if they can only get them to understand that they will stop their destructive behavior. Guilting, shaming, threatening, and controlling the wounding partner in order to get them to stop engaging in their infidelity-related behavior will not produce the desired effect. Neither will insisting that the wounding partner recommit to the relationship 100% immediately. Although it makes sense that the wounded partner would engage in these behaviors in an attempt to ease their suffering and save the relationship, they usually have an effect opposite of what was intended. Engagement in these behaviors are likely to drive an unrepentant wounding partner further away from the relationship, especially if limerence is an issue. Demanding and threatening on the wounded partner's part only serves to fuel the remorseless wounding partner's forbidden behavior because it increases the excitement.

As much as the behaviors listed above do nothing to resolve the issue, neither does giving the wounding partner everything they want. When the wounded partner gives the wounding partner more sex, more patience, accepts responsibility that isn't theirs, or engages in sexual behavior that feels uncomfortable to them, they wind up hurting themselves and allowing the unrepentant wounding partner to have their cake and eat it too. Instead, it is better for the wounded partner to draw boundaries with the wounding partner that show them that, if they continue to engage an affair partner, pornography, etc., they can't have both the infidelity-related behavior and the benefits associated with the relationship.

The best advice we can give the wounded partner when the wounding partner is acting out and still in the midst of their turmoil is this: Place your emotions and energy into praising God! He knows ALL that is going on. It is best to cooperate with Him, set your healthy boundaries and allow God to work in your situation.

Phil 4: 4-9 MSG

4-5 Celebrate God all day, every day. I mean, revel in him! Make it as clear as you can to all you meet that you're on their side, working with them and not against them. Help them see that the Master is about to arrive. He could show up any minute!

6-7 Don't fret or worry. Instead of worrying, pray. Let petitions and praises shape your worries into prayers, letting God know your concerns. Before you know it, a sense of God's wholeness, everything coming together for good, will come and settle you down. It's wonderful what happens when Christ displaces worry at the center of your life.

8-9 Summing it all up, friends, I'd say you'll do best by filling your minds and meditating on things true, noble, reputable, authentic, compelling, gracious—the best, not the worst; the beautiful, not the ugly; things to praise, not things to curse. Put into practice what you learned from me, what you heard and saw and realized. Do that, and God, who makes everything work together, will work you into his most excellent harmonies.

For the wounding partner who refuses to disengage from their infidelity-related behavior, they are unlikely to change until the pain of the consequences associated with their actions supersedes the benefits derived from it. The wounded partner's boundaries can play a pivotal role in helping an unrepentant wounding partner see the error of their ways. That being said, we feel it is important to stress that boundaries should never be used to manipulate the wounding partner's behavior. However, the absence of boundaries will surely enable it. Instead of using a boundary to try and get the wounding partner to stop their behavior, the wounded partner should consider personal boundaries as a way to keep themselves safe. A personal boundary is an imaginary line that separates people from one another in terms of personal space, feelings, needs, and responsibilities. Appropriate boundaries are a critical component to maintaining healthy connections and are especially important to use when dealing with a remorseless wounding partner.

Wounded partner, it is best to remember that a remorseless wounding partner is first cheating God. They continually cross God's boundaries and ignore His standards. It is vital that you set boundaries for your own safety when the wounding partner is still operating in a sinful way. Understand God's perspective on how He deals with those who cross His boundaries and assist Him with this process.

James 4: 1-10 MSG

4 1-2 Where do you think all these appalling wars and quarrels come from? Do you think they just happen? Think again. They come about because you want your own way, and fight for it deep inside yourselves. You lust for what you don't have and are willing to kill to get it. You want what isn't yours and will risk violence to get your hands on it.

2-3 You wouldn't think of just asking God for it, would you? And why not? Because you know you'd be asking for what you have no right to. You're spoiled children, each wanting your own way.

4-6 You're cheating on God. If all you want is your own way, flirting with the world every chance you get, you end up enemies of God and his way. And do you suppose God doesn't care? The proverb has it that "he's a fiercely jealous lover." And what he gives in love is far better than anything else you'll find. It's common knowledge that "God goes against the willful proud; God gives grace to the willing humble."

7-10 So let God work his will in you. Yell a loud no to the Devil and watch him make himself scarce. Say a quiet yes to God and he'll be there in no time. Quit dabbling in sin. Purify your inner life. Quit playing the field. Hit bottom and cry your eyes out. The fun and games are over. Get serious, really serious. Get down on your knees before the Master; it's the only way you'll get on your feet.

As we stated previously, a boundary is not a way for the wounded partner to try to coerce the wounding partner into behaving the way that they want them to, nor is it a way to punish them. When we work with wounded partners, it is not uncommon for them to misuse boundaries, especially if they aren't used to setting them. Here are some examples of where boundaries often go awry:

- Using boundaries to get your way
- Using boundaries in an attempt to guarantee safety
- Using boundaries as threats
- Drawing boundaries for someone else
- Becoming rigid around boundaries
- Creating boundaries around almost everything

While it is important that the wounded partner not misuse boundaries, it is just as important that they start to put boundaries in where needed. Here are some common areas associated with boundaries in romantic relationships:

Physical Boundaries

Physical boundaries encompass our need for personal space, physical touch, and physical needs such as rest, nourishment, etc. To put it plainly, physical boundaries are about how we want our bodies to be treated. Sharing your physical boundaries with your partner can be helpful to your relationship. Boundaries such as when you need to rest and when you need to be alone are also important to share. Physical boundaries can be violated when someone touches you in unwanted or harmful ways (such as hugging you when you don't want a hug or hitting you) and when a person invades your personal space. An example of a common physical boundary for the wounded partner when betrayal has taken place is when they don't want the wounding partner to touch them.

Emotional Boundaries

Emotional boundaries are all about respecting feelings and emotional energy. They also let us know where we end, and another person begins. For example, if your partner is feeling agitated and you take this feeling on, you may need to put an emotional boundary in place. You can also limit conversations that take emotional energy by setting a boundary around where and when you talk about certain subjects. Emotional boundaries can be violated when someone criticizes, belittles, or invalidates your feelings.

Sexual Boundaries

Sexual boundaries are vital to any healthy romantic relationship. The idea of sexual boundaries in a relationship encompasses a mutual understanding and respect of limitations and desires between partners as well as overall consent. Sexual boundaries can be violated when we are touched in unwanted ways, coerced or pressured into sexual acts that we are uncomfortable with, guilted into having sex, or physically forced. Additionally, the act of sexual infidelity violates healthy sexual boundaries in two ways. First, it violates the agreement of sexual exclusivity between partners. Second, it violates the wounded partner's body when the wounding partner has sex with them after having sex with someone outside of the relationship. Sexual boundaries can also be violated in open relationships when the rules that the couple agrees upon regarding engaging outside parties are not followed.

Intellectual Boundaries

Intellectual boundaries are boundaries that we set around our thoughts, beliefs, and ideas. Respecting the thoughts of others, even if they are different than our own, and asking that ours are respected is important. An awareness of appropriate discussion around beliefs, thoughts, and ideas is also encompassed by the idea of intellectual boundaries. Much like emotional boundaries, intellectual boundaries are violated when a person refuses to respect our beliefs, thoughts, and ideas as well as when we don't respect another person's. This can come in the form of belittling, dismissing, or ridiculing.

Material Boundaries

The idea of material boundaries encompasses money and possessions. Healthy boundaries in this area involve setting limitations around how much of what you possess is shared with others as well as with whom it is shared. Material boundaries are violated when someone takes something that belongs to you without permission or uses something you own in ways and with people that you never agreed to. The most common ways material boundaries are violated when it comes to betrayal are when the wounding partner spends money on their infidelity-related behavior, gives gifts to an affair partner, or invites the affair partner into the family home, car, vacation properties, etc.

Time Boundaries

This type of boundary refers to how someone spends their time. We often violate our own time boundaries when we don't set aside the proper amount of time for different areas of our life or don't prioritize our time. Some ways others can violate our time boundaries are by demanding too much of our time or controlling our time by dictating how we must spend it. Another way our time boundaries can be violated is by someone who continually makes us late for things or keeps us waiting.

Non-negotiables and Ultimatums

Non-negotiables, or "dealbreakers", are important when setting boundaries when the wounding partner refuses to stop engaging in infidelity-related behavior. Where betrayal is concerned, common non-negotiables include:

- Ending the affair and cutting off all contact with the affair partner (often involves giving proof)
- Willingness to take full responsibility for their actions (now and ongoing)
- Willingness to take a polygraph (now and ongoing)
- Willingness to enter counseling or coaching (now and ongoing)
- Willingness to join an accountability group (now and ongoing)
- Willingness to open full access to phone, computer, emails, etc. (now and ongoing)

It is important for wounded partners to understand that it will take a significant amount of time (months and even years) before a relationship can be completely restored after betrayal. Many changes need to take place in both partners, and this takes time and patience. The wounding partner will need to take a hard look at themselves and put much effort into figuring out their reasons for the infidelity-related behavior without blaming their partner. The wounded partner will eventually have to forgive if the relationship is to be truly reconciled—provided that the wounding partner enters recovery. This is why we have included the words "now and ongoing" on so many of the items above. Recovery is a process.

Ultimatums are also an important part of the recovery process. You may have heard that ultimatums are unhealthy and can hurt a relationship. Although this is true in many cases, we believe that ultimatums are appropriate when it comes to ongoing infidelity-related behavior. For example, if the wounded partner has set up healthy boundaries and non-negotiables and the wounding partner keeps crossing them, it may be time for an ultimatum. Ultimatums should be considered last-resort responses to serious boundary violations. Here are some examples of appropriate ultimatums:

- "If you continue the affair, I am going to end the relationship."
- "If you continue to contact the affair partner, I will move out of the bedroom."
- "If you continue to verbally abuse me, I'm moving out."
- "If you discontinue your counseling, coaching, or accountability group I can't trust you, so I need a separation until you resume those things."

The key with non-negotiables and ultimatums is to use them sparingly. Otherwise, the wounded partner runs the risk of their words falling on deaf ears. It is also important to note that the wounded partner should not say they are going to do something in response to a boundary violation if they are not prepared to follow through with it.

Stating boundaries

When it comes to stating a boundary, we like the DESC method of communication created by Sharon and Gordon Bower as outlined in their book *Asserting Yourself*. The letters DESC break down as follows:

Describe the situation.

Express your feelings and observations about the behavior.

Specify what the ideal outcome would be.

Consequences or compromise. If the behavior persists, explain what the consequences will be. Depending on the situation, a compromise could be appropriate as well.

Here's an example of how to use the DESC method:

"I notice that when I say something you don't like you give me the silent treatment. This is hurtful to me, and I don't think it helps our relationship. Ideally, I would like to be able to have an open discussion with you about things that bother me without being given the silent treatment afterwards. If you continue doing this, I'm going to leave the house and do something fun because I don't want to experience that."

Another easy formula for stating boundaries is:

When you (insert behavior)

I feel (insert feeling)

If you (continued behavior)

I will (consequence)

Here's an example of a statement using this formula:

"When you continue communication with your affair partner I feel hurt and betrayed. If you continue to communicate with her, I will go to my mom's for a while until you can show me that you've ceased all communication."

These methods are similar to each other and can both be used to effectively communicate boundaries.

The role of consequences

You may have noticed that the methods referenced above contain consequences. Consequences play an important role when setting boundaries and should be thought of ahead of time. The proper time to use a consequence is after a boundary has been clearly stated and a person refuses to acknowledge it or honor it.

When first communicating a new boundary, we prefer to communicate it without using the consequence portion of the formula. We find that the person being communicated with usually receives what is being said better without the threat of a consequence. However, we still find it helpful to use the formulas in order to decide what the consequence will be beforehand if the boundary is repeatedly violated. Using the DESC method above, this is what the statement would look like when leaving off the "C" portion:

"I notice that when I say something you don't like you give me the silent treatment. This is hurtful to me, and I don't think it helps our relationship. Ideally, I would like to be able to have an open discussion with you about things that bother me without being given the silent treatment afterwards. Can we please agree that you will stop doing this?"

This type of statement with a request at the end gives the person a chance to respond without threat. If they honor your request, that is wonderful. If not, you can always add in the consequence portion when restating the boundary.

Enforceable consequences

When using consequences, make sure that they are something that you have the power to enforce. This means that the consequence: a) doesn't require the other person to do something, b) is something that you are ready and able to follow through on, and c) isn't overly harsh for the situation. If a consequence of a boundary violation requires the other person to do something, it is not enforceable because you can't control what someone else will and will not do. If you aren't prepared to enforce a consequence, pick a different one. By not following through, you are teaching the person that you don't really mean what you say. If your consequences are overly harsh, you may be able to enforce them, but you risk damaging your relationship by building barriers to intimacy.

Common boundary mistakes

Here are a few common mistakes that we see wounded partners make when trying to implement and enforce boundaries:

- Failing to ask for exactly what they want out of fear
- Setting boundaries that they don't believe in or aren't ready to enforce
- Setting boundaries based on what someone else thinks they should do
- Compromising their boundaries as a response to violations (changing boundaries solely based on the fact that the other person refuses to acknowledge or respect them)
- Creating too many boundaries
- Withdrawing love from the person they set a boundary with
- Failing to model the boundary themselves

The goal of boundaries is to give clear communication as to what you will and will not accept. By avoiding these mistakes, you can help ensure that you get your point across in the way you intended.

The Bible is clear about what a life without boundaries looks like.

Galatians 5: 19-21 MSG

19-21 It is obvious what kind of life develops out of trying to get your own way all the time: repetitive, loveless, cheap sex; a stinking accumulation of mental and emotional garbage; frenzied and joyless grabs for happiness; trinket gods; magic-show religion; paranoid loneliness; cutthroat competition; all-consuming-yet-never-satisfied wants; a brutal temper; an impotence to love or be loved; divided homes and divided lives; small-minded and lopsided pursuits; the vicious habit of depersonalizing everyone into a rival; uncontrolled and uncontrollable addictions; ugly parodies of community. I could go on. This isn't the first time I have warned you; you know. If you use your freedom this way, you will not inherit God's kingdom.

This is what a life with boundaries looks like.

Galatians 5: 22-26 MSG

22-23 But what happens when we live God's way? He brings gifts into our lives, much the same way that fruit appears in an orchard—things like affection for others, exuberance about life, serenity. We develop a willingness to stick with things, a sense of compassion in the heart, and a conviction that a basic holiness permeates things and people. We find ourselves involved in loyal commitments, not needing to force our way in life, able to marshal and direct our energies wisely.

23-24 Legalism is helpless in bringing this about; it only gets in the way. Among those who belong to Christ, everything connected with getting our own way and mindlessly responding to what everyone else calls necessities is killed off for good—crucified.

***25-26** Since this is the kind of life we have chosen, the life of the Spirit, let us make sure that we do not just hold it as an idea in our heads or a sentiment in our hearts, but work out its implications in every detail of our lives. That means we will not compare ourselves with each other as if one of us were better and another worse. We have far more interesting things to do with our lives. Each of us is an original.*

Prayer for the wounded partner:

Father, give me the grace to celebrate You every day and all day long! I am working with You and with my wounding partner when I cooperate with You and keep myself in an attitude of thankfulness and worship. This proves to You that I am grateful for what You are working on in the heart and emotions of my wounding partner behind the scenes. Instead of worrying, I will pray. I will present my petitions and praises before You. As I do this, You will take action on my concerns. Your word insures that You are working everything for my good. This settles my spirit and calms my emotions. I displace worry with Christ because HE is the center of my life! I fill my mind with truth, noble, reputable, authentic, compelling and gracious thoughts and subject matter. I meditate on the beautiful and not the ugly, I think of things to praise and not to curse or cause me pain. I will put self-discipline into practice and keep myself in boundaries that will maintain my spiritual, emotional, and physical health in optimal condition. I am a temple of the Holy Spirit and I take care of my temple. As I do this, You, Father, will bring everything in my life into harmony and make everything work together for my good. In Jesus' name, Amen.

Prayer for wounding partner:

Father, give me the grace to live Your way. Cause me to have affection for my wounded partner. Cause me to have exuberance about life and to live with serenity. Provide me grace with the willingness to stick with things, to gain a sense of compassion in my heart and a conviction that basic holiness permeates things and people. Give me the grace to be loyal and committed to my wounded partner, and to be able to marshal and direct my energies wisely. Remove my heart of stone and replace it with a heart of flesh. By Your grace, I willingly crucify the evil I once determined was a necessity of my life. I will live the life of the Spirit and will work out its implications in every detail of my life. In Jesus' name, Amen.

PART 11

Trust-Breaking Behavior #2
Refusing to Acknowledge Lies, Gaslighting, and Minimizing

The second trust-breaking behavior is a refusal on the wounding partner's part to acknowledge past or ongoing lies, gaslighting, and minimizing. It is not uncommon for us to hear statements from wounding partners such as, "I'm being honest now, why can't my partner just get over it?" or, "It meant nothing to me, I don't understand why it's such a big deal!" When we hear statements like these, it is clear to us that the person making them has no clue as to how their actions have affected their partner. And, if it is clear to us, it will definitely be clear to the wounded partner. These types of statements scream to the wounded partner that the wounding partner is still protecting themselves and is, therefore, untrustworthy.

Gaslighting

When a wounded partner is gaslighted, it causes them to feel confused, powerless, and sometimes downright crazy. This is because gaslighting involves the wounding partner deliberately trying to get the wounded partner to question their reality. For wounded partners, being in a long-term relationship with someone who gaslights creates a prison of psychological trauma, anxiety, isolation, and depression. A refusal by the wounding partner to acknowledge past gaslighting is the same as refusing to give their partner a key by which their prison door can be opened. Eventually, the wounded partner will need to find their own way out of the prison, and that often means leaving the relationship. If you as a wounding partner think that gaslighting your partner is a way to get them to stay with you, think again. Additionally, a refusal to acknowledge past gaslighting is, in and of itself, continued gaslighting. In essence, your refusal to acknowledge the problem denies your partner's reality that something occurred. This is a common tactic known as withholding (more on withholding below). Here are some common gaslighting tactics:

- Countering: Countering involves the questioning of someone's memory of events
- Withholding: Pretending not to understand what someone is talking about or refusing to accept the validity of someone's experience

- Forgetting: Pretending to have forgotten something or denying that something happened
- Trivializing: Making someone's concerns or feelings seem unimportant or irrational
- Diverting/Blocking: Changing the subject or focusing on the credibility of what is being said instead of the content (Medical News Today, 2020)

Common statements associated with gaslighting include:

- "You never remember things correctly."
- "I never said that."
- "You're being too sensitive."
- "That never happened."
- "I never understand what you're talking about."
- "Your memory is bad. You need to see someone."
- "You seem off. You need help."
- "You're crazy."
- "The kids think you're crazy."
- "This is why you don't have any friends."
- "You can never take a joke."
- "You're the one gaslighting me."

It is important to note that gaslighting is intentional. Therefore, if you are trying to determine whether or not someone is gaslighting you, you need to understand the person's motives surrounding what they are saying. Gaslighting is an *intentional* **behavior directed at diminishing someone's sense of reality or denying their experiences as a way of helping the gaslighter save face**, avoid responsibility, protect ego, or win an argument. "The crux of gaslighting involves a sense of *malice*, i.e., an intentional attempt to deny someone's reality for the gaslighter's gain (even if this gain is subtle or unacknowledged)." (Guha, 2021)

Here is an account of Naboth, who owned a vineyard by his family inheritance and would not sell out to the king because it would be a shameful action. Since he was an integrous man, Jezebel and Ahab gaslighted the community by using religion as a tool. They created a day of "fasting", hired two scoundrels who "heard from God" and accused Naboth of cursing both God and King. The punishment for such an action was death. Once Naboth was stoned to death by the community, thereby keeping their hands "clean", Jezebel and Ahab took possession of his vineyard and considered their malicious action justified for their personal gain.

1 Kings 21 NIV- Naboth's Vineyard

21 Sometime later there was an incident involving a vineyard belonging to Naboth the Jezreelite. The vineyard was in Jezreel, close to the palace of Ahab, king of Samaria. 2 Ahab said to Naboth, "Let me have your vineyard to use for a vegetable garden, since it is close to my palace. In exchange I will give you a better vineyard or, if you prefer, I will pay you whatever it is worth."

3 But Naboth replied, "The Lord forbid that I should give you the inheritance of my ancestors."

4 So Ahab went home, sullen and angry because Naboth the Jezreelite had said, "I will not give you the inheritance of my ancestors." He lay on his bed sulking and refused to eat.

5 His wife Jezebel came in and asked him, "Why are you so sullen? Why won't you eat?"

6 He answered her, "Because I said to Naboth the Jezreelite, 'Sell me your vineyard; or if you prefer, I will give you another vineyard in its place.' But he said, 'I will not give you my vineyard.'"

7 Jezebel his wife said, "Is this how you act as king over Israel? Get up and eat! Cheer up. I'll get you the vineyard of Naboth the Jezreelite."

8 So she wrote letters in Ahab's name, placed his seal on them, and sent them to the elders and nobles who lived in Naboth's city with him. 9 In those letters she wrote:

"Proclaim a day of fasting and seat Naboth in a prominent place among the people. 10 But seat two scoundrels opposite him and have them bring charges that he has cursed both God and the king. Then take him out and stone him to death."

11 So the elders and nobles who lived in Naboth's city did as Jezebel directed in the letters she had written to them. 12 They proclaimed a fast and seated Naboth in a prominent place among the people. 13 Then two scoundrels came and sat opposite him and brought charges against Naboth before the people, saying, "Naboth has cursed both God and the king." So they took him outside the city and stoned him to death. 14 Then they sent word to Jezebel: "Naboth has been stoned to death."

15 As soon as Jezebel heard that Naboth had been stoned to death, she said to Ahab, "Get up and take possession of the vineyard of Naboth the Jezreelite that he refused to sell you. He is no longer alive, but dead." 16 When Ahab heard that Naboth was dead, he got up and went down to take possession of Naboth's vineyard.

17 Then the word of the Lord came to Elijah the Tishbite: 18 "Go down to meet Ahab king of Israel, who rules in Samaria. He is now in Naboth's vineyard, where he has gone to take possession of it. 19 Say to him, 'This is what the Lord says: Have you not murdered a man and seized his property?' Then say to him, 'This is what the Lord says: In the place where dogs licked up Naboth's blood, dogs will lick up your blood—yes, yours!'"

20 Ahab said to Elijah, "So you have found me, my enemy!"

"I have found you," he answered, "because you have sold yourself to do evil in the eyes of the Lord. 21 He says, 'I am going to bring disaster on you. I will wipe out your descendants and cut off from Ahab every last male in Israel—slave or free.[a] 22 I will make your house like that of Jeroboam son of Nebat and that of Baasha son of Ahijah, because you have aroused my anger and have caused Israel to sin.'

23 "And also concerning Jezebel the Lord says: 'Dogs will devour Jezebel by the wall of[b] Jezreel.'

24 "Dogs will eat those belonging to Ahab who die in the city, and the birds will feed on those who die in the country."

25 (There was never anyone like Ahab, who sold himself to do evil in the eyes of the Lord, urged on by Jezebel, his wife. 26 He behaved in the vilest manner by going after idols, like the Amorites the Lord drove out before Israel.)

God considers gaslighting vile. Walk in the fear of the Lord, it is the beginning of wisdom. Knowledge of the Holy One brings understanding.

Minimizing

"Arguments of convenience lack integrity and inevitably trip you up."— Donald Rumsfeld

In the quote above, Donald Rumsfeld uses the term "arguments of convenience" to describe the type of arguments that arise from a person's need to argue something that they don't even completely believe themselves because it suits their needs in the moment. Arguments that include minimization on the part of the wounding partner are often arguments of convenience. Although we will concede that wounding partners tend to be unempathetic early in recovery, it is not uncommon for them to eventually acknowledge that they minimize their partner's feelings in an attempt to escape feeling the full consequences of their actions.

The trouble with minimizing is that it essentially tells the wounded partner that their experience, and what they feel as a result, is not a big deal. The definition of the word "minimize" is "to represent at the lowest possible amount, value, importance, influence, etc.—especially in a disparaging way." (Dictionary. com) When the wounding partner minimizes the wounded partner's experience, they are reducing that experience to the lowest possible importance level. Typically, the wounding partner engages in minimization in order to escape feelings of guilt and shame. While this is understandable, it is ill-advised. Some wounding partners who minimize do so because they believe that the consequences of their actions won't be as bad if they can reduce the value of their impact. They think if they can get their partner to concede to the idea that what they did was no big deal, they can get them to move on. This is a way of trying to escape one of the largest consequences of their actions—a troubled and tumultuous relationship. When the wounding partner minimizes the impacts of their behavior, they are taking on a defensive stance. Minimization is only one step away from complete denial of any personal responsibility for the situation.

Whatever the reason for using minimization as a tactic, it sends a bad message to the wounded partner for the following reasons:

- It says you are unwilling/unable to accept the consequences of your actions. This sets off an alarm bell with the wounded partner because, if you can't accept consequences, you aren't likely to learn from the situation.

- It shows that you just don't get it. Minimization shows a lack of empathy. It tells the wounded partner that you simply don't understand how your actions have impacted them.

- It says you are willing to throw them under the bus. When you minimize your partner's experience, you are essentially trading the validation of their feelings (something that would help them in their pain) for your own comfort.

- It says that, on some level, you are rationalizing your behavior. In order to minimize the impact of your infidelity-related behavior, you have to rationalize some of it away as not being important.

- It says that you lack the ability to self-reflect. Since minimization is a defensive tactic, it can keep you from doing the self-reflection necessary to truly change your ways.

Minimization is detrimental to the rebuilding trust process because it tells the wounded partner that the wounding partner is still selfishly motivated. When the wounding partner uses minimization as a defensive strategy, the wounded partner receives the message that they are much more interested in saving themselves than they are in saving the relationship. Additionally, minimization tells the wounded partner that the wounding partner lacks integrity. When a wounding partner minimizes, they essentially tell the wounded partner that their lack of follow through on their commitment to the relationship was no big deal. Commitments *are* a big deal. They are an indicator of important character traits such as self-discipline, self-sacrifice, and persistence. A person who is committed is focused and, as a result, is willing to go outside of their comfort zone in order to honor their commitments. A person who lacks commitment lacks focus and, as a result, can end up making hazy choices. When the wounding partner engages in minimization, they show that they haven't changed and that the same character defects that led them to make the decision to engage in infidelity-related behavior are still present.

Potiphar's wife minimized the act of adultery by attempting to convince Joseph that having sex with her is the equivalent of performing just another household task.

Genesis 39:6-20 NIV

Now Joseph was well-built and handsome, 7 and after a while his master's wife took notice of Joseph and said, "Come to bed with me!"

8 But he refused. "With me in charge," he told her, "my master does not concern himself with anything in the house; everything he owns he has entrusted to my care. 9 No one is greater in this house than I am. My master has withheld nothing from me except you, because you are his wife. How then could I do such a wicked thing and sin against God?" 10 And though she spoke to Joseph day after day, he refused to go to bed with her or even be with her.

11 One day he went into the house to attend to his duties, and none of the household servants was inside. 12 She caught him by his cloak and said, "Come to bed with me!" But he left his cloak in her hand and ran out of the house.

13 When she saw that he had left his cloak in her hand and had run out of the house, 14 she called her household servants. "Look," she said to them, "this Hebrew has been brought to us to make sport of us! He came in here to sleep with me, but I screamed. 15 When he heard me scream for help, he left his cloak beside me and ran out of the house."

16 She kept his cloak beside her until his master came home. 17 Then she told him this story: "That Hebrew slave you brought us came to me to make sport of me. 18 But as soon as I screamed for help, he left his cloak beside me and ran out of the house."

19 When his master heard the story his wife told him, saying, "This is how your slave treated me," he burned with anger. 20 Joseph's master took him and put him in prison, the place where the king's prisoners were confined.

God considers minimizing abhorrent.

Lying

Most wounded partners tell us that, as hard as it is to forgive betrayal, it's even harder to forgive the deception surrounding the betrayal. The fact that the wounding partner had a secret life that they knew nothing about can be a hard thing to get over. It is even harder to get over when someone keeps lying. After a while, the wounded partner begins to wonder if the wounding partner is even capable of telling the truth. This can seriously affect their willingness to move forward with the relationship. Additionally, when the wounding partner repeatedly lies, they send the message that they are more interested in protecting themselves than they are in caring for their partner's broken heart.

This is an account of Gehazi, the attendant to the prophet Elisha. In a space of a few hours, he lied to himself, to Naaman, and to Elisha. He just wouldn't stop lying!!

Kings 5: 15, 16, 19-27 NIV

15 Then Naaman and all his attendants went back to the man of God. He stood before him and said, "Now I know that there is no God in all the world except in Israel. So please accept a gift from your servant."

16 The prophet answered, "As surely as the Lord lives, whom I serve, I will not accept a thing." And even though Naaman urged him, he refused.

After Naaman had traveled some distance, 20 Gehazi, the servant of Elisha the man of God, said to himself, "My master was too easy on Naaman, this Aramean, by not accepting from him what he brought. As surely as the Lord lives, I will run after him and get something from him."

21 So Gehazi hurried after Naaman. When Naaman saw him running toward him, he got down from the chariot to meet him. "Is everything all right?" he asked.

22 "Everything is alright," Gehazi answered. "My master sent me to say, 'Two young men from the company of the prophets have just come to me from the hill country of Ephraim. Please give them a talent[d] of silver and two sets of clothing.'"

23 "By all means, take two talents," said Naaman. He urged Gehazi to accept them, and then tied up the two talents of silver in two bags, with two sets of clothing. He gave them to two of his servants, and they carried them ahead of Gehazi. 24 When Gehazi came to the hill, he took the things from the servants and put them away in the house. He sent the men away and they left.

25 When he went in and stood before his master, Elisha asked him, "Where have you been, Gehazi?"

"Your servant didn't go anywhere," Gehazi answered.

26 But Elisha said to him, "Was not my spirit with you when the man got down from his chariot to meet you? Is this the time to take money or to accept clothes—or olive groves and vineyards, or flocks and herds, or male and female slaves? 27 Naaman's leprosy will cling to you and to your descendants forever." Then Gehazi went from Elisha's presence and his skin was leprous—it had become as white as snow.

Lying brings on the judgment of God.

Prayer for wounding partner:

Father, I repent of living in an attitude of disrespect and disregard towards You and towards my wounded partner. I will no longer engage in sins that feed my addiction. I will no longer use my body, mind, will and emotions as weapons of wickedness. Gaslighting, minimizing and lying are an abomination to You, degrades me to something that is less than human and traumatizes my wounded partner. Forgive me for taking on the attitude of a prostitute, reveling in evil and then asking who is next in line to sin with. I am now a weapon of righteousness and I live in the Kingdom of Your dear Son. I will do everything in my power to live a life that is worthy of You and to promote trust and healing into the life of my wounded partner. In Jesus' name, Amen.

Trust is pivotal to all healthy relationships. The whole reason we wrote this book was to help couples rebuild the trust that has been torn down by betrayal. Lying and deception not only break trust, but they also lead to more lies and deception to cover up the initial lying and deception. This results in a never-ending, downward spiral that ultimately leads to the complete breakdown of the relationship. Lying also prevents the deep, important conversations that are at the core of committed relationships from happening because distrust can often lead to withdrawal on the wounded partner's part. A lack of communication will also lead to a breakdown of the relationship. Outright lying, half- truths, lies by omission, and even carelessness with seemingly minor details will hamper momentum toward the recovery of the relationship.

PART 12

Trust-Building Belief #1

"I am 100% responsible for my choices."

Now that we have gone through the most common and detrimental trust-breaking behaviors that we see in our practice, let's talk about trust-building beliefs that we consider to be integral to the rebuilding trust process.

The first trust-building belief is the wounding partner's belief that they are 100% responsible for their choice to engage in infidelity-related behavior. Until the wounding partner can accept responsibility for the choices that contributed to their betrayal, progress in the rebuilding trust process will stall out. Many of the behaviors that hamper the rebuilding of trust in a relationship stem from the wounding partner's need to blame, at least in part, others for their choices. This creates a victim mentality (more on that shortly) that hampers connection to self and others. Here are some reasons why accepting responsibility is important:

- It increases confidence. Although many people who refuse to take responsibility for their actions act grandiose, they usually feel the opposite way inside. Working through our mistakes allows us to become free from the guilt, shame, and regret associated with bad choices.

- It allows us to fix your mistakes. It may feel momentarily better to refuse taking responsibility, but we actually disempower ourselves when we do it. Accepting responsibility is the only way to give ourselves back the power to change things.

- It keeps us from damaging others. When we blame other people for our actions, especially a wounded partner, we hurt them emotionally. Taking responsibility keeps us from unnecessarily hurting others that we say we care about.

- It allows us more control over our life. When we take responsibility for our life choices, we can become the author of our own life instead of a victim to everything that happens to us.

When we encounter a lack of willingness to accept responsibility in the clients we work with, it is typically driven from a place of shame. Most of us will profess the fact that we believe the statement that "no one is perfect". However, so many of us don't live it out. Perfectionism and blame can stem from a deep seated fear of people seeing us for who we are. The shame-driven person believes that if anyone knew who they really were, they would not be loved. As a result, if we are shame-based, we feel unlovable unless we are perfect. This is where a refusal to accept responsibility comes in. If we can blame others for our actions, we hope to look faultless and, therefore, better in the eyes of others. Deceiving ourselves into believing that we are less culpable for our actions than we truly are as an attempt to look better in our own eyes can lead to an inflated ego. Instead of understanding that we make mistakes just like everyone else, we tell ourselves that we somehow make less mistakes than everyone else does and are, therefore, better.

In the case of betrayal, it is not uncommon for a certain percentage of wounding partners to blame the wounded partner, at least in part, for their infidelity-related behavior. This is especially common within the first six months of recovery. We want to state in no uncertain terms that **blame toward the wounded partner for any portion of the wounding partner's infidelity-related behavior is entirely inappropriate and highly damaging to both the wounded partner and to the relationship.** We understand that wounded partners have limitations and imperfections as all human beings do. However, when the wounding partner focuses on these limitations and imperfections as a way to blame shift, they are re-wounding their partner in an attempt to make themselves feel better. Infidelity is always a choice. The wounding partner could have dealt with whatever feelings, disappointments, etc. that they were experiencing in a multitude of different ways, and they *chose* to be unfaithful. Even if they were driven by addiction, it was still their choice to not deal with the addiction that led to the infidelity-related behavior. The choice to indulge any behavior at the expense of someone we claim to love is always wrong. This includes infidelity, but can also include blame-shifting, gaslighting, and defensiveness as well.

This is an account of David who committed adultery. We all know all the blame shifting, gaslighting and defensiveness he acted upon. This is what it took for him to finally admit the truth.

2 Samuel 12: 1-13 NIV

12 The Lord sent Nathan to David. When he came to him, he said, "There were two men in a certain town, one rich and the other poor. 2 The rich man had a very large number of sheep and cattle, 3 but the poor man had nothing except one little ewe lamb he had bought. He raised it, and it grew up with him and his children. It shared his food, drank from his cup and even slept in his arms. It was like a daughter to him.

4 "Now a traveler came to the rich man, but the rich man refrained from taking one of his own sheep or cattle to prepare a meal for the traveler who had come to him. Instead, he took the ewe lamb that belonged to the poor man and prepared it for the one who had come to him."

5 David burned with anger against the man and said to Nathan, "As surely as the Lord lives, the man who did this must die! 6 He must pay for that lamb four times over, because he did such a thing and had no pity."

7 Then Nathan said to David, "You are the man! This is what the Lord, the God of Israel, says: 'I anointed you king over Israel, and I delivered you from the hand of Saul. 8 I gave your master's house to you, and your master's wives into your arms. I gave you all Israel and Judah. And if all this had been too little, I would have given you even more. 9 Why did you despise the word of the Lord by doing what is evil in his eyes? You struck down Uriah the Hittite with the sword and took his wife to be your own. You killed him with the sword of the Ammonites. 10 Now, therefore, the sword will never depart from your house, because you despised me and took the wife of Uriah the Hittite to be your own.'

11 "This is what the Lord says: 'Out of your own household I am going to bring calamity on you. Before your very eyes I will take your wives and give them to one who is close to you, and he will sleep with your wives in broad daylight. 12 You did it in secret, but I will do this thing in broad daylight before all Israel.'"

13 Then David said to Nathan, "I have sinned against the Lord."

David suffered over this sin for the rest of his life. The consequences spilled over into the next generation. Learn from David's mistakes!

Proverbs 21:11 MSG

Simpletons only learn the hard way, but the wise learn by listening.

We get asked by many wounding partners when it is that they can finally talk about the wounded partner's issues instead of theirs. Our answer to that is a challenge. If the wounding partner can go a number of months and take responsibility without defending, then they can check with us to see if it is time to talk about the wounded partner's problems. The length of the challenge varies depending on the individual's propensity to defend and blame. However, generally speaking, the average time is about six months. We don't do this to be mean. Instead, we challenge the wounding partner in this way in order to let the relationship breathe and give the wounded partner time to heal—which cannot happen if blame is constantly being hurled their way. The truth is that a wounded partner is highly unlikely to look at any of their shortcomings until the wounding partner has completely accepted responsibility for their actions without defense for quite some time. When this challenge is completed correctly, it isn't uncommon for the wounded partner to become completely willing to look at other parts of the relationship in order to understand what changes they can personally make to strengthen it. However, it is never appropriate for a wounded partner to accept blame in any way for their partner's choice to betray them. The wounding partner must accept that they are 100% responsible for their actions, and the devastation that those actions have caused if true recovery is to happen within themselves and within the relationship.

Trust-Building Belief #2

"People can change."

The second trust-building belief is that people can change. We want to preface this section by stating that some people *won't* change because they continue to make destructive choices for a myriad of reasons. However, the idea that people *can't* change is an erroneous one. People change all the time. That is not to imply that change comes easily. In the case of mindsets that lead to infidelity and/or addiction, the changes that lead to good relationships with self and others are hard won. They require a vast amount of difficult work in the areas of self-reflection and behavior modification. They also require humility and a willingness to be mentored by someone who has succeeded in the area(s) where success is desired. However, to say that these changes aren't possible just because they aren't easy is entirely false. People do change. How else could we explain the success stories of famous people like Robert Downey Jr. and Jamie Lee Curtis who found their way out of the struggle of substance abuse? Or the countless number of everyday people all over the world who find help for issues such as overeating, sex addiction, and gambling through 12-step programs.

Our Heavenly Father transforms us from caterpillars to butterflies! He makes everything possible! A great example of this is Saul of Tarsus who transformed into Paul the Apostle.

Acts 9: 1-22 NIV

9 Meanwhile, Saul was still breathing out murderous threats against the Lord's disciples. He went to the high priest 2 and asked him for letters to the synagogues in Damascus, so that if he found any there who belonged to the Way, whether men or women, he might take them as prisoners to Jerusalem. 3 As he neared Damascus on his journey, suddenly a light from heaven flashed around him. 4 He fell to the ground and heard a voice say to him, "Saul, Saul, why do you persecute me?"

5 "Who are you, Lord?" Saul asked.

"I am Jesus, whom you are persecuting," he replied. 6 "Now get up and go into the city, and you will be told what you must do."

7 The men traveling with Saul stood there speechless; they heard the sound but did not see anyone. 8 Saul got up from the ground, but when he opened his eyes he could see nothing. So they led him by the hand into Damascus. 9 For three days he was blind and did not eat or drink anything.

10 In Damascus there was a disciple named Ananias. The Lord called to him in a vision, "Ananias!"

"Yes, Lord," he answered.

11 The Lord told him, "Go to the house of Judas on Straight Street and ask for a man from Tarsus named Saul, for he is praying. 12 In a vision he has seen a man named Ananias come and place his hands on him to restore his sight."

13 "Lord," Ananias answered, "I have heard many reports about this man and all the harm he has done to your holy people in Jerusalem. 14 And he has come here with authority from the chief priests to arrest all who call on your name."

15 But the Lord said to Ananias, "Go! This man is my chosen instrument to proclaim my name to the Gentiles and their kings and to the people of Israel. 16 I will show him how much he must suffer for my name."

17 Then Ananias went to the house and entered it. Placing his hands on Saul, he said, "Brother Saul, the Lord—Jesus, who appeared to you on the road as you were coming here—has sent me so that you may see again and be filled with the Holy Spirit." 18 Immediately, something like scales fell from Saul's eyes, and he could see again. He got up and was baptized, 19 and after taking some food, he regained his strength.

Saul spent several days with the disciples in Damascus. 20 At once he began to preach in the synagogues that Jesus is the Son of God. 21 All those who heard him were astonished and asked, "Isn't he the man who raised havoc in Jerusalem among those who call on this name? And hasn't he come here to take them as prisoners to the chief priests?" 22 Yet Saul grew more and more powerful and baffled the Jews living in Damascus by proving that Jesus is the Messiah.

Stanford Professor of Psychology Dr. Carol Dweck has completed multiple studies on students in order to help determine why some people thrive in the face of adversity where others fail. What she discovered is what she refers to as the difference between a growth and a fixed mindset. In her book *Mindset: The New Psychology of Success*, Dr. Dweck attributes the following attitudes to a fixed mindset:

- A focus on validation
- A belief that potential is fixed and pre-determined
- Threatened by the success of others
- A need for certainty
- A reluctance to put in extra effort
- A tendency to crumble under pressure

Whereas those with a growth mindset present the following attitudes:

- A focus on learning
- A desire for ongoing improvement
- A willingness to accept challenges
- A willingness to accept effort as a measure of success
- A willingness to learn from the success of others
- A willingness to learn and grow from failure

In one of her TED Talks, Dr. Dweck makes the statement that the students who had fixed mindsets were "gripped by the tyranny of the now instead of empowered by the 'not yet'". ("Developing a Growth Mindset with Carol Dweck", 2014, TED Talks)

So, how does this apply to recovery from betrayal? The answer is that the belief on both the wounding and the wounded partners' part that change is possible is crucial to the recovery process. If either partner is gripped by the tyranny of the now, it could impede progress that could be made toward the future. When people let go of the idea that abilities are fixed traits, they can open their minds up to the possibility that abilities can, instead, be developed through things like hard work, perseverance, and mentorship. The core belief of a fixed mindset is that everyone has a fixed amount of skills and, therefore, a fixed potential. If someone then fails in a certain area, such as upholding the commitment to be faithful, they have failed altogether and, therefore, do not have what it takes to ever be faithful. This is not necessarily true. Although the phrase, "once a cheater, always a cheater" has some research to back it up, we would submit to you that serial cheaters are such not because of lack of potential, but because of the lack of willingness to do what is necessary to change. People don't engage in infidelity-related behavior because they lack potential. They engage in it because they lack personal and relationship skills and make choices that provide them with what they think of as an easy way out of those challenges. Instead of putting in the hard work necessary to make lasting change, they take what they think is the easier path of self-indulgence and self-gratification.

We encourage wounding partners to take a close look at what might be holding them back from making the changes necessary to help their partner heal and, hopefully, help mend the relationship. If you find yourself resisting change, evaluate your thoughts to see if your resistance could be due to a fixed mindset.

How we respond to the following issues can make the difference between making personal growth and staying stuck:

- Criticism. How we respond to criticism is indicative of our mindset. Those who respond by defending and blaming are typically responding that way because they think if they admit to faults, that makes them less than other people. Instead, try asking yourself if there is any truth to what is being said. If there is, try to make the changes necessary to fix the issue.
- Challenges. When those with a fixed mindset are challenged, they tend to give up almost immediately. Instead of giving up, commit to figuring out what you need to do (not what others need to do) in order to overcome the challenge.
- Setbacks. When those with a fixed mindset encounter a setback, they tend to not only give up but take it as a sign that they don't have what it takes to try again. A growth mindset says that setbacks are valuable learning experiences that can help us do better the next time.

- The skills of others. How we respond to another person being better at something than us says a lot about which mindset we are operating from. Those operating from fixedmindsets will often be threatened by the idea of someone being better than them at something because they thinkit means that they aren't good enough. Instead of feeling threatened, ask yourself what you can learn from that personin order to increase your own skills.

When we see wounded partners operate from a fixed mindset, it typically shows up as a rigidness toward the wounding partner even if they have truly engaged in recovery. This fixed mindset comes out in statements like, "they will never change" and, "I still don't trust them", even though the wounding partner has been consistent for a significant period of time with recovery work. We would like to qualify this by stating that it is completely normal to have a healthy amount of skepticism about a wounding partner's willingness to change early on in recovery—particularly in the first 6-9 months. In fact, we get concerned when wounded partners extend trust to the wounding partner right away. As we stated previously, trust has to be earned and the wounding partner must show that they are willing to do whatever it takes over an extended period of time to help heal the damage they have caused. Extending trust too quickly, especially without requiring the wounding partner to be ongoingly accountable, is imprudent and could set the wounded partner up for hurt and disappointment later on. Of course it is also possible that the wounding partner is checking "all of the right boxes" of recovery but there has been no change of heart. However, if the couple is well into recovery and the wounding partner has an attitude conducive to rebuilding trust, the wounded partner could be struggling with a fixed mindset.

In the Book of Philemon, first we see Paul praising Philemon for his work for the Lord, his love for other Christians and his gift of hospitality. Then he addresses Philemon about his runaway slave, Onesimus. Paul notes the change in Onesimus, so much so that to return him to Philemon would cost him a great personal loss of comfort and companionship. Onesimus must have truly metamorphosized from his former self into a man of honor. Paul discipled him and it was probably a long and arduous process, but finally, he was confident in the development of Onesimus' Christian character. He used his influence over Philemon to remove any rigidity of attitude he had towards Onesimus and requested that he would accept him back into his household. Paul rebuilt Philemon's trust in Onesimus.

Philemon 8-22 MSG

8-9 In line with all this I have a favor to ask of you. As Christ's ambassador and now a prisoner for him, I wouldn't hesitate to command this if I thought it necessary, but I'd rather make it a personal request.

10-14 While here in jail, I've fathered a child, so to speak. And here he is, hand-carrying this letter—Onesimus! He was useless to you before; now he's useful to both of us. I'm sending him back to you, but it feels like I'm cutting off my right arm in doing so. I wanted in the worst way to keep him here as your stand-in to help out while I'm in jail for the Message. But I didn't want to do anything behind your back, make you do a good deed that you hadn't willingly agreed to.

15-16 Maybe it's all for the best that you lost him for a while. You're getting him back now for good—and no mere slave this time, but a true Christian brother! That's what he was to me—he'll be even more than that to you.

17-20 So if you still consider me a comrade-in-arms, welcome him back as you would me. If he damaged anything or owes you anything, chalk it up to my account. This is my personal signature—Paul—and I stand behind it. (I don't need to remind you, do I, that you owe your very life to me?) Do me this big favor, friend. You'll be doing it for Christ, but it will also do my heart good.

21-22 I know you well enough to know you will. You'll probably go far beyond what I've written.

Paul understood the power of a healthy mindset when someone is going through recovery. He was supportive and encouraging to Onesimus and even willing to pay for any damages Onesimus had caused. Paul understood God's transforming power that was at work in Onesimus because Paul experienced it personally.

Prayer for the wounding partner:

Father, transform me into the image of Your dear Son, Jesus Christ. I will feed myself with Your holy word and allow You to do your work in my mind and my heart. I will not be a simpleton and learn only the hard way, through the school of hard knocks. But I will be wise and learn by listening and doing what my counselors and Your word says to do. In Jesus' name Amen.

Prayer for wounded partner:

Father, give me the grace to be like Paul. He knew and understood when real change took place. Give me that ability to know and understand when real change has taken place, so I can trust my wounding partner once again. Help me to encourage them in this long and arduous process so we can all have victory in this situation. In Jesus' name, Amen.

PART 13

Trust-Breaking Belief #1

"I am a victim."

Now that we have covered the two most important trust- building beliefs, let's discuss the most common trust- breaking beliefs. When we see these beliefs in our practice, we can accurately predict that both the individual with these beliefs along with the relationship will stall out in recovery.

The first trust-breaking belief is when the wounding partner believes that they are a victim. We all know someone who frequently plays the victim card. The self-pity, the "everything is everyone else's fault", the "poor me". When it comes to working with wounding partners, we often see the victim card played out as blame toward the wounded partner. It can also come out when they seek pity from other members of our coaching groups for what they are having to "endure" at home regarding their partner's anger. We often see it in individual coaching sessions as well; when a wounding partner tries to justify their infidelity-related behavior by talking about how the wounded partner wasn't meeting their needs prior to the affair, to the pornography, or whatever. Some even try to get us to believe that they are the double victim—first of their partner's "neglect", that "made" them act out, and now of their partner's anger toward them because of the betrayal. What they fail to see is that they are the author of their own circumstances.

When wounding partners play the victim card, they try to get everyone around them to accept the fact that they were somehow driven to their infidelity-related behavior out of necessity. They want people to believe that they are somehow faultless victims of cruel partners who neglected them so much that they were driven to cheat, lie, and deceive. That their partner practically forced them to engage in infidelity. When a wounding partner plays the victim card, their sole focus is on image management. They think that by playing the victim that they will somehow look better. That if people will just accept the fact that they were simply being driven to infidelity by valid human needs such as love, attention, sexual intimacy, and affirmation, they will understand how the wounding partner really had no other choice and is, therefore, not to blame for their actions. But they did have a choice, and they chose to betray their partner.

Some wounding partners who play the victim card sound self-righteous. We think this happens because to play the victim, they have to justify their bad behavior in their own mind first. Once the behavior has been justified, they fool themselves into believing that they are somehow the wronged party, and this leads them to self-righteous indignation. The problem is that most of us, especially the wounded partner, aren't buying what they are selling. Playing the victim is unattractive. All it does is highlight to the wounded partner, and almost everyone else, the true depth of that person's self-absorption.

When wounding partners play the victim card, they typically do so out of fear. Many times they want to be rescued or excused from having to do the hard work of recovery because it is daunting due to their lack of skills. The problem is that no one can do the work for another person. While we will admit that the work that needs to be done by the wounding partner in order to rebuild trust in a relationship is difficult, they are the only one who can do it. If they continue to play the victim card instead of doing the work, it makes them unsafe for the wounded partner. The result is often that the wounded partner pulls away in self-protection because they know that, while the wounding partner is busy wallowing in self-pity, they have been completely forgotten.

What wounding partners who play the victim card don't realize is that they are missing a chance to help heal the relationship. By seeing something intimidating like recovery and moving toward it out of a commitment to the relationship, the wounding partner is showing courage which could, over time, win them the respect of the wounded partner. Even if the relationship cannot be restored, the wounding partner still needs to do the work so that they don't carry their issues into a new relationship down the road.

A Word About Resentments

If you are a wounded partner reading this, please don't take what we have to say about the wounding partner's resentments toward you as us condoning their behavior. As we have stated many times, the decision to engage in infidelity-related behavior is 100% the responsibility of the wounding partner. You did nothing to make your partner choose to betray you instead of dealing with issues in a constructive way. That being said, we do need to address the issue of the wounding partner's resentments toward the wounded partner because these resentments often represent justifications in their mind for their behavior and can lead to victim mentality.

When we work with wounding partners, it is not uncommon for them to have resentments that they hold against the wounded partner. While we encourage that all wounding partners take 100% responsibility for their poor choices, we understand that it is unwise to leave these resentments undealt with. Whether the wounding partner has built up resentments out of unrealistic expectations, entitlement, or real issues, they will need to deal with these if recovery is to take place. From our standpoint, it isn't the wounding partner's resentment and anger that are truly the problem. It is the fact that they often use those feelings to justify bad behavior. If you are a wounding partner reading this, it is of utmost importance that you surround yourself with people that do not reinforce your need to justify in any way. You should not share your resentments with your partner within the first six to twelve months of recovery because this will be extremely hurtful to them and come off as blaming. However, if you are a wounding partner with resentments, you will need somewhere safe to work through your feelings. We recommend that you engage a trained coach or counselor in order to work on anger and resentment toward your partner. Your coach or counselor can also help you decide when the right time would be for you to share your issues with your partner, should the need arise. If you hold onto your anger and resentment, you will not only stall out in your own recovery process, but you will likely continue to engage in defending, blaming, and playing the victim, which will further damage your relationship.

Genesis 4:2-12 NIV

Now Abel kept flocks, and Cain worked the soil. 3 In the course of time Cain brought some of the fruits of the soil as an offering to the Lord. 4 And Abel also brought an offering—fat portions from some of the firstborn of his flock. The Lord looked with favor on Abel and his offering, 5 but on Cain and his offering he did not look with favor. So Cain was very angry, and his face was downcast.

6 Then the Lord said to Cain, "Why are you angry? Why is your face downcast? 7 If you do what is right, will you not be accepted? But if you do not do what is right, sin is crouching at your door; it desires to have you, but you must rule over it."

8 Now Cain said to his brother Abel, "Let's go out to the field."[d] While they were in the field, Cain attacked his brother Abel and killed him.

9 Then the Lord said to Cain, "Where is your brother Abel?"

"I don't know," he replied. "Am I my brother's keeper?"

10 The Lord said, "What have you done? Listen! Your brother's blood cries out to me from the ground. 11 Now you are under a curse and driven from the ground, which opened its mouth to receive your brother's blood from your hand. 12 When you work the ground, it will no longer yield its crops for you. You will be a restless wanderer on the earth."

Commentators note that the reason everyone realized that Abel's offering was favored is that God burned his offering with fire from heaven, so this was a very public display of God's pleasure with Abel and displeasure with Cain. Cain's public image was BAD!

Cain saw himself as the victim. It was Abel's fault that God didn't favor him! Abel was God's favorite! Abel was showing off and giving God his very best lambs and sheep from his herd! That's why God wasn't satisfied with this perfectly good vegetable/fruit offering Cain made. Abel, Abel, Abel!!! BUT God gives Cain instructions on how to stop playing the victim.

1) Understand the cause of his anger

2) Do what is expected and right

3) The attitude of rebellion against the right course of action will result in a wrong course of action

4) Do not feed rebellious desires

5) You could rule over dark desires and replace it with right godly desires that will result in God's favor

But Cain portrays himself as the 'faultless' victim of a cruel God. He wants everyone to know that he was neglected by God's love, attention and affirmation. Cain was not willing to do the work to heal and carry his relationship with his brother forward into the future. So, Cain nursed his evil emotions and mentally justified his course of action. He resented Abel and had no other choice but to murder him because he was driven by the need of the public affirmation of God's favor on his life.

When God 'caught' him in the act, Cain was very haughty and hung on to his anger and resentment. Cain engaged in defending, blaming and playing the victim and that further damaged his relationship with God and was eventually evicted from his homeland and was regarded as a criminal by the entire community.

Trust-Breaking Belief #2

"The grass is greener on the other side."

We hear this occasionally from both partners when infidelity has become an issue in their relationship. For the wounding partner, it is often because they are romanticizing their affair partner, the pornography, etc. because it helped them escape from their issues. For the wounded partner, this can look like reminiscing about an old flame, wondering if they should find another relationship, or, even worse, have an affair of their own.

Regardless of your situation, if you are entertaining the idea that the grass is greener somewhere else, we can assure you that it is not.

When wounding partners complain about the grass being greener elsewhere, they are usually trying to justify their actions by explaining how bad their relationship was prior to their engagement in infidelity-related behavior. While all relationships have issues, we often find that the grass wasn't green in the relationship because the wounding partner was failing to water it. If they had invested half of the time, effort, money, and attention in their relationship as they did in their infidelity- related behavior, they would have found that the garden of their relationship would have blossomed from their efforts. Sadly, they were, and still are, so busy indulging the "what ifs" they neglect the "what is". As a result, the grass directly beneath their feet has begun to wither and die.

In the case of sexual or emotional infidelity, it is often the allure of getting instead of giving that trips wounding partners up. When life with their partner becomes hectic or troubled, they feel the urge to escape, and an affair seems to offer all the reward with none of the work. What they fail to understand is that affairs happen outside of the realities of life and that, sooner or later, their troubles will resurface. This is especially true if they end up leaving the wounded partner for an affair partner. As we stated previously, research shows that approximately 75% of marriages based on affairs end in divorce. In the case of the wounding partner who wants to keep their current relationship, they have now increased the magnitude of the relationship's problems a hundredfold.

Numbers 11: 4-6, 10-15, 18-20, 31-34 NIV

4 The rabble with them began to crave other food, and again the Israelites started wailing and said, "If only we had meat to eat! 5 We remember the fish we ate in Egypt at no cost—also the cucumbers, melons, leeks, onions and garlic. 6 But now we have lost our appetite; we never see anything but this manna!"

10 Moses heard the people of every family wailing at the entrance to their tents. The Lord became exceedingly angry, and Moses was troubled. 11 He asked the Lord, "Why have you brought this trouble on your servant? What have I done to displease you that you put the burden of all these people on me? 12 Did I conceive all these people? Did I give them birth? Why do you tell me to carry them in my arms, as a nurse carries an infant, to the land you promised on oath to their ancestors? 13 Where can I get meat for all these people? They keep wailing to me, 'Give us meat to eat!' 14 I cannot carry all these people by myself; the burden is too heavy for me. 15 If this is how you are going to treat me, please go ahead and kill me—if I have found favor in your eyes—and do not let me face my own ruin."

18 "Tell the people: 'Consecrate yourselves in preparation for tomorrow, when you will eat meat. The Lord heard you when you wailed, "If only we had meat to eat! We were better off in Egypt!" Now the Lord will give you meat, and you will eat it. 19 You will not eat it for just one day, or two days, or five, ten or twenty days, 20 but for a whole month—until it comes out of your nostrils, and you loathe it—because you have rejected the Lord, who is among you, and have wailed before him, saying, "Why did we ever leave Egypt?"'"

31 Now a wind went out from the Lord and drove quail in from the sea. It scattered them up to two cubits[b] deep all around the camp, as far as a day's walk in any direction. 32 All that day and night and all the next day the people went out and gathered quail. No one gathered less than ten homers. [c] Then they spread them out all around the camp. 33 But while the meat was still between their teeth and before it could be consumed, the anger of the Lord burned against the people, and he struck them with a severe plague. 34 Therefore the place was named Kibroth Hattaavah, [d] because there they buried the people who had craved other food.

1) Much like a wounding partner, the Israelites yearned for Egypt, the place where they were enslaved by a tyrant pharaoh and lived under such harsh conditions it caused them to moan and cry to the Lord for a way of escape. Egypt was now paradise, the place where all of their needs and appetite were satisfied. When in fact they were now a free nation having all of their needs met supernaturally by a God who made the other nations tremble.

2) Much like a wounded partner, Moses experienced the backlash of a people who mentally and verbally energized past brutal experiences as intense cravings of amazing pleasure and was terrified that these people would take his life because he could not satisfy their romanticized needs.

3) When there is no way to change a person's mind from craving something evil, God will permit them to satiate themselves with their desires and allow it to destroy them.

2 Samuel 16:15-23 NIV

The Advice of Ahithophel and Hushai

15 Meanwhile, Absalom and all the men of Israel came to Jerusalem, and Ahithophel was with him. 16 Then Hushai the Arkite, David's confidant, went to Absalom and said to him, "Long live the king! Long live the king!"

17 Absalom said to Hushai, "So this is the love you show your friend? If he's your friend, why didn't you go with him?"

18 Hushai said to Absalom, "No, the one chosen by the Lord, by these people, and by all the men of Israel—his I will be, and I will remain with him. 19 Furthermore, whom should I serve? Should I not serve the son? Just as I served your father, so I will serve you."

20 Absalom said to Ahithophel, "Give us your advice. What should we do?"

21 Ahithophel answered, "Sleep with your father's concubines whom he left to take care of the palace. Then all Israel will hear that you have made yourself obnoxious to your father, and the hands of everyone with you will be more resolute." 22 So they pitched a tent for Absalom on the roof, and he slept with his father's concubines in the sight of all Israel.

23 Now in those days the advice Ahithophel gave was like that of one who inquires of God. That was how both David and Absalom regarded all of Ahithophel's advice.

We see many levels of retaliation here. Absalom retaliated against his father, David. Hushai, David's adviser, severed his friendship with David and joined Absalom's illegitimate advisory team. Ahithophel, also no longer David's adviser, retaliated against him by giving Absalom advice on how to destroy David in the eyes of Israel on a deeply personal level. In the Old Testament, raping the wife of another man was an object lesson of dominance over their manhood. It was the greatest insult that could be given to another human, and that's not even mentioning the devastation that is happening to the spouse's partner. Absalom not only disgraced King David, but he also destroyed the lives of these innocent concubines.

Retaliation comes from the pit of hell. This vengeful act not only complicated the process of restoration, but it also made it impossible.

Proverbs 20:22 NIV

Do not say, "I'll pay you back for this wrong!" Wait for the Lord, and he will avenge you.

A Word About Retaliatory Affairs

In our coaching practice, we run across a fair number of wounded partners who entertain thoughts of having an affair or who actually have an affair themselves after they discover that their partner has been unfaithful. Although this isn't particularly surprising, it is concerning to us since we witness the devastation that infidelity causes to individuals and relationships on a daily basis.

When the wounded partner discovers that their partner has been unfaithful, it is one of the most immensely painful events that a person can go through. As a result, it's not surprising that many wounded partners entertain thoughts of getting back at their partner one way or another by having an affair or imagine that their pain would be lessened if they had the distraction of an affair of their own. If you think about it, a "revenge" affair can seem like the perfect way to do that…at least on the surface.

When we hear that someone has had an affair or is entertaining thoughts of one in response to their partner's infidelity-related behavior, it is typically for one of the following four reasons:

1. To hurt their partner as much as they were hurt or "even the score"

2. To teach their partner a lesson

3. To make their partner empathize with or understand the pain they are in

4. To provide themselves with a distraction from the immense pain that they are feeling

Although we certainly understand the reasoning, our experience working with betrayed partners and couples working through betrayal has shown us that the outcome is usually the exact opposite of what the wounded partner had in mind. This is for four main reasons:

1. The bond has already been severed. When your partner engaged in their affair or other infidelity-related behavior, one of the reasons it hurt you so badly is because there was an active bond between you and your partner, at least on your side of things. If you engage in a revenge affair, you will be unable to even the score because the impact of your actions won't have nearly the same effect on your partner asthey did on you.

2. It can make the wounding partner feel better. There's something about human nature that yearns for the scales tobe balanced when a wrong has been committed. We

have heard wounding partners tell us that knowing their partner did the same thing as they did absolved them of their guilt.

3. It can make the wounding partner feel justified. For some wounding partners, especially the unrepentant ones, the fact that their partner engaged in a revenge affair gives them just the excuse they need to carry on with their own bad behavior. For some, this means an excuse to continue their affair or other infidelity-related behavior. For others, it means giving them an excuse to minimize their actions, refuse to accept responsibility, or minimize the wounded partner's feelings.

4. It often makes the wounded partner feel bad about themselves. In most cases, the wounded partner is not the one who would normally engage in an affair. If the wounded partner has not cheated up to this point, they probably value their relationship and are concerned with hurting other people. As a result, the wounded partner ends up feeling terrible about themselves because they had to compromise their values in order to engage in their affair.

What makes us sad about these situations is that, if reconciliation is the goal, revenge affairs complicate the process so much that it can take years to untangle all of the issues. The adage "two wrongs don't make a right" definitely applies in this situation. In the case of infidelity, two wrongs only make it worse.

If you are a wounded partner and reconciliation is not your goal or is not possible, we still encourage you to think long and hard before retaliating with an affair of your own. Engagement in a revenge affair can hurt your individual recovery in the following ways:

- The feeling of betrayal doesn't go away, but is now compounded with guilt and shame
- Respect for yourself can go down because you become like the person who betrayed you
- It distracts from emotions and trauma that need to be dealt with
- As mentioned previously, it can cause you to go against your own morals and values
- If you have children, you set a poor example

Affairs and infidelity-related behavior leave a debt that simply can't be repaid. If you are a wounded partner and your partner is willing to do the work, please take some time to decide if you think reconciliation is a possibility before making decisions and, please, don't engage in an affair of your own based on an emotionally charged situation. If, over time, your partner is still "not getting it" or hasn't chosen you, moving on in your life will be much easier without the guilt and shame that can result from retaliation and/or decisions made from pain.

We would also like to mention the "grass is greener" syndrome when it comes to intimacy avoidance and intimacy anorexia®. According the book *Intimacy Anorexia: Healing the Hidden Addiction in Your Marriage,* the author, Dr. Doug Weiss, explains that one of the tactics that intimacy anorexics use in order to maintain distance is "the fantasy person". According to Weiss, the fantasy person is a real or imagined person that the IA keeps in their mind and compares their partner to. This "fantasy person" typically has attributes that the IAs partner does not and, oftentimes, these attributes are completely unattainable for the IAs partner. For example, the IA may be in a relationship with a short person yet talk about how they are attracted to people who are tall. These unfair comparisons to the "fantasy person" provides the IA with an excuse to withdraw from their partner because, in their mind, the partner is faulty. Distance within the relationship happens with the wounded partner, who never feels good enough, withdraws and/or when the IA withdraws in silent judgement. This particular take on the "grass is greener" syndrome deeply damages the wounded partner mentally and emotionally.

Trust-Breaking Belief #3

"My partner should complete me."

We blame this one on Hollywood. If you watch any number of movies, you will soon realize that the message being sent is that, somehow, all it takes is the right person to come along and—poof—we will be complete. Whether it is the fairytale princess waiting for her prince to save her, or the bad boy who suddenly changes when he meets the right woman, the message is clear: the pain of life will be cured when we meet the right person.

There are a few problems with this idea, but the main one is that it is completely false. We can never be completed by another person, and we can never complete another person. Our deep-rooted issues and pain do not magically disappear once we find the right relationship. In fact, our shortcomings will often be magnified in our interactions with our partner. The traumatized princess will still have issues even if her prince does come. The Hollywood "bad boy" will not magically cease all his behaviors once in a relationship. He will almost surely repeat them.

When a person believes that their partner should be the be-all, end-all solution to their issues, they are heavily disappointed when this is not the case. This often leads them to become disillusioned and blame their partner for falling short. The truth, however, is that the expectation of their partner meeting their every need and desire was completely unrealistic to begin with. In the case of infidelity, wounding partners often use these unrealistic expectations to justify their actions. This can be reinforced within a culture that overvalues sexuality, which in turn creates entitlement around sex that can lead to ego injury if a person perceives they are being rejected. Additionally, although the wounded partner has every right to expect the wounding partner to be faithful, their pain caused by betrayal cannot be fixed solely by their partner. Although the wounding partner will need to help the recovery process by committing to honesty and transparency without blame or defensiveness moving forward, this will only go partway to healing the wounded partner's pain. The wounded partner will need to take responsibility for their own recovery if complete healing is to occur.

In a 2014 interview for TED Radio entitled *Are We Asking Too Much of Our Spouses?*, renowned psychologist Ether Perel puts it this way:

> "So we come to one person, and we basically are asking them to give us what once an entire village used to provide. Give me belonging, give me identity, give me continuity, but give me transcendence and mystery all in one. Give me comfort. Give me edge. Give me novelty. Give me familiarity. Give me predictability. Give me surprise."

The truth of the matter is that we all need to understand where our responsibilities lie and step up to the plate. This holds true for the wounding partner who justifies their infidelity-related behavior with their partner's real or perceived shortcomings. It also holds true for the wounded partner who refuses to engage in recovery because they are waiting for the wounding partner to fix it all. This last statement is not meant to minimize the fact that the wounding partner has caused many of the issues the wounded partner is now facing. However, regardless of how the wounds came about, the wounded partner is now responsible for doing the work necessary to ensure that they are not permanently damaged from their partner's behavior. Accountability and responsibility for each person's issues is imperative if recovery after betrayal is to take place. This may require one or both parties to adjust their expectations. Relationships should, of course, bring us happiness. However, they are not a fix for our own personal issues.

1 Corinthians 7:7 MSG

7 Sometimes I wish everyone were single like me—a simpler life in many ways! But celibacy is not for everyone any more than marriage is. God gives the gift of the single life to some, the gift of the married life to others.

This verse speaks of the Apostle Paul. Paul never married and managed to write a good portion of the New Testament. In fact, He turned the entire world upside down by spreading the Good News of the Gospel. Paul did NOT have a partner to make him complete, he was a complete person all by himself.

Jesus was the MOST complete person that ever walked the face of the earth. He reconciled mankind to His Father without a wife!

Genesis 1:26 NIV

26 Then God said, "Let us make mankind in our image, in our likeness, so that they may rule over the fish in the sea and the birds in the sky, over the livestock and all the wild animals,[a] and over all the creatures that move along the ground."

"Let US" ... Us refers to the Godhead, The Father, The Son and The Holy Spirit.

Ecclesiastes 4:12 MSG

By yourself you're unprotected. With a friend you can face the worst. Can you round up a third? A three-stranded rope isn't easily snapped.

The number for completion in Hebrew is always three, NOT two. The number two always refers to union, the joining of one to another, not completion.

Trust-Breaking Belief #4

"I caused my partner's infidelity."

This last one is not a trust-breaking belief per se. However, it is a belief that can hold the wounded partner back from making progress in their recovery. If we have not been clear up to this point, we never blame the wounded partner for the wounding partner's infidelity-related behavior. The choice to betray is 100% the responsibility of the wounding partner. Thus, the wounded partner shares none of the blame.

If you are a wounded partner reading this, and you feel that your partner's behavior is your fault, we want to help you understand that it isn't. Many wounded partners feel this way because they realize that they haven't been perfect in the relationship. The fact of the matter is that no one is perfect, but that never excuses infidelity. If your conscience is bothering you about something you have done and you want to look at where you might do better in order to improve your relationship, that is commendable. However, owning a facet of how the relationship could be improved is completely different than taking on fault for your partner's infidelity-related behavior.

Many wounded partners start to believe that the betrayal was their fault because the wounding partner overtly or subtly blames them for it. Oftentimes, especially early in recovery, the wounding partner is adamant that the wounded partner should share some of the blame for their infidelity-related behavior. They will often cite the fact that the wounded partner was not meeting their emotional needs, not giving them enough sex, or not being available enough. This can be extremely confusing when the wounding partner believes their own justifications so whole-heartedly that the accusations come off as true. This scenario is especially prevalent in relationships where intimacy avoidance is present. Since gaslighting, blaming, and minimization have been part of the relationship for so long, the wounded partner's mind may be cloudy and confused as to what is actually real. The result is that they may take on blame that isn't theirs to take on.

No relationship is 100% satisfying, and no person is 100% perfect. If those things were valid justifications for infidelity, then everyone would be unfaithful. The truth is that the wounding partner could have dealt with their feelings in a number of ways, and they *chose* infidelity-related behavior as their option. Furthermore, many of the attitudes of a wounding partner are often based in unrealistic expectations and entitlement. These attitudes are based on the wounding partner's flawed way of thinking and, as such, are solely their responsibility to deal with. When a wounding partner blames their partner, they are trying to push off their guilt and the responsibility to change onto the other person so that they don't have to look at themselves. Wounding partners do not engage in infidelity-related behaviors because the wounded partner is faulty. They engaged in infidelity because they *chose* to do so based on a sense of entitlement, self-centeredness, and justifications.

In the beginning of time, Adam and Eve played the blame game.

Genesis 3:1-13 MSG

3 *The serpent was clever, cleverer than any wild animal God had made. He spoke to the Woman: "Do I understand that God told you not to eat from any tree in the garden?"*

2-3 *The Woman said to the serpent, "Not at all. We can eat from the trees in the garden. It's only about the tree in the middle of the garden that God said, 'Don't eat from it; don't even touch it or you'll die.'"*

4-5 *The serpent told the Woman, "You won't die. God knows that the moment you eat from that tree, you'll see what's really going on. You'll be just like God, knowing everything, ranging all the way from good to evil."*

6 *When the Woman saw that the tree looked like good eating and realized what she would get out of it—she'd know everything! —she took and ate the fruit and then gave some to her husband, and he ate.*

7 *Immediately the two of them did "see what's really going on"—saw themselves naked! They sewed fig leaves together as makeshift clothes for themselves.*

8 *When they heard the sound of God strolling in the garden in the evening breeze, the Man and his Wife hid in the trees of the garden, hid from God.*

9 *God called to the Man: "Where are you?"*

10 *He said, "I heard you in the garden and I was afraid because I was naked. And I hid."*

11 *God said, "Who told you that you were naked? Did you eat from that tree I told you not to eat from?"*

12 *The Man said, "The Woman you gave me as a companion, she gave me fruit from the tree, and, yes, I ate it."*

God said to the Woman, "What is this that you've done?"

13 *"The serpent seduced me," she said, "and I ate."*

EVERYONE was blaming everyone else!!!

The snake blamed God for hindering Eve's curiosity.

The snake blamed God for limiting Eve's intelligence and power.

The snake blamed God for specifically withholding the power to know good and evil by making it appear that it is the greatest power of all!

Eve blamed God for taking away her rights to know good from evil.

Adam blamed God for having them make a choice between knowing good and evil or getting the negative consequence if they disobey.

Adam blamed God for becoming naked in the garden.

Adam blamed his nakedness and his disobedience on Eve.

Eve blamed the serpent for making her eat the forbidden fruit.

The reality is that Adam and Eve engaged in infidelity against God. The center of the garden, the core of their belief system, was challenged by an option that was "different" from the one predetermined as "very good" for them. The unknown and forbidden titillated their souls. Their hunger for the powers contained in the forbidden fruit superseded their love and fidelity to God. Very decisively, they switched loyalties from their wondrous, powerful and loving Creator and transferred their allegiance to the despicable, deceptive, hateful lowest level of God's creation. Deception is the false appearance of a thing that is the least inferior option made to appear into something far superior to all other options. They had to blame someone else for their rationale because they were deeply ashamed of the poor choice they made. They chose to be self-entitled, self-centered and justified in their course of action in order for others to believe they made the right choice. Well, we all know how that worked out. Truth unveils deception and categorizes everything in its proper place. That is why truth sets us free!

Prayer for wounding partner:

Father, help me. I own up to my responsibility and admit that I am NOT a victim. I am 100% responsible for my infidelity related behavior. Give me the grace to nurture my own relationship and not look for titillating opportunities to selfishly feed my own ego. Give me the ears to hear the truth that sets me free and give me the heart to choose wisely. I accept that what You say is "very good" for me is, in fact, VERY GOOD for me!!! You love me and will never deceive me. The deceiver is maniacal, and his intent is to destroy me and all that is connected with me. That is why he makes the most inferior option appear as the best option. I am a complete person united with another complete person and I will not break my vows. The deceiver is the third strand that wants to tear apart my union with my partner. When You are the third strand of a three-stranded cord, our union can't help but be watertight and will not easily be broken. Your thoughts are higher than my thoughts and

Your ways are higher than my ways. I submit to You and Your ways. I take responsibility for my own actions. I repent of self-entitlement, self-centeredness and of the immaturity to justify evil choices. You love me and my partner and everything about You is VERY GOOD! In Jesus' name, Amen.

Prayer for wounded partner:

Father, I understand that my wounding partner made a destructive choice to break our vows. I understand that there is no excuse for the wounding partner to break our covenant with You. None. If there are resentments against me, I will forgive the wounding partner and ask You to deal with their heart and soul.

If there are resentments in me that need to be dealt with, I ask that You reveal it to me. I will not entertain the thoughts of retaliatory affairs. (or I ask forgiveness for my retaliatory affairs). Affairs and retaliatory affairs leave a debt that cannot be repaid. My wounding partner is a complete person united to me as another complete person. The deceiver is the third strand that wants to tear apart my union with my partner. When You are the third strand, our union can't help but be watertight. Your thoughts are higher than my thoughts and Your ways are higher than my ways. I submit to You and Your ways. I accept that what You say is "very good" for me is in fact, VERY GOOD for me! You love me and will never deceive me. In Jesus' name, Amen.

PART 14

Rebuilding Trust Pyramid Layer #2

Safety

Most of the couples that we work with report a lack of safety in their relationship once betrayal has been discovered or disclosed. This feeling of unsafety is especially prevalent for the wounded partner. This makes sense since the agreements that the couple entered the relationship with were violated when the wounding partner engaged in the infidelity- related behavior. Any time a person breaks a promise to their partner, whether that be sexual exclusivity or just making the relationship a priority in their life, it calls the safety of the relationship into question. This is because, for safety to exist, trust must exist. If a person is not true to their word, trust is broken.

When we refer to the word "safety", we are referring to two main types of safety that have been affected by the wounding partner's actions. The primary type of safety that gets affected is what we refer to as emotional safety. When a person is emotionally safe in a relationship, it means that they feel that their emotional experience is cared about and validated. Without emotional safety, a person will have a hard time sharing their fears, dreams, hopes, and pain. In fact, they will be highly unlikely to share anything remotely resembling vulnerability with their partner for fear of being discounted. Betrayal creates emotional unsafety for the wounded partner because, through their actions, the wounding partner showed a complete disregard of how those actions would affect their partner. In the case of the intimacy avoidant relationship, the wounded partner feels a lack of emotional safety at all times because the IAs actions invalidate the wounded partner's emotional experience on a regular basis. In the case of sexual infidelity, the wounded partner's sexual safety is also affected. When the wounding partner goes outside of the relationship, it is not uncommon for them to continue to have sexual relations with the wounded partner as well. This is a complete violation of the wounded partner's body and indicates a profound lack of respect on the wounding partner's part.

All of the couples that we work with are dealing with the unsafety caused by a massive breach of trust due to betrayal. However, as we work with them over time, it becomes apparent in many of the cases that trust has been broken down through other infractions as well. Let's use, for example, the case of childcare. If one partner feels that the other one does not take good care of the children when they are away, this can lead to a frustrating situation in which the responsible partner now feels they have to babysit their partner. Or, if one partner refuses to take ownership over normal chores associated with running the household and the other partner is constantly having to remind them, it wears on the fabric of the relationship over time. This lack of prioritization can result in a breakdown of trust because the partner sees this as a lack of reliability. Other examples could be overspending, poor time management (making someone late all the time) or throwing someone under the bus in order to look good. Once a partner questions another partner's reliability, trust becomes fragile. If enough infractions happen over time, the result is broken trust.

Perhaps the best example of this phenomenon can be seen in the intimacy avoidant relationship. In the case of intimacy avoidance, the IA's actions are considered to be unfaithful because they have chosen to put themselves first. In the intimacy avoidant relationship, there can certainly be sexual infidelity, emotional infidelity, and infidelity through pornography. However, even if these things aren't present, trust is almost always missing. This is because the IA uses multiple ways to withhold from their partner in order to create an imbalance of power in their own favor. They then use minimization, defensiveness, and gaslighting to keep the wounded partner from gaining equal footing in the relationship. This combination, often present even at the beginning of the relationship, causes a situation in which trust cannot be fostered. One common example of this is when the IA overworks or acts too preoccupied to pay real attention to their partner. When the partner brings this up, their feelings are usually minimized with statements such as, "you're being overly sensitive." Or worse, they are gaslighted and told that the IA does, in fact, make plenty of time for them. This creates a void of safety. As opposed to the abrupt break in safety that we see in other types of betrayal, in many cases, almost every area of the intimacy avoidant relationship feels unsafe to the wounded partner.

When we address the subject of safety with the couples we work with, we typically talk about it in two parts. The first part of safety is built through a commitment to recovery and the attitudes and demeanor of both parties in the relationship. Additionally, the first stage of building safety requires that we work with a couple to outline the actual plans that need to be put into place that address that relationship's particular issues. We will be covering those things in this section. The second part of safety is built through consistently working the plans put in place, the wounding partner consistently being accountable for their time and whereabouts, and, again, consistency in showing a demeanor conducive to the rebuilding of trust. This is applicable to both parties in the relationship but is especially applicable to the wounding partner. We will cover this important part of building and maintaining safety in the next section on consistency.

Judges 6:11-24 MSG

11-12 One day the angel of God came and sat down under the oak in Ophrah that belonged to Joash the Abiezrite, whose son Gideon was threshing wheat in the winepress, out of sight of the Midianites. The angel of God appeared to him and said, "God is with you, O mighty warrior!"

13 Gideon replied, "With me, my master? If God is with us, why has all this happened to us? Where are all the miracle-wonders our parents and grandparents told us about, telling us, 'Didn't God deliver us from Egypt?' The fact is, God has nothing to do with us—he has turned us over to Midian."

14 But God faced him directly: "Go in this strength that is yours. Save Israel from Midian. Haven't I just sent you?"

15 Gideon said to him, "Me, my master? How and with what could I ever save Israel? Look at me. My clan's the weakest in Manasseh and I'm the runt of the litter."

16 God said to him, "I'll be with you. Believe me, you'll defeat Midian as one man."

17-18 Gideon said, "If you're serious about this, do me a favor: Give me a sign to back up what you're telling me. Don't leave until I come back and bring you my gift."

He said, "I'll wait till you get back."

19 Gideon went and prepared a young goat and a huge amount of unraised bread (he used over half a bushel of flour!). He put the meat in a basket and the broth in a pot and took them back under the shade of the oak tree for a sacred meal.

20 The angel of God said to him, "Take the meat and unraised bread, place them on that rock, and pour the broth on them." Gideon did it.

21-22 The angel of God stretched out the tip of the stick he was holding and touched the meat and the bread. Fire broke out of the rock and burned up the meat and bread while the angel of God slipped away out of sight. And Gideon knew it was the angel of God!

Gideon said, "Oh no! Master, God! I have seen the angel of God face-to-face!"

23 But God reassured him, "Easy now. Don't panic. You won't die."

24 Then Gideon built an altar there to God and named it "God's Peace." It's still called that at Ophrah of Abiezer.

What did God do for Gideon?

>1) Verse 11- God met Gideon where he was at. He met Gideon at his workplace, hiding from the enemy, and doing what he had to do to feed himself and his family.
>
>2) Verse 12- God did not call Gideon by his current character, someone who was fearful and full of resentment, but called Gideon the man He saw him to be by telling him that He was with him and that he was a mighty warrior.
>
>3) Verse 14- God answered Gideon's question. Gideon didn't understand why Israel was suffering such tyranny when God did so many incredible signs and wonders in the past. God tells him the past is over but that He was with him now and that he will be the answer to his own questions.
>
>4) Verse 15- God soothes Gideon's self-doubts.
>
>5) Verse 16 - God reassures Gideon that He will be with him and that his inadequacies will not get in the way of victory against Mideon.

6) Verse 17, 18, 19- God allowed Gideon to choose how he could gain confidence in what God was telling him.

7) Verse 20- God wanted Gideon to understand just how much He will accept his sacrifice by drenching it in broth and making it impossible to burn. Divine fire that torched the sacrifice was the sign of God's respect and favor.

8) Verse 21, 22- God accepted Gideon's sacrifice and supernaturally torched it on the altar. This was THE sign that Gideon had God's respect and favor!

9) Verse 23 - God reassured Gideon that he will not die for having doubts but will live and through God's grace, bring salvation to his people.

10) Vs 24- Safety brings peace, the reassurance of tranquility, calmness and repose.

God wants us to be an imitator of Him!

Ephesians 5:1 & 2 MSG

5 1-2 Watch what God does, and then you do it, like children who learn proper behavior from their parents. Mostly what God does is love you. Keep company with him and learn a life of love. Observe how Christ loved us. His love was not cautious but extravagant. He didn't love in order to get something from us but to give everything of himself to us. Love like that.

Demeanor

Until the wounded partner feels a great deal of safety within the relationship, little-to-no progress will be made toward rebuilding trust. One of the main ways that safety can begin to be reestablished—or established for the first time in the case of the intimacy avoidant relationship— is through the demeanor of the wounding partner. If the wounding partner continues to be resistant to recovery or acts prideful, defensive, and/or arrogant, the wounded partner will not feel safe enough to engage in the recovery of the relationship. It is not enough to end the infidelity- related behavior, although this is extremely important. The wounding partner needs to be able to show true remorse for their actions. Arrogance, pride, and defensiveness send the wounded partner the message that the wounding partner is not truly sorry for what they have done and/or does not understand the effect that their actions have had on their partner.

When a wounding partner engages in infidelity-related behavior, they selfishly set the wounded partner aside in favor of something else. As a result, the wounded partner feels disrespected, unimportant, and forgotten. This is why it is of the utmost importance that the wounding partner show that they will do whatever it takes to win their partner back. If the wounding partner continues to display a lack of humility by acting defensive, arrogant, or prideful, the message that is inadvertently conveyed to the wounded partner is that they should not ask for what they need in order to heal. Instead, they should just be happy with whatever the wounding partner is willing to give. A defensive, prideful, or arrogant demeanor on the wounding partner's part sends the message that they do not value their partner. Someone with this type of demeanor needs to ask themselves why anyone would want to stay with someone who shows them this type of disrespect. Why should anyone stay with a person who could cast them aside in an act of unfaithfulness and then continue to act remorseless about it and/or protect their own self-interest?

When we view things in this light, we begin to understand how gracious the wounded partner is being by offering the wounding partner another chance. This chance is a gift of high value and should be taken very seriously by the wounding partner. If the wounding partner casts it aside in the interest of their own pride and comfort, it is highly unlikely that they are truly sorry for their behavior or understand the effects of their actions.

If you are a wounding partner reading this and your partner is continuing to emotionally flood, chances are that you are engaging in behavior that is causing them to feel unsafe. If you cannot or will not do everything you can to create a safe environment for your partner, any advances toward the restoration of the relationship will be slow to non-existent. If you do not know what it is that you need to do, you should ask your partner at a time when they are not emotionally flooded. Typically, the things that make a wounded partner feel most safe are prioritization of the relationship, accountability for your actions and whereabouts, your availability to listen to them and meet their needs, and the consistency at which you behave in a manner that they interpret as loving. However, your partner may have other requirements. If these requirements are reasonable, agree to meet them. If you are not sure if they are reasonable, engage the help of a trained professional to help you understand.

As the wounding partner, earning back trust will require a great deal of patience on your part. You may tell your partner time and time again that you are "all in", but it takes much more than words to prove to them that you mean it. Rushing your partner toward "recovery" by complaining about their need to talk about it or shutting them down is not only unfair and inappropriate, but it comes across as controlling and uncaring. You need to remember that their reactions are in response to your deception. It is going to take quite a while before they believe that you are no longer engaged in a double life. A word of caution: we see many wounding partners, especially intimacy avoidants, insist that their partner stop bringing the up betrayal in conversation. This will backfire if you are at all interested in the restoration of trust in the relationship. Wounded partners who are shut down in this way share with us that they continue to feel a profound lack of trust and safety, even if they aren't voicing it. The only thing that shutting the conversation down does is ensure that the wounded partner does not share their feelings with you. This erodes trust even further over the long run and often results in the relationship ending.

Here is an example of Gideon not having the correct demeanor, while his father, Joash did. Joash put his life on the line and defended his son and God. In the end, Gideon followed his father's example and changed his demeanor so much that the community *changed his name* because he was so bold in his stand against Baal! Our demeanor is important to God and to our partner.

Judges 6:25-32 MSG

"Take your father's best seven-year-old bull, the prime one. Tear down your father's Baal altar and chop down the Asherah fertility pole beside it. Then build an altar to God, your God, on the top of this hill. Take the prime bull and present it as a Whole-Burnt-Offering, using firewood from the Asherah pole that you cut down."

27 Gideon selected ten men from his servants and did exactly what God had told him. But because of his family and the people in the neighborhood, he was afraid to do it openly, so he did it that night.

28 Early in the morning, the people in town were shocked to find Baal's altar torn down, the Asherah pole beside it chopped down, and the prime bull burning away on the altar that had been built.

29 They kept asking, "Who did this?"

Questions and more questions, and then the answer: "Gideon son of Joash did it."

30 The men of the town demanded of Joash: "Bring out your son! He must die! Why, he tore down the Baal altar and chopped down the Asherah tree!"

31 But Joash stood up to the crowd pressing in on him, "Are you going to fight Baal's battles for him? Are you going to save him? Anyone who takes Baal's side will be dead by morning. If Baal is a god in fact, let him fight his own battles and defend his own altar."

32 They nicknamed Gideon that day Jerub-Baal because after he had torn down the Baal altar, he had said, "Let Baal fight his own battles."

Ambivalence

Ambivalence is the state of having mixed feelings or contradictory ideas about someone or something. (Oxford Languages) Ambivalence on the part of either partner creates a lack of safety in the relationship. This is because, in order to work on the relationship, both partners need to be committed to doing the work. Notice that we did not say that both partners must know for certain that recovery for the relationship is possible. For many couples, it is normal for one or both parties to not know if the relationship will recover or if reconciliation is truly even what they want. However, a commitment to doing the work necessary to see if the relationship can survive is vital to creating enough safety to move forward with recovery work. If one or both partners remain frozen in inaction due to ambivalence, recovery will stall out.

Ambivalence, although a normal part of the rebuilding trust process for many people, is often painful experience—especially to the wounded partner. Ambivalence on the part of a wounding partner is often excruciating for the wounded partner because it is like pouring salt into a cut. It was hard enough finding out about their partner's betrayal, but to watch the wounding partner vacillate between wanting to stay in the relationship and wanting to leave it is almost unbearable. For the wounding partner with empathy, it can be a hard situation to be in. They don't want to further injure their partner, but they can't help how they feel. It can also be hard for a wounded partner to feel ambivalent about their relationship, especially if the wounding partner is truly sorry for their actions. Unless the wounded partner is using ambivalence to gain back power in the relationship, it doesn't feel good to hurt the wounding partner even though they were hurt themselves by the betrayal.

If you are a wounding or wounded partner who is trying to elicit pain from your partner by acting ambivalent, we urge you to stop. If you are using ambivalence to manipulate the other person, it will do nothing but damage to your already-damaged relationship. For most people, however, ambivalence is an unwelcome feeling. It is often frightening because many people take the presence of ambivalence as a sign that the relationship is doomed. Although prolonged ambivalence on the part of either partner stalls recovery which can ultimately lead to the relationship's demise, we want to tell you that, when handled correctly, it doesn't have to end in separation.

If you are feeling ambivalent about your relationship, it is important that you deal with this feeling head on. If you run from it, it will only prolong the recovery process and could end up backfiring. We realize that it might be scary for you to admit to feelings of ambivalence. However, ignoring your feelings will not make them go away. To quote Dr. Phil McGraw, *"you can't change what you don't acknowledge."* A word of caution: you will need some help dealing with ambivalence. If you had the answers within yourself, you would have come to a decision by now. We recommend enlisting the help of a trained professional in order to help you sift through the intense feelings that create ambivalence. Feelings of ambivalence create an opportunity for a person to truly look at why they want to stay and why they want to leave.

We recommend making a pro's and con's list that includes the consequences of either choice—not only to the partners involved in the relationship, but to children (if any), friends, and family members as well.

We also recommend that you do not make any decisions in your ambivalent state. Instead, we recommend that you set a date in the near future (no more than twelve months) and work diligently toward it. When we say work diligently toward it, we mean embrace the work that you need to do in order to do recovery. If you don't, you are likely to remain in your ambivalent state for an extended period. You don't have to decide about the entire future of the relationship now. Of course, you will have to eventually decide. However, for now, we encourage you to make a choice about working as hard as you can on recovery. This includes engaging, on a frequent basis, the professional help that you enlist to deal with your ambivalence. There is a lot at stake here, and that should not be taken lightly. Commit to working on recovery with your partner in order to see whether the relationship can be saved. The only way out of ambivalence is through it.

If you are a wounded partner dealing with prolonged ambivalence on the part of the wounding partner, it may be time to evaluate your response to the situation. For example, a common tactic of a partner that wants the relationship to work is for them to try to reason with, beg, and even threaten the ambivalent partner into action. Most of the time, this pushes the ambivalent partner further away. It also creates a situation in which the "chaser" gives away their power to the "chasee" every time they chase them. If you are a partner experiencing this, we suggest that you pull back from the situation and possibly put some boundaries in place. We aren't suggesting this tactic as a way to manipulate the ambivalent partner into making the decision to stay in the relationship. Instead, we recommend the "hands- off" approach for the following reasons:

1. It is empowering. There is nothing more defeating than chasing someone around who acts like they don't want you. Although it can be painful to accept the reality that your partner may not want to stay, accepting the truth can empower you to make decisions based on the situation you are currently facing.

2. It conserves emotional energy. Chasing an ambivalent partner around takes emotional energy from the partner that they can't spare. This energy would be better used if the partner put it toward their own recovery instead.

3. It helps stop the insanity. Chasing an ambivalent partner is crazy-making and painful. This can be especially infuriating if the ambivalent partner is the one who was unfaithful. Taking a hands-off approach can help stop the insanity.

If things are going to change, the non-ambivalent partner needs to stop doing the things that are leading them nowhere. When we work with couples, we often find that the dynamics in the relationship before the betrayal were similar to the way they are afterwards. This is to say that it is not uncommon for one of the partners to traditionally be the "chaser" and the other one to be the "chasee". If either partner wants things to change, one or both are going to have to stop doing things the way they have always done them. In this case, the ambivalent partner is unlikely to enact the change. This leaves it up to the non-ambivalent partner to put a stop to the situation. The ambivalent partner is blind to the need for change because their ambivalence has them frozen. When the non-ambivalent partner pulls back, it often creates an urgency for the ambivalent partner to act.

We want to stress that pulling back does not guarantee that the ambivalent partner will make a decision in favor of the relationship. However, chasing them around will surely push them away. If the non-ambivalent partner pulls away and the ambivalent partner does not respond within a few months of the new situation, it may be time for the non-ambivalent partner to put a boundary in place until the ambivalent partner commits to making a choice. Common boundaries in this scenario include separation and even divorce if the partners are married. We recommend that the boundary be time-bound and be stated using one of the two methods shared regarding boundaries in the previous section on honesty.

God addresses ambivalence. We cannot win any battle going in with fear and doubts, not in any arena! Remember, that the enemy of our souls uses ambivalence to keep us helpless and weak. Ambivalence is a chokehold to victory and guarantees total loss. This is an example of Gideon being reassured that God will move on his behalf and on the behalf of His people. God dealt with all of his inadequacies and built him up in the faith so he could perform mighty exploits! Armed with faith, he won the battle before he even fought it!

Judges 7:8-15 MSG

8 After Gideon took all their provisions and trumpets, he sent all the Israelites home. He took up his position with the three hundred. The camp of Midian stretched out below him in the valley.

9-12 That night, God told Gideon: "Get up and go down to the camp. I've given it to you. <u>If you have any doubts</u> about going down, go down with Purah, your armor bearer; when you hear what they're saying, you'll be bold and confident." He and his armor bearer Purah went down near the place where sentries were posted. Midian and Amalek, all the easterners, were spread out on the plain like a swarm of locusts. And their camels! Past counting, like grains of sand on the seashore!

13 Gideon arrived just in time to hear a man tell his friend a dream. He said, "I had this dream: A loaf of barley bread tumbled into the Midianite camp. It came to the tent and hit it so hard it collapsed. The tent fell!"

14 His friend said, "This has to be the sword of Gideon son of Joash, the Israelite! God has turned Midian—the whole camp! —over to him."

15 When Gideon heard the telling of the dream and its interpretation, he dropped to his knees before God in prayer. Then he went back to the Israelite camp and said, "Get up and get going! God has just given us the Midianite army!"

Prayer for the wounding partner:

Father, You provide me with safety, and it is my job to provide my partner with safety. Your demeanor towards me is always compassionate and ready to hear and answer me. My attitude towards my partner must also be compassionate and ready to hear and answer them. You are never ambivalent towards me, and I will not be ambivalent towards my partner. I will not do anymore damage to this already fragile relationship but will constantly build it up and bring peace to my partner. In Jesus' name, Amen.

PART 15

Wounded Partner Pitfalls Pitfall #1
Telling too many people

For this next section, we would like to highlight some common pitfalls that wounded and wounding partners can fall into both individually and as a couple. These pitfalls erode safety within the relationship and make it nearly impossible for recovery to gain any traction. We will start by outlining five common pitfalls wounded partners experience.

Although it can be tempting for the wounded partner to tell whoever they want to about the pain their partner has caused them, we don't recommend it. We have worked with many wounded partners who regularly tell us that they regret telling so many people about their partner's infidelity-related behavior. Telling the wrong people can destroy relationships, damage children, and damage the wounding partner. It is often counterproductive to the recovery of the relationship as well.

Although it is not uncommon for wounded partners not to care who they tell in the beginning because they are determined to leave the relationship, it is our experience that many of them change their mind once some time goes by. This can lead to a situation that the wounded partner comes to regret. One extreme example of this is when a woman we worked with got her husband fired from his job because she wanted to punish him. She later came to regret that decision and realized that she had shot holes in her own boat by doing so.

Although telling a large number of people is not advisable, we don't recommend that wounded partners go it alone either. It is not a healthy situation for the wounded partner to process all their emotions with the wounding partner. We recommend that both the wounding and the wounded partners identify two or three people each that they are going to lean on for support during this time. It is best if both partners can agree on each other's lists so that neither feels betrayed through the sharing of information. However, we understand that sometimes this isn't possible. The purpose of identifying support people ahead of time is that it reduces the likelihood that one or both partners will share with random people out of pain. Sharing the pain of betrayal randomly is not advisable since a person may inadvertently tell someone who will give them bad advice, gossip about their situation, or leave them abandoned in their pain because they don't know how to respond. Hurtful gossip as a result of sharing the pain from betrayal with the wrong person can set an already- fragile relationship up for more damage.

The wounded partner should be careful not to share their experience out of bad motives. Here are some questions to ask when deciding when to share emotions and with whom:

- Am I trying to punish my partner?
- Am I trying to manipulate my partner or the outcome of the relationship?
- Am I feeling self-righteous by sharing this information?
- Will sharing this information serve a positive benefit?

If the wounded partner takes the time to ask themselves these questions before sharing and limits the number of people they share with, they are likely to save themselves a lot of trouble down the road.

The Bible is clear. Don't let anger and rage lead you into destructive behavior.

James 1:19-21 MSG Act on What You Hear

19-21 Post this at all the intersections, dear friends: Lead with your ears, follow up with your tongue, and let anger straggle along in the rear. God's righteousness doesn't grow from human anger. So throw all spoiled virtue and cancerous evil in the garbage. In simple humility, let our gardener, God, landscape you with the Word, making a salvation-garden of your life.

Proverbs 10:14 NIV

The wise store up knowledge, but the mouth of a fool invites ruin.

Pitfall #2

Not dealing with underlying issues

We want to preface this by stating that we are not implying that a wounded partner should take on any responsibility for the wounding partner's behavior. The choice to engage in infidelity- related behavior is 100% the responsibility of the wounding partner. That being said, we have seen many wounded partners create a lack of safety in the recovery process by continuing to lash out at their partner through raging, humiliation, threatening, and shaming. Although it is normal for a wounded partner to engage in some of these behaviors (especially within the first three months of disclosure or discovery), a continuous and/or prolonged engagement in these behaviors is an indication that something is going on underneath the pain.

Trauma from betrayal affects multiple areas of a wounded partner's life. It has a way of bringing up past painful experiences as well. Here are some common areas of underlying issues:

- Self-worth
- Control
- Past traumatic events and abuse
- Depression or anxiety
- Co-dependency
- Abandonment

Healing from trauma happens in stages. Thus, it is not uncommon for new trauma to trigger feelings from past trauma and emotional pain. The underlying issues that betrayal brings up are signals that the wounded partner may have unresolved issues and/or needs to go deeper into recovery. This can be frustrating for the wounded partner, who is already dealing with so much. It can be especially frustrating when the wounded partner is being plagued with past issues that they thought were already resolved. Our goal in sharing this information is not to discourage you, but to help prepare you. Dealing with past issues is a normal part of the recovery process.

Let's take a look at how Jesus dealt with His past issues.

Hebrews 12:1-3 MSG

12 1-3 Do you see what this means—all these pioneers who blazed the way, all these veterans cheering us on? It means we'd better get on with it. Strip down, start running—and never quit! No extra spiritual fat, no parasitic sins. Keep your eyes on Jesus, who both began and finished this race we're in. Study how he did it. Because he never lost sight of where he was headed—that exhilarating finish in and with God—he could put up with anything along the way: Cross, shame, whatever. And now he's there, in the place of honor, right alongside God.

How does God expect us to deal with our past issues?

Hebrews 12:3-17 MSG

3 When you find yourselves flagging in your faith, go over that story again, item by item, that long litany of hostility he plowed through. That will shoot adrenaline into your souls!

4-11 In this all-out match against sin, others have suffered far worse than you, to say nothing of what Jesus went through—all that bloodshed! So don't feel sorry for yourselves. Or have you forgotten how good parents treat children, and that God regards you as his children?

My dear child, don't shrug off God's discipline, but don't be crushed by it either. It's the child he loves that he disciplines; the child he embraces, he also corrects.

God is educating you; that's why you must never drop out. He's treating you as dear children. This trouble you're in isn't punishment; it's training, the normal experience of children. Only irresponsible parents leave children to fend for themselves. Would you prefer an irresponsible God? We respect our own parents for training and not spoiling us, so why not embrace God's training so we can truly live? While we were children, our parents did what seemed best to them. But God is doing what is best for us, training us to live God's holy best. At the time, discipline isn't much fun. It always feels like it's going against the grain. Later, of course, it pays off big-time, for it's the well-trained who find themselves mature in their relationship with God.

12-13 So don't sit around on your hands! No more dragging your feet! Clear the path for long-distance runners so no one will trip and fall, so no one will step in a hole and sprain an ankle. Help each other out. And run for it!

14-17 Work at getting along with each other and with God. Otherwise you'll never get so much as a glimpse of God. Make sure no one gets left out of God's generosity. Keep a sharp eye out for weeds of bitter discontent. A thistle or two gone to seed can ruin a whole garden in no time. Watch out for the Esau syndrome: trading away God's lifelong gift in order to satisfy a short-term appetite. You well know how Esau later regretted that impulsive act and wanted God's blessing—but by then it was too late, tears or no tears.

Pitfall #3

Not enforcing boundaries

Boundaries are an important part of the recovery process for wounded partners. Much of the anger that results from betrayal is because the wounding partner has crossed so many boundary lines. Because boundaries keep us and others safe, a lack of boundary enforcement can lead to an unsafe situation for the wounded partner and for the relationship overall.

We often see wounded partners start out with firm boundaries, only to move their boundary lines when they meet with resistance from the wounding partner or when things start to go better in the relationship. One example of this is when the wounding partner won't honor communication boundaries and continues to rage, hurl insults, threaten, or refuses to honor constraints on the length of time conversations around the betrayal should last. Another example of this is when the wounded partner lets go of insisting on the wounding partner's need to be ongoingly accountable. We will cover both of these issues later. For now, we want to stress that not enforcing boundaries and/or getting lax on boundaries is a mistake.

Sometimes wounded partners let go of their boundaries in an attempt to let go of the past and move on. While it is understandable that neither partner wants to live in the aftermath of betrayal forever, letting go of boundaries is not the way to achieve lasting recovery. In fact, the opposite is true. Boundaries are vital to any healthy relationship. They help others understand how we want to be respected, help us gain a strong sense of identity, and bring focus and attention to our own well-being. A lack of boundaries creates a lack of safety and can cause us to build up some hefty resentments that can eventually lead to the demise of our relationships.

Titus was a young missionary who was trained by the Apostle Paul. Paul instructed Titus to set boundaries for persons in various positions in life. Expectations bring security and ensure order.

Titus 2: 1-15 MSG -A God-Filled Life

2 1-6 Your job is to speak out on the things that make for solid doctrine. Guide older men into lives of temperance, dignity, and wisdom, into healthy faith, love, and endurance. Guide older women into lives of reverence so they end up as neither gossips nor drunks, but models of goodness. By looking at them, the younger women will know how to love their husbands and children, be virtuous and pure, keep a good house, be good wives. We don't want anyone looking down on God's Message because of their behavior. Also, guide the young men to live disciplined lives.

7-8 But mostly, show them all this by doing it yourself, trustworthy in your teaching, your words solid and sane. Then anyone who is dead set against us, when he finds nothing weird or misguided, might eventually come around.

9-10 Guide slaves into being loyal workers, a bonus to their masters—no back talk, no petty thievery. Then their good character will shine through their actions, adding luster to the teaching of our Savior God.

11-14 God's readiness to give and forgive is now public. Salvation's available for everyone! We're being shown how to turn our backs on a godless, indulgent life, and how to take on a God-filled, God-honoring life. This new life is starting right now, and is whetting our appetites for the glorious day when our great God and Savior, Jesus Christ, appears. He offered himself as a sacrifice to free us from a dark, rebellious life into this good, pure life, making us a people he can be proud of, energetic in goodness.

15 Tell them all this. Build up their courage, and discipline them if they get out of line. You're in charge. Don't let anyone put you down.

Pitfall #4

Over-Responsibility

We feel that this one falls into the category of boundaries. However, we see it so often that we think it deserves a section of its own. Although we sometimes see this in both partners, we most often see it in the wounded partner—especially when the wounding partner is ambivalent and/or does not seem to be taking recovery seriously. Due to how significant the effects of betrayal are, it is no wonder that over responsibility would show up. If the wounding partner fails to do the work necessary for the relationship to heal, it can create a situation that feels quite frightening to the wounded partner because there is so much on the line.

The term "over responsibility" can be described as a situation in which a person manages another person in such a way that they take on the responsibility for that person's choices and behaviors. Typically, this situation happens because the over responsible person wants to minimize or avoid pain—particularly rejection, disappointment, and loss. In the case of wounded partners, it often comes across as "babysitting" the recovery process. They frequently check in with their partner and offer reminders in the form of questions such as, "are you doing the reading?", "did you make that appointment yet?", or "you do realize that your group starts in 15 minutes, right?"

We are not unsympathetic to the wounded partner's pain and acknowledge that it may be the cause of much of over responsible behavior. However, it typically backfires in the following ways:

- The wounded partner continues to feel unsafe because they are unsure of the wounding partner's motives for recovery.
- They never give the wounding partner the opportunity to own their own recovery.
- They use up emotional energy that they can't spare, which can lead to being overwhelmed in multiple areas of life.
- One or both of the partners become resentful.

Although it can be tempting for the wounded partner to engage in behavior that is over responsible, it most often creates frustration for them. It is also important to note that, although managing the wounding partner's recovery process can be tempting and even seem necessary, it is of utmost importance that the wounding partner own the recovery for themselves. They can't be forced into it. If they are, it typically will not last. This can be very difficult for the wounded partner to face, but it's true. If the wounded partner continues to have to do all of the work for recovery, the question is whether or not the wounding partner is really committed in the first place. Conversely, if the wounding partner is simply slow to get going on recovery, over responsibility on the wounded partner's part could push them in the opposite direction.

So what can an over-responsible person do to help the situation? Although overcoming over responsibility is often a long process, especially if the tendency to be over responsible was present prior to the betrayal, here are some things that can help:

- **Own it.** The first step to overcoming an obstacle like over responsibility is to acknowledge that it is an issue.
- **Dig deeper.** Oftentimes, there are deeper issues driving over responsibility that a person needs to discover and work on if they are to stop engaging in this behavior. Common areas include pain, worry, pride, fear, and childhood issues.
- **Self-care.** For many wounded partners, the thought of not being over responsible for their partner's recovery is stressful. It can be nerve wracking to pull back and wait to see if the wounding partner is going to take responsibility for their own recovery. Self-care is critical to help combat this potentially stressful situation.
- **Accountability.** For some, pulling back and taking a "wait and see" attitude when it comes to the wounding partner's recovery is extremely difficult. It can help to put accountability in place so that the wounded partner does not feel tempted to reengage in over responsibility.
- **Self-compassion.** The stakes are high when it comes to recovery from betrayal. Wounding partners should be patient with themselves during this difficult process. If you reengage in the over responsible behavior, get back on track by admitting to it and offer yourself compassion.

Tamar, the daughter in law of Judah, was in a covenant. She lost her two husbands, both sons of Judah. Judah gave her a promise for her to marry his third son when he came of age so she could have children. He didn't follow through, so she took matters into her own hands. She acted over responsible. She managed Judah's end of the deal and chose the way that this covenant would be fulfilled.

Genesis 38 6-26 MSG

6-7 Judah got a wife for Er, his firstborn. Her name was Tamar. But Judah's firstborn, Er, grievously offended GOD and GOD took his life.

8-10 So Judah told Onan, "Go and sleep with your brother's widow; it's the duty of a brother-in-law to keep your brother's line alive." But Onan knew that the child wouldn't be his, so whenever he slept with his brother's widow he spilled his semen on the ground so he wouldn't produce a child for his brother. GOD was much offended by what he did and also took his life.

11 So Judah stepped in and told his daughter-in-law Tamar, "Live as a widow at home with your father until my son Shelah grows up." He was worried that Shelah would also end up dead, just like his brothers. So Tamar went to live with her father.

12 Time passed. Judah's wife, Shua's daughter, died. When the time of mourning was over, Judah with his friend Hirah of Adullam went to Timnah for the sheep shearing.

13-14 Tamar was told, "Your father-in-law has gone to Timnah to shear his sheep." She took off her widow's clothes, put on a veil to disguise herself, and sat at the entrance to Enaim which is on the road to Timnah. She realized by now that even though Shelah was grown up, she wasn't going to be married to him.

15 Judah saw her and assumed she was a prostitute since she had veiled her face. He left the road and went over to her. He said, "Let me sleep with you." He had no idea that she was his daughter-in-law.

16 She said, "What will you pay me?"

17 "I'll send you," he said, "a kid goat from the flock."

She said, "Not unless you give me a pledge until you send it."

18 "So what would you want in the way of a pledge?"

She said, "Your personal seal-and-cord and the staff you carry."

He handed them over to her and slept with her. And she got pregnant.

19 She then left and went home. She removed her veil and put her widow's clothes back on.

20-21 Judah sent the kid goat by his friend from Adullam to recover the pledge from the woman. But he couldn't find her. He asked the men of that place, "Where's the prostitute that used to sit by the road here near Enaim?"

They said, "There's never been a prostitute here."

22 He went back to Judah and said, "I couldn't find her. The men there said there never has been a prostitute there."

23 Judah said, "Let her have it then. If we keep looking, everyone will be poking fun at us. I kept my part of the bargain—I sent the kid goat but you couldn't find her."

24 Three months or so later, Judah was told, "Your daughter-in-law has been playing the whore—and now she's a pregnant whore."

Judah yelled, "Get her out here. Burn her up!"

25 As they brought her out, she sent a message to her father-in-law, "I'm pregnant by the man who owns these things. Identify them, please. Who's the owner of the seal-and-cord and the staff?"

26 Judah saw they were his. He said, "She's in the right; I'm in the wrong—I wouldn't let her marry my son Shelah." He never slept with her again.

Pitfall #5

Going on the attack after the wounding partner shares information

This is a tough one for many wounded partners. On the one hand, the wounded partner desperately needs to understand what their partner has done in order to process the information. On the other hand, they typically feel extremely angry and hurt when they find the information out. This can lead many wounded partners to attack the wounding partner. Although it is completely understandable why the wounded partner would do this, it is counterproductive to recovery and creates a lack of safety in the relationship.

For some wounded partners, the information shared with them can cause such great pain that they lash out physically against their partners. For others, they engage in verbal assaults. As we said, this is understandable but counterproductive. As hard as it may be to accept, the wounded partner needs to provide a safe space for the wounding partner to share information regarding their infidelity-related behavior. If they don't, the wounding partner is likely to withhold information which will stall recovery. We feel it important to say that we never advocate for the wounding partner to hold back information just because this is happening. As we have said previously, the wounding partner needs to be forthcoming with information regarding infidelity-related behavior regardless of the circumstances.

We want anyone reading this to understand that we are not saying that the wounded partner shouldn't be angry or express anger. However, expressing anger, disappointment, hurt, disgust, etc. in an appropriate way is of the utmost importance if the wounded partner wants the dialogue between them and their partner to continue. Name calling, threatening, physically attacking, or throwing things at the wounding partner will create a lack of safety in the relationship. Although it is understandable that the wounded partner would be angry and hurt by the wounding partner's actions, they must work hard at keeping that anger in check. Time outs, which we will cover at length later on in this section, are a good way to ensure that displays of anger are kept at appropriate levels.

If you are a wounded partner and have been in the habit of doing this, you may be facing a situation in which your partner is hesitant or refuses to give you the information you need regarding their infidelity-related behavior. In order to reestablish safe communication, we would advise you to commit to not reacting to the information your partner gives you right away. Instead, we recommend that you commit to not acting on the information for a certain period of time after you have received it. Depending on the circumstances and the type of information received, this could be anything from 24 hours to one year participating in a couple's recovery program.

Haman, an Aggagite, got angry at a certain Jew named Mordecai. When Mordecai dishonored Haman because he would only bow down to the One True God, Haman set into motion a diabolical plan to destroy all Jews and called for their annihilation. His hatred and rage controlled him. In the end, it was Hamen and his ten sons who were impaled/hanged in the place where he intended to murder Mordecai.

Esther 3:1-6 MSG

3 1-2 Sometime later, King Xerxes promoted Haman son of Hammedatha the Agagite, making him the highest-ranking official in the government. All the king's servants at the King's Gate used to honor him by bowing down and kneeling before Haman—that's what the king had commanded.

2-4 Except Mordecai. Mordecai wouldn't do it, wouldn't bow down and kneel. The king's servants at the King's Gate asked Mordecai about it: "Why do you cross the king's command?" Day after day they spoke to him about this, but he wouldn't listen, so they went to Haman to see whether something shouldn't be done about it. Mordecai had told them that he was a Jew.

5-6 When Haman saw for himself that Mordecai didn't bow down and kneel before him, he was outraged. Meanwhile, having learned that Mordecai was a Jew, Haman hated to waste his fury on just one Jew; he looked for a way to eliminate not just Mordecai but all Jews throughout the whole kingdom of Xerxes.

Esther 7:9-10 MSG

9 Harbona, one of the eunuchs attending the king, spoke up: "Look over there! There's the gallows that Haman had built for Mordecai, who saved the king's life. It's right next to Haman's house—seventy-five feet high!"

The king said, "Hang him on it!"

10 So Haman was hanged on the very gallows that he had built for Mordecai. And the king's hot anger cooled.

Proverbs 16:32 TLB

32 It is better to be slow tempered than famous; it is better to have self-control than to control an army.

Prayer for the wounded partner:

Father, I will lead with my ears, follow up with my tongue and let my anger straggle along in the rear. I will deal with underlying issues and strip down anger and resentment. I refuse to quit! I will keep my eyes on Jesus who both began and finished this race that we are in. He never lost sight of where he was headed, he put up with everything along the way, the Cross and all of its shame. And now He's in the place of honor, right alongside God. I will establish godly boundaries in my life and keep them in place. I will not be over responsible and take action for someone else. I will not attack my wounding partner when they disclose information about the betrayal. I will allow You to deal with them. No one could deal with them better than You, Lord. I will be slow tempered, and practice self-control and You will work on my behalf!. In Jesus' name, Amen.

PART 16

Wounding Partner Pitfalls

Since we have already explained the major mistakes of not ending the infidelity-related behavior and defending and blaming, we will not detail those here. Instead, we would like to offer you information on other common mistakes that wounding partners make that sabotage safety in the recovery process.

Pitfall #1: Lying (about anything)

It goes without saying that the wounding partner should never lie about what their infidelity-related behavior entails. However, it is also important to remember that lying about anything will leave the wounded partner wondering if there is any hope for safety in the relationship.

According to Merriam-Webster, the definitions of lying best suited to the purposes of this book are as follows:

1. To make an untrue statement with the intent to deceive

2. To create a false and/or misleading impression

There are three common types of lies that people tell. These are:

1. Lies of commission. Lying by intentionally using falsestatements.

2. Lies of omission. Lying by failing to disclose relevant information.

3. Lies of influence (a.k.a. "character lies"). Lying by not directly answering the question but, instead, offering astatement about your character that implies that you wouldnever do such a thing.

When a couple is working through the aftermath of betrayal, even seemingly innocuous lies are a huge deal to the wounded partner. Because the wounding partner engaged in deception when they engaged in their infidelity-related behavior, every lie told from here on out could constitute a reason why the wounded partner feels they cannot trust the wounding partner. This includes "white lies" and leaving out seemingly unimportant details.

Luke 8:16 & 17 TLB

"Who ever heard of someone lighting a lamp and then covering it up to keep it from shining? No, lamps are mounted in the open where they can be seen. 17 This illustrates the fact that someday everything in men's hearts shall be brought to light and made plain to all.

Proverbs 14:25 MSG

"Souls are saved by truthful witnesses and betrayed by the spread of lies."

Pitfall #2: Checking boxes

When we work with wounded partners who feel unsafe in the relationship, we are often told that this is because they feel that the wounding partner is simply "checking boxes" when it comes to recovery. What they mean by this is that the wounding partner is only going through the motions when it comes to their recovery work, but there has been very little change in their demeanor and attitudes. If you are a wounding partner reading this and this describes your situation, we challenge you to dig deep within yourself in order to discover why. If it is because of ambivalence on your part, we encourage you to deal with that head-on. Until you do, your relationship will stall out in terms of recovery.

It is important for the wounding partner to understand that the wounded partner is not interested in having items on a list checked off—especially if it is only being done to placate them or to make the wounding partner look good. What the wounded partner is looking for from the wounding partner are signs of a change of heart. If the wounding partner is disengaged from the process of true recovery, it sends the message to the wounded partner that the relationship is not a priority.

Here are some common ways that wounding partners come across as if they are merely "checking boxes":

- Getting information but failing to apply it to their actions.
- Setting themselves up as the exception to the rule when it comes to what they should be doing.
- Making the wounded partner do all of the work when it comes to making counseling/coaching appointments, finding self-help books to read, etc.
- Making their recovery work dependent on their partner changing.

Jesus addressed the Pharisees who were famous at checking boxes and having the appearance of holiness and not possessing the power to change themselves or others for good.

Luke 11: 37-52 MSG

37-41 When he finished that talk, a Pharisee asked him to dinner. He entered his house and sat right down at the table. The Pharisee was shocked and somewhat offended when he saw that Jesus didn't wash up before the meal. But the Master said to him, "I know you Pharisees buff the surface of your cups and plates, so they sparkle in the sun, but I also know your insides are maggoty with greed and secret evil. Stupid Pharisees! Didn't the One who made the outside also make the inside? Turn both your pockets and your hearts inside out and give generously to the poor; then your lives will be clean, not just your dishes and your hands.

42 "I've had it with you! You're hopeless, you Pharisees! Frauds! You keep meticulous account books, tithing on every nickel and dime you get, but manage to find loopholes for getting around basic matters of justice and God's love. Careful bookkeeping is commendable, but the basics are required.

43-44 "You're hopeless, you Pharisees! Frauds! You love sitting at the head table at church dinners, love preening yourselves in the radiance of public flattery. Frauds! You're just like unmarked graves: People walk over that nice, grassy surface, never suspecting the rot and corruption that is six feet under."

45 One of the religion scholars spoke up: "Teacher, do you realize that in saying these things you're insulting us?"

46 He said, "Yes, and I can be even more explicit. You're hopeless, you religion scholars! You load people down with rules and regulations, nearly breaking their backs, but never lift even a finger to help.

47-51 "You're hopeless! You build tombs for the prophets your ancestors killed. The tombs you build are monuments to your murdering ancestors more than to the murdered prophets. That accounts for God's Wisdom saying, 'I will send them prophets and apostles, but they'll kill them and run them off.' What it means is that every drop of righteous blood ever spilled from the time earth began until now, from the blood of Abel to the blood of Zechariah, who was struck down between altar and sanctuary, is on your heads. Yes, it's on the bill of this generation and this generation will pay.

52 "You're hopeless, you religious scholars! You took the key of knowledge, but instead of unlocking doors, you locked them. You won't go in yourself and won't let anyone else in either."

Matthew 7:21-23 MSG

21-23 "Knowing the correct password—saying 'Master, Master,' for instance—isn't going to get you anywhere with me. What is required is serious obedience—*doing* what my Father wills. I can see it now—at the Final Judgment thousands strutting up to me and saying, 'Master, we preached the Message, we bashed the demons, our super-spiritual projects had everyone talking.' And do you know what I am going to say? 'You missed the boat. All you did was use me to make yourselves important. You don't impress me one bit. You're out of here.'

Pitfall #3: A lack of humility

"Pride makes us artificial, and humility makes us real."— Thomas Merton

When couples are trying to recover from the effects of betrayal, a lack of humility on the wounding partner's part creates a lack of safety in the relationship that brings recovery to a grinding halt. When we work with wounding partners who lack humility, we often feel like we are talking to a brick wall. It is unfortunate because their pride keeps them from benefitting from the information that is vital to both their personal recovery and the recovery of the relationship.

Here are some signs that pride is an issue:

- Being defensive
- Being argumentative
- Talking over the top of people
- A focus on being heard instead of hearing other people
- Excuse-making
- Hiding flaws
- Blaming

When wounding partners lack humility, they are unsafe. They put themselves and their relationship in danger because the wounded partner will feel that they can't freely talk about the issues that would help them recover. And the wounded partner isn't the only one who suffers. Wounding partners who lack humility set themselves up for future failure because they don't understand their ability to engage in infidelity-related behavior in the future. Instead, they often tell themselves that they will never do it again because their pride clouds their understanding of their own vulnerability. Additionally, wounding partners who lack humility cut themselves off from a community of people who could help them with the issues they are dealing with.

A lack of humility (or pride) is always accompanied by wicked character traits.

Proverbs 8: 12-21 MSG

"I am Lady Wisdom, and I live next to Sanity, Knowledge and Discretion live just down the street. The Fear-of-God means hating Evil, whose ways I hate with a passion— pride and arrogance and crooked talk. Good counsel and common sense are my characteristics; I am both Insight and the Virtue to live it out. With my help, leaders rule, and lawmakers legislate fairly; With my help, governors govern, along with all in legitimate authority. I love those who love me; those who look for me find me. Wealth and Glory accompany me— also substantial Honor and a Good Name. My benefits are worth more than a big salary, even a very big salary; the returns on me exceed any imaginable bonus. You can find me on Righteous Road—that's where I walk— at the intersection of Justice Avenue, Handing out life to those who love me, filling their arms with life—armloads of life!

God takes arrogance very seriously. Remember, it is pride that kicked Lucifer out of heaven!

Ezekiel 28:11-19 MSG

11-19** God's Message came to me: "Son of man, raise a funeral song over the king of Tyre. Tell him, A Message from God, the Master: "You had everything going for you. You were in Eden, God's garden. You were dressed in splendor, your robe studded with jewels: Carnelian, peridot, and moonstone, beryl, onyx, and jasper, Sapphire, turquoise, and emerald, all in settings of engraved gold. A robe was prepared for you the same day you were created. You were the anointed cherub. I placed you on the mountain of God. You strolled in magnificence among the stones of fire. From the day of your creation you were sheer perfection . . . and then imperfection—evil! —was detected in you. In much buying and selling you turned violent, you sinned! I threw you, disgraced, off the mountain of God. I threw you out—you, the anointed angel-cherub. No more strolling among the gems of fire for you! Your beauty went to your head. You corrupted wisdom by using it to get worldly fame. I threw you to the ground, sent you sprawling before an audience of kings and let them gloat over your demise. By sin after sin after sin, by your corrupt ways of doing business, you defiled your holy places of worship. So I set a fire around and within you. It burned you up. I reduced you to ashes. All anyone sees now when they look for you is ashes, a pitiful mound of ashes. All who once knew you now throw up their hands 'This can't have happened! This has happened!'

Pitfall #4: Expecting the wounded partner to "just get over it"

Although it can seem like it would be beneficial for the relationship to have everyone, particularly the wounded partner, move on, dismissing the gravity of the situation with a quick fix is a mistake of huge proportions. If you are a wounding partner reading this, and you are interested in saving your relationship, we cannot stress enough the fact that you should immediately stop. When you engage in this type of behavior, you marginalize your because an attitude of "just get over it" implies that the issue is not as big of a deal as they are making it out to be. If you continue to marginalize your partner in this way, you are acting disrespectfully and risk pushing them away from you completely and permanently.

Here are a few of the statements that wounding partners make that marginalize wounded partners:

- "Why can't we just move on?"
- "It meant nothing to me. I don't see what the big deal is."
- "When are you going to stop bringing this up?"
- "I said I was sorry. You need to forgive me."
- "Haven't we talked about this enough already?"
- "I don't see why you're still upset."

Unfortunately, we hear these types of statements in our offices on a regular basis. The dismissive attitude that typically accompanies these statements is not only harmful to the wounded partner, but it can also create huge barriers to the recovery of the relationship. Additionally, it can be an indication of denial on the wounding partner's part. Instead of choosing to look at the evidence that suggests that their infidelity-related behavior was, in fact, a VERY big deal, they choose to believe that it wasn't. However, denying the truth does not change the facts of the situation. The wounded partner is doing and saying the things they are because the infidelity-related behavior was extremely damaging, violating, and world-changing. The wounded partner's pain should be all the evidence the wounding partner needs to acknowledge that their betrayal was, and is, a big deal.

Another take on the "just get over it" situation is when we see the wounding partner engage in recovery and expect that this is enough to fix the wounded partner's pain. If you are a wounding partner reading this, we would remind you that individual recovery, while great for everyone involved, is not enough to immediately fix the situation. This is especially true for wounding partners involved in pornography addiction, sex addiction, and/ or intimacy avoidant behavior. In our programs, people working the 12-steps for these issues often get a sobriety date. While this is fantastic, and we want to commend those of you entering into sobriety on their efforts, you need to understand that your sobriety date is likely a painful reminder to your partner of the date that you last acted out. As such, they are highly unlikely to feel the same sense of pride about it as you do.

What is important for wounding partners to remember is that they should not expect a large amount of praise from the wounded partner for good behavior, or simply for a lack of bad behavior. Expecting praise for behaving better than when they were acting out is a lot like expecting praise for not hitting the wounded partner in the head with a hammer. While it is great that they aren't hitting them in the head with a hammer anymore, the fact remains that they once did hit them in the head with the "hammer" of infidelity-related behavior. Expecting them to be overly grateful for this is unrealistic. While we understand that recovery is difficult and encouragement is often helpful to sustained self-improvement, we encourage wounding partners to remember that expecting praise for a *lack of bad behavior* is not only unrealistic but can come off as self-serving and unempathetic. Instead, it is better for the wounding partner to join a workgroup such as the ones we offer at Becoming Well in order to gain insight and encouragement from other group members.

In recovery, we use the term "pink clouding" to describe a situation in which the wounding partner feels excited about their own recovery. Pink clouding is most common when the wounding partner has been engaged in addictive behavior and is marked by the following:

- Feelings of joy and/or excitement
- A hopeful outlook
- Optimism

- Confidence
- Calmness
- A heavy focus on recovery-related behaviors
- Commitment to change
- A tendency to overlook the hard work needed to maintain recovery
- Increased awareness of their own emotions

While pink clouding offers a much-needed shift of focus, it can be difficult for the wounded partner to see the wounding partner respond this way. We have been told by many wounded partners that they often feel jealous of the wounding partner's ability to feel optimistic and joyful because the situation is quite different for them. For a wounded partner who has experienced betrayal, they are left struggling through the aftermath of shattered hopes and dreams. Feelings of comfort and safety are gone, and the wounded partner is left staring into the unknown. This often leaves the wounded partner with a bleak sense of hopelessness that they will have to work through if they are to feel joy within the relationship once more. If you are a wounding partner reading this and are pink clouding, we advise you to keep this in mind. Although it is wonderful that you have fully engaged in recovery, and we don't want to discourage you from that, we want to encourage you to balance out the excitement you feel at your own recovery with the perspective that your partner is likely struggling. Please do not adopt the attitude that they should "just get over it" and come along in recovery with you. Instead, acknowledge that their path is different than yours and commit to listening to, empathizing with, and acknowledging their pain, because it is pain that you created for them.

The natural born brothers of Jesus had absolutely no empathy for Him and certainly wanted Him to 'get over' Himself! All this nonsense about His life being in danger! Who does He think He is anyway? Look at this scripture passage.

John 7:1-11 MSG

7 1-2 Later Jesus was going about his business in Galilee. He didn't want to travel in Judea because the Jews there were looking for a chance to kill him. It was near the time of Tabernacles, a feast observed annually by the Jews.

3-5 His brothers said, "Why don't you leave here and go up to the Feast so your disciples can get a good look at the works you do? No one who intends to be publicly known does everything behind the scenes. If you're serious about what you are doing, come out in the open and show the world." His brothers were pushing him like this because they didn't believe in him either.

6-8 Jesus came back at them, "Don't pressure me. This isn't my time. It's your time—it's always your time; you have nothing to lose. The world has nothing against you, but it's up in arms against me. It's against me because I expose the evil behind its pretensions. You go ahead, go up to the Feast. Don't wait for me. I'm not ready. It's not the right time for me."

9-11 He said this and stayed on in Galilee. But later, after his family had gone up to the Feast, he also went. But he kept out of the way, careful not to draw attention to himself.

Jesus did not have the support of his family. They minimized his work and publicly disrespected him.

When people asked Jesus for help, he didn't tell them to get over it!

Luke 18:35-43 MSG

35-37 He came to the outskirts of Jericho. A blind man was sitting beside the road asking for handouts. When he heard the rustle of the crowd, he asked what was going on. They told him, "Jesus the Nazarene is going by."

38 He yelled, "Jesus! Son of David! Mercy, have mercy on me!"

39 Those ahead of Jesus told the man to shut up, but he only yelled all the louder, "Son of David! Mercy, have mercy on me!"

40 Jesus stopped and ordered him to be brought over. When he had come near, Jesus asked, "What do you want from me?"

41 He said, "Master, I want to see again."

42-43 Jesus said, "Go ahead—see again! Your faith has saved and healed you!" The healing was instant: He looked up, seeing—and then followed Jesus, glorifying God. Everyone in the street joined in, shouting praise to God.

Pitfall #5: Not supporting the wounded partner's recovery

If you are a wounding partner reading this, we need to stress that it is important that you support your partner's individual recovery. In our work with wounding partners, we have discovered that a certain percentage of them seem to have trouble with this concept for the following reasons:

- It embarrasses them to have their secrets revealed to other people. While we understand that it can be embarrassing for the wounding partner to have someone else know what they have done, it is important that this is dealt with as a separate issue and not projected onto the wounded partner. It is important to the wounded partner's recovery that they have people to process emotions with who will give them sound advice and caring support. If this is an issue, we urge you to deal with it in order to resolve the issue for yourself. Putting your own comfort before the well-being of your partner sends the message that you aren't prioritizing the relationship.

- It costs them money. Yes, recovery can be expensive— especially recovery from betrayal because the process takes a long time. We understand that not everyone is financially able to engage in every single experience that would help them recover. However, the wounding partner needs to make recovery for both themselves and the wounded partner a priority. Our advice is for the wounding partner to prioritize spending on recovery-related activities.

- The wounded partner's autonomy threatens them. Unfortunately, we see this on a regular basis—especially in relationships where intimacy avoidance is an issue. Some relationships are defined by the wounding partner's need to control the wounded partner's autonomy in order to avoid abandonment and/or rejection. For others, it can be scary because they know their infidelity-related behavior may cause their partner to leave them. If you are feeling threatened by your partner's autonomy in this situation, we urge you to deal with this as a separate issue.

- They want to minimize the problem. Sadly, some wounding partners care more about looking bad than they do about their partner's recovery. Minimizing in any way is self-serving and will hurt the wounded partner and the relationship. We urge wounding partners who minimize to stop putting themselves and their feelings above the needs of their partner to heal.

- They do not consider their partner's needs to be important or as important as theirs. We see this occasionally in intimacy avoidant and narcissistic relationships. For some wounding partners, their needs, feelings, desires, etc. come before anyone else's and especially before the wounded partner's. The root of this issue is usually a fragile sense of self-worth. Many wounding partners who feel this way actually feel bad about themselves and mistakenly think that acknowledging the importance of someone else's needs somehow diminishes their own importance.

As we stated previously, it is imperative that the wounded partner get their own individual recovery after betrayal has been discovered or disclosed. Supporting their recovery is a way that the wounding partner can show remorse for their actions as well as love toward the wounded partner.

Jesus actually taught us how to show love towards those who are wounded, and He expects us to do it. He stated that it will give us life.

Luke 10: 25-37 MSG: Defining "Neighbor"

25 Just then a religion scholar stood up with a question to test Jesus. "Teacher, what do I need to do to get eternal life?"

26 He answered, "What's written in God's Law? How do you interpret it?"

27 He said, "That you love the Lord your God with all your passion and prayer and muscle and intelligence—and that you love your neighbor as well as you do yourself."

28 "Good answer!" said Jesus. "Do it and you'll live."

29 Looking for a loophole, he asked, "And just how would you define 'neighbor'?"

30-32 Jesus answered by telling a story. "There was once a man traveling from Jerusalem to Jericho. On the way he was attacked by robbers. They took his clothes, beat him up, and went off leaving him half-dead. Luckily, a priest was on his way down the same road, but when he saw him he angled across to the other side. Then a Levite religious man showed up; he also avoided the injured man.

33-35 "A Samaritan traveling the road came on him. When he saw the man's condition, his heart went out to him. He gave him first aid, disinfecting and bandaging his wounds. Then he lifted him onto his donkey, led him to an inn, and made him comfortable. In the morning he took out two silver coins and gave them to the innkeeper, saying, 'Take good care of him. If it costs any more, put it on my bill—I'll pay you on my way back.'

36 "What do you think? Which of the three became a neighbor to the man attacked by robbers?"

37 "The one who treated him kindly," the religion scholar responded.

Jesus said, "Go and do the same."

1 Timothy 5:8 NLT

8 But those who won't care for their relatives, especially those in their own household, have denied the true faith. Such people are worse than unbelievers.

Prayer for wounding partner:

Father, Lying is an abomination to You. I want to save the soul of my wounded partner and stop the damage that I have caused. I do not want to be pharisaical and check boxes. I want to change my heart. My heart belongs to You and my wounded partner. I also repent of arrogance and pride. I want to be a person of good counsel, common sense and virtue. I want to have an excellent reputation for myself and to pass it on to my future generations. I repent of my 'get over it' attitude. My actions have caused damage and destruction to my wounded partner, and I will not minimize the disastrous effects of my past wicked behavior. I will support the healing process of my wounded partner. I will do everything in my power to accelerate their recovery. I ask for Your abundant grace to help me. In Jesus' name, Amen.

PART 17

Pitfalls As a Couple

Pitfall #1: Failing to prioritize ongoing accountability

One of the biggest mistakes a couple can make in recovery is for one or both of partners to fail making accountability a priority. Typically, we see this happen for one of the following reasons:

1. The wounding partner is being lax with recovery.

2. The wounded partner gets tired of pushback when they ask for accountability.

3. The wounded partner fails to understand ways in which they themselves need to be accountable.

4. One or both partners feel the relationship has improved so much that accountability is no longer needed.

Reasons one and two indicate that there is a lack of true recovery on the wounding partner's part. This is problematic because, if true recovery does not take place, the relationship is not a safe place because the infidelity-related behavior has a high likelihood of resurfacing at some point. As for reason number three, it isn't uncommon for wounded partners to feel that it is their partner that needs recovery—not them. One of our goals in working with wounded partners is to help them understand that they need their own recovery due to the fact that experiencing trauma from betrayal is like being hit by a bus. Although it was through no fault of their own, they will still need to heal and recover from their injuries. Additionally, the wounded partner will need ongoing accountability for any behaviors they are engaging in that hurt the relationship.

Reason number four is, perhaps, the most dangerous reason for not prioritizing ongoing accountability because it is the hardest one to explain to couples who are finally doing better. Most couples who have struggled through infidelity and come out the other side just want to put everything behind them and move on. While this is certainly understandable, we would like to point out that there is a difference between talking about the betrayal all of the time (which is not recommended) and keeping good recovery habits in place.

Oftentimes, wounding partners have every intention of holding true to their promises. Unfortunately, it is one thing for a person to say that they would never do something again and another to keep the necessary guardrails in place to keep them from running off the track. When it comes to recovery from betrayal, especially when addiction is in the mix, good intensions simply aren't enough. Habits, especially ones related to infidelity- related behavior, are like ruts in the road of life. It only takes a person getting a little bit off track before they realize that their wheels have slipped into those ruts, and they are now following an all-too-familiar path to destruction.

As human beings, when we travel down a good road for a long period of time it is easy for us to forget about the ruts in the road that lead down a bad path. We can tell ourselves that we aren't the same person we used to be, that we can bend the rules and still be fine, or that we are so far away from the ruts that lead to the bad path that there is no way we could ever go back there again. Unfortunately, life doesn't work like that. It is a journey, not a destination. To think that we have arrived is to set ourselves up for possible relapse.

What we recommend is that each partner outline the behaviors that are non-optional, the behaviors that are life-giving, and the questionable, or "slippery", behaviors. Each person should do this for themselves, although it can be a good couple's exercise to do as well. An easy way to outline these behaviors is to use a 3-Circle Exercise:

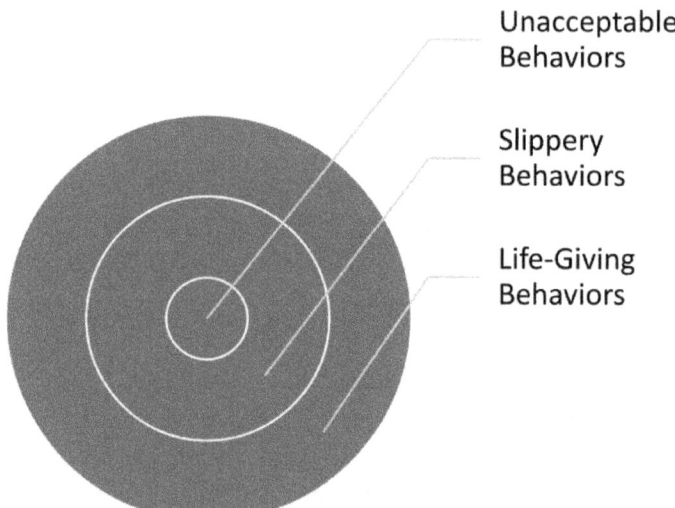

Figure 3: 3-Circle Exercise

Next, outline the accountability you are going to put into place in order to sustain each one. Although this exercise can be somewhat time consuming, it is highly valuable because it can help the relationship, and the individuals in it, to stay on track. Taking a proactive approach to accountability is vital to recovery. We have known many people who have done well in recovery for years who seem to suddenly slip off the rails due to stressors in their life. What we discover is that most of them gave up on the daily routine of accountability long before they acted out. As opposed to simply reacting when things get hard, proactively engaging in ongoing accountability will help ensure that the necessary guardrails are in place if and when times get stressful.

In The Message Bible, this parable is labeled The Story About Investment. Investment made into prioritizing ongoing accountability easily fits into this category.

Matthew 25: 14-30 MSG

The Story About Investment

14-18 "It's also like a man going off on an extended trip. He called his servants together and delegated responsibilities. To one he gave five thousand dollars, to another two thousand, to a third one thousand, depending on their abilities. Then he left. Right off, the first servant went to work and doubled his master's investment. The second did the same. But the man with the single thousand dug a hole and carefully buried his master's money.

19-21 "After a long absence, the master of those three servants came back and settled up with them. The one given five thousand dollars showed him how he had doubled his investment. His master commended him: 'Good work! You did your job well. From now on, be my partner.'

22-23 "The servant with the two thousand showed how he also had doubled his master's investment. His master commended him: 'Good work! You did your job well. From now on, be my partner.'

24-25 "The servant given one thousand said, 'Master, I know you have high standards and hate careless ways, that you demand the best and make no allowances for error. I was afraid I might disappoint you, so I found a good hiding place and secured your money. Here it is, safe and sound down to the last cent.'

26-27 "The master was furious. 'That's a terrible way to live! It's criminal to live cautiously like that! If you knew I was after the best, why did you do less than the least? The least you could have done would have been to invest the sum with the bankers, where at least I would have gotten a little interest.

28-30 "'Take the thousand and give it to the one who risked the most. And get rid of this "play-it-safe" who won't go out on a limb. Throw him out into utter darkness.'

Pitfall #2: Using children as pawns

Unfortunately, this is common enough that we had to include it in this book. When one parent bad-mouths another parent, can create a harmful situation for the child(ren) involved. Although most parents we work with understand why it is not in their children's best interest to do this, we occasionally run across it in the following scenarios:

1. The wounded partner is so disgusted with the wounding partner's behavior that they try to get the child(ren) on their side by telling them the sordid details.

2. The wounding partner, not wanting to look bad, gets the child(ren) on their side by telling them bad things about the wounded partner.

3. One partner purposely hurts their child(ren) as a way to get back at the other partner.

Studies have shown that alienation by a parent can create mental health, relationship, self-esteem, trust, anger, substance abuse, and learning issues for children. Although it is only human to want the empathy of others during this difficult time, we implore you to leave your child(ren) out of it. Additionally, we do not recommend that either partner use even their older child(ren) as confidantes, although it is okay to tell them the truth. Please keep in mind that the details given need to be age appropriate. For example, telling a young child that the wounding partner did not treat the wounded partner in a loving way is truthful, but still age appropriate. It is okay to tell a grown child more details such as, "Mom had an affair". However, we still recommend that you err in giving children, no matter what age, as little detail as possible and not involving them in what is going on.

Colossians 3:21 MSG

21 Parents don't come down too hard on your children or you'll crush their spirits.

Ephesians 6:4 MSG - parenthesis mine

4 Fathers (parents) don't frustrate your children with no-win scenarios. Take them by the hand and lead them in the way of the Master.

1 Samuel 3: 11-18 MSG

11 And the Lord said to Samuel: "See, I am about to do something in Israel that will make the ears of everyone who hears about it tingle. 12 At that time I will carry out against Eli everything I spoke against his family—from beginning to end. 13 For I told him that I would judge his family forever because of the sin he knew about; his sons blasphemed God,[a] and he failed to restrain them. 14 Therefore I swore to the house of Eli, 'The guilt of Eli's house will never be atoned for by sacrifice or offering.'"

15 Samuel lay down until morning and then opened the doors of the house of the Lord. He was afraid to tell Eli the vision, 16 but Eli called him and said, "Samuel, my son."

Samuel answered, "Here I am."

17 "What was it he said to you?" Eli asked. "Do not hide it from me. May God deal with you, be it ever so severely, if you hide from me anything he told you." 18 So Samuel told him everything, hiding nothing from him. Then Eli said, "He is the Lord; let him do what is good in his eyes."

Do NOT put your children into the position that Eli placed Samuel. The Lord had to speak through Samuel in order for Eli to be warned and corrected on how he didn't deal with his sons. Be a responsible parent and don't dump the role of 'responsible adult' upon them. Protect your children from harm!

Pitfall #3: Marathon conversations

A marathon conversation is a conversation that should take 45 minutes or less to discuss but ends up turning into a conversation that lasts for hours, and even days. We've had couples report that some discussion marathons have lasted all night into the wee hours of the morning, rendering both parties exhausted and barely able to function during the daytime. Although this is bound to happen occasionally, it is not uncommon for this to become a regularly occurring issue for some couples.

This term can also be used to describe a situation in which a couple is having multiple conversations per day about the betrayal. This situation usually happens when a wounded spouse is trying to "connect the dots" of information in order to wrap their head around how the betrayal happened. Agony, fear, and pressure are usually felt by the wounded spouse during this time. The person who has been unfaithful often feels a sense of dread and helplessness.

Other situations in which marathon conversations occur are:

1. When the wounded partner asks a question, and the wounding partner seems evasive or even outright refuses to answer.

2. The wounding partner tries to defend their behavior or blame shift

3. The wounded partner refuses to believe the answers they are given and decides to keep digging. This can possibly indicate that the wounded spouse has given relational meaning to certain infidelity-related behavior.

4. The wounded partner is verbally attacking the wounding partner out of pain and/or a need for punishment or revenge.

In all of the above-described scenarios, the wounded partner needs to understand the totality of the situation and is unlikely or unable to stop until they feel satisfied. Some of the reasons for this can include:

1. They want to get to the bottom of a particular issue

2. They are emotionally out of control and can't stop

3. They need to prove and point and/or be validated

4. They want to teach the wounding partner a lesson and/or use the information to get the wounding partner to "wake up" to what they have done

Wounding partners can get caught up in marathon conversations because:

1. They want to minimize or defend their behavior, so they don't feel so badly

2. They want the wounded partner to take at least part of the blame

3. They want the wounded partner to understand that they are actually wrong about something they are saying, thinking that "if they only understood, they would feel better"

4. They are triggered and/or angry

5. They are afraid to end the conversation for fear of being seen as uncaring or unwilling to try

It may seem counterintuitive, but the couples that are the most successful with navigating triggers and conversations around betrayal place time limits on their interactions around the subject. Short conversations (around 30-45 minutes in length) can be productive, while longer conversations are generally exhausting and typically get the couple nowhere. Also, the time you have your discussions will determine how productive they will be. We never recommend having discussions directly before bedtime.

At some point, conversations around the infidelity need to end because constantly digging up the past keeps the relationship from being able to move forward. However, this can vary depending on several different factors. If marathon conversations continue to be an issue for you, we highly recommend enlisted the help of a trained professional to assist you in getting past it.

Proverbs 10: 19-21 MSG

The more talk, the less truth; the wise measure their words. The speech of a good person is worth waiting for; the blabber of the wicked is worthless. The talk of a good person is rich fare for many, but chatterboxes die of an empty heart.

The Word of God states we are to measure our words and trust God to move on the wounding partner. We know we have gone over this verse before, but it is worth repeating over and over again. It will bring you true peace.

Philippians 4: 6-9 MSG

6-7 Don't fret or worry. Instead of worrying, pray. Let petitions and praises shape your worries into prayers, letting God know your concerns. Before you know it, a sense of God's wholeness, everything coming together for good, will come and settle you down. It's wonderful what happens when Christ displaces worry at the center of your life.

8-9 Summing it all up, friends, I'd say you'll do best by filling your minds and meditating on things true, noble, reputable, authentic, compelling, gracious—the best, not the worst; the beautiful, not the ugly; things to praise, not things to curse. Put into practice what you learned from me, what you heard and saw and realized. Do that, and God, who makes everything work together, will work you into his most excellent harmonies.

No one can remove a heart of stone, except God. Not only is He willing, but He is able!

Ezekiel 36: 26-28 MSG

I'll remove the stone heart from your body and replace it with a heart that's God-willed, not self-willed. I'll put my Spirit in you and make it possible for you to do what I tell you and live by my commands. You'll once again live in the land I gave your ancestors. You'll be my people! I'll be your God!

Pitfall #4: Staying in denial

Although we don't see this as frequently as some of the other issues we have outlined here, we see it often enough that it warrants mentioning. We typically become concerned that this may be an issue for a couple when we hear reports of the following:

- One or both partners drops out of recovery early on
- Thinking the relationship is suddenly better because one or both partners knows more about recovery than they used to
- The couple is not talking about, or hardly ever talks about, the infidelity
- Infidelity-related behavior was discovered but there has been no real disclosure process or discussions since
- One or both partners seem overly distracted with work, activities, etc.
- The couple is engaging in "normal" behavior such as sex, vacations, family get togethers, etc. despite discovery or disclosure being new and reports that it is upsetting to the wounded partner

The truth is that betrayal in a relationship drastically changes things. While it doesn't have to mean that the relationship is doomed, it is important that both partners accept the fact that their reality has now changed. Couples and individuals struggling with denial are attempting to avoid the grief associated with the painful losses that betrayal represents. For wounded partners, these losses often include a loss of trust, safety, and a feeling of being able to depend on the wounding partner. For wounding partners, these losses can include the loss of the comfort associated with the infidelity-related behavior, the loss of positive self-image and a sense of honor, or a loss of the wounded partner's respect and admiration.

Although we understand that it may be tempting for one or both partners to remain in denial about the new situation that the discovery or disclosure of infidelity has created, here are some reasons why staying in denial isn't a good idea:

- It can cause one or both partners to ignore deeper personal issues that need to be dealt with.
- It can cause preexisting issues to be ignored.
- It can cause partners to become frustrated with themselves or the other person when any issues related to the betrayal arise.
- It can cause marathon fights because, once triggered, all of the issues come out at once.
- It can contribute to the wounding partner's relapse.
- It can set one or both partners up for physical and mental health issues due to the suppression of emotions.
- It can lead to distance between partners.
- It can deny both partners an opportunity for true intimacy.

Even though it can be tempting to pretend everything is "business as usual", each partner must be willing to deal with the challenges that betrayal presents if recovery is truly to take place. Although the idea of having tough conversations can be anxiety- producing, avoidance of those conversations will only serve to maintain that anxiety to the detriment of each partner and to the relationship overall.

God is light and light dispels darkness. If denial persists, we will continue nurturing an atmosphere of sin and depravity that will create a momentum of destruction and devastation in our lives.

1 John 1: 5- 10 MSG

Walk in the Light

5 This, in essence, is the message we heard from Christ and are passing on to you: God is light, pure light; there's not a trace of darkness in him.

6-7 If we claim that we experience a shared life with him and continue to stumble around in the dark, we're obviously lying through our teeth—we're not living what we claim. But if we walk in the light, God himself being the light, we also experience a shared life with one another, as the sacrificed blood of Jesus, God's Son, purges all our sin.

8-10 If we claim that we're free of sin, we're only fooling ourselves. A claim like that is errant nonsense. On the other hand, if we admit our sins—simply come clean about them—he won't let us down; he'll be true to himself. He'll forgive our sins and purge us of all wrongdoing. If we claim that we've never sinned, we out-and-out contradict God—make a liar out of him. A claim like that only shows off our ignorance of God.

Pitfall #5: Believing that the process should be quick

While we wish we could tell you that recovery from betrayal is a quick process, we can't. The truth is that recovery often takes couples an average of eighteen months to two years to achieve. In many cases, depending on the circumstances, it can take even longer. The rebuilding of trust is a long and time-consuming process. It is also an ongoing process that can be derailed if one or both partners fail to nurture it. This is not to say that a couple will not experience victories in communication and intimacy along the way. However, most couples report that it takes at least a solid eighteen months before they feel the relationship has begun to stabilize. Additionally, it is not uncommon for new realizations to hit the wounded partner years down the line and/or for anniversaries to continue to trigger intense emotions. Engaging in honest and safe communication around these issues and getting professional help when needed is the best way to move past this.

We don't write this to discourage you, but we want you to be prepared to have patience with yourself and with the process. There is simply no way to shortcut the rebuilding of trust after betrayal. There are, however, some ways that will prolong it or make it impossible. These are:

- Defending, blaming, or minimizing on the part of the wounding partner
- Explosive or inappropriate displays of anger on the part of the wounded partner
- Dribbling disclosure
- Continued mind-reading or unsubstantiated accusations on the part of the wounded partner
- Refusal to talk about the betrayal on the part of the wounding partner
- Marathon conversations that exhaust both partners
- Continued lying or engagement in infidelity-related behavior on the part of the wounding partner

Research shows that couples who can talk about infidelity in a constructive way on a regular basis tend to recover more quickly than those who don't. Therefore, it is imperative that the wounding partner engage in the recovery process and not shut the wounded partner down or refuse to answer questions. Although rebuilding trust is not a quick process, it can be done if both partners are committed to providing safety in the relationship.

God promised Adam and Eve in Genesis 3:15 MSG

"I'm declaring war between you and the woman, between your offspring and hers. He'll wound your head, you'll wound his heel."

It took 4000 years to bring that promise (Jesus' crucifixion and resurrection) to fruition. It was a long and arduous process. And many many times, it seemed impossible for God to bring that promise to pass. And yet He did! And we are still celebrating the victory of those numerous and intense battles today!

Ecclesiastes 3: 1-8 MSG

3 There's an opportune time to do things, a right time for everything on the earth:

2-8

A right time for birth and another for death,
A right time to plant and another to reap,
A right time to kill and another to heal,
A right time to destroy and another to construct,
A right time to cry and another to laugh,
A right time to lament and another to cheer,
A right time to make love and another to abstain,
A right time to embrace and another to part,
A right time to search and another to count your losses,
A right time to hold on and another to let go,
A right time to rip out and another to mend,
A right time to shut up and another to speak up,
A right time to love and another to hate,
A right time to wage war and another to make peace.

Life is a process and everything in this life is a process. Process brings opportunity for growth and maturity. If we allow it, we will discover the treasure that God deposited in our spirit as we face ourselves, our partner and our situation at hand. His resurrection power is at work in our lives as He makes His home in our hearts.

Ephesians 3:14-19 MSG

14-19 My response is to get down on my knees before the Father, this magnificent Father who parcels out all heaven and earth. I ask him to strengthen you by his Spirit—not a brute strength but a glorious inner strength—that Christ will live in you as you open the door and invite him in. And I ask him that with both feet planted firmly on love, you'll be able to take in with all followers of Jesus the extravagant dimensions of Christ's love. Reach out and experience the breadth! Test its length! Plumb the depths! Rise to the heights! Live full lives, full in the fullness of God.

20-21 God can do anything, you know—far more than you could ever imagine or guess or request in your wildest dreams! He does it not by pushing us around but by working within us, his Spirit deeply and gently within us.

Prayer for both the wounding and the wounded partner:

Father, strengthen us by Your Spirit. Give us Your glorious inner strength. Remove all pollution, corruption, manipulation, misconceptions and ties to ungodly thoughts, feelings and purposes. Unite us in Your love. Christ lives in us, we have opened the door and invited Him in. Both of our feet are planted firmly in Your word. Help us to understand the extravagant dimensions of Your love. Help us to comprehend the breadth, its length, the depths, and the heights of Your love! Help us to live fully healed and productive lives! You can do anything, far more than we could ever imagine, beyond our wildest dreams! Thank you for working inside of us by Your Holy Spirit. In Jesus' name, Amen.

PART 18

Recovery Plans

In order to help rebuild trust in a relationship after betrayal, recovery plans are essential when a couple is trying to reestablish safety. During our group and individual intensives, we work with couples to help them develop both relationship and individual recovery plans. These plans provide boundaries for both the wounding and wounded partner and can help keep the relationship on track. The plans that we discuss during intensives include:

- Communication Plan Ground Rules (Part I of the Communication Plan)
- Trigger Plan (Part II of the Communication Plan)
- Time-Out Protocol (Part III of the Communication Plan)
- Self-Care Plan
- Individual Recovery Plans

In the next few chapters, we will take a look at each of these in greater detail. First, let's look at the ground rules for the communication plan:

Recovery Plan #1: Communication plan (ground rules)

This is the first part of a three-part Communication Plan. Communication can be a challenge even for couples who aren't trying to recover from betrayal. However, when infidelity enters the mix, even the best communicators often have trouble. Although establishing safe communication can be difficult, it is worth the effort. Once both partners can express themselves and be understood, a deep sense of intimacy can be experienced, and the relationship can be strengthened.

If intimacy is to be restored, it is important that both partners agree on some ground rules for communication. This typically includes a system for both speaking and listening as well as a list of off-limit behaviors. We find that the Speaker-Listener technique is a simple and effective tool for couples who want to avoid conversations that spin out of control and go nowhere.

Speaker/Listener Technique

Each person takes turns speaking. You can have a "speaker object" if you are the speaker (such as a ball or a card), or just trade off.

Speaker Rules:

1. Use I statements only, such as "I felt sad when…."

2. Speak only for yourself (don't interject opinion, assumptions, or "mind reading")

3. Be respectful

4. Keep your statements brief and to the point (your partner can't paraphrase you if you go on and on)

5. Stop frequently to let the listener paraphrase

Listener Rules:
1. Paraphrase what you heard by saying, "what I heard you say is_. Is that correct?"

2. If you weren't correct with what you paraphrased, the speaker should say "no" and say it again

3. Keep repeating this process until you get the paraphrasing correct.

4. Once the paraphrasing is correct, ask, "is there more?"

5. DO NOT rebut

6. DO NOT problem solve

7. When the speaker is done, validate what they said by saying something like, "It makes sense you could feel that way because…."

8. Show empathy for their experience

Rules for Both People:
1. The speaker always has the floor.

2. The speaker keeps the floor until they have said what they have to say.

3. Equal time should be given to each person to have the floor and to be heard.

4. Be respectful

5. After the speaker has said what they have to say and feels heard, the partners should switch roles.

6. WARNING: If the next speaker uses their turn to invalidate, rebut, or defend, all communication progress will be lost.

When using the Speaker-Listener technique, the object is to listen to, empathize with, and care about what the other person is saying.

In addition to using an effective system for speaking and listening, we also recommend that couples make a list of behaviors that they agree will be off-limits in terms of communication. Some of the more common of these include:

- Name-calling and insults
- Defending and blame-shifting
- Stonewalling
- Acting annoyed or inconvenienced
- Threatening
- Eye-rolling and other non-verbal signs of disrespect
- Character assassinations
- Always and never statements
- Predicting what the other person is going to say or do or saying things like, "I knew you would do that".

This is only a partial list of some of the most common mistakes couples make when trying to communicate. We recommend that couples make a list of specific things that pertain to them and agree ahead of time that these behaviors will be off limits.

Well-known author and psychotherapist Terrence Real outlines his five winning and losing strategies when it comes to communication in his book *The New Rules of Marriage*. According to Real, the five losing strategies are:

1. Right fighting. An argument about who is more right in the situation.

2. Controlling your partner. An argument where at least one partner is trying to control the other one. This is often done through aggression (yelling, threatening, blaming, etc.) or manipulation (guilting, shaming, twisting words, playing the victim, etc.)

3. Unbridled self-expression. An argument where at least one partner says whatever they are thinking in the heat of the moment to the other partner with no filter of kindness, compassion, or respect.

4. Retaliation. An argument where at least one partner says something to purposely hurt the other one as a way of paying the person back for hurting them in some way. This can be overt or passive aggressive.

5. Withdrawal. An argument that leads to one or both partners withdrawing out of frustration, resignation, or retaliation (silent treatment). Not to be confused with taking a proper time out.0

Terrence Real's five winning strategies are:

1. Shift from complaint to request. It is often easier to complain about someone than to make requests for what we need. Requesting requires vulnerability while complaining puts the speaker in a one-up position. Switch from complaints to requests and make your requests behavioral and reasonable.

2. Speak to repair with love and respect. Commit, along with your partner, to the repair process. Remember love when speaking.

3. Respond with generosity. Listen to understand (this doesn't mean you have to agree). Clarify to make sure you understand what your partner is saying. Acknowledge whatever you can without rebuttal. Give whatever you can to your partner.

4. Empower each other. Acknowledge any gifts your partner has brought to the conversation. Ask how you can help your partner. Give whatever you can.

5. Cherish each other. Give your partner feedback and positive affirmations daily. Practice generosity. Nourish the relationship with your time and energy.

Listen to what the word of God says about communication!

Ephesians 4:29 MSG

29 Watch the way you talk. Let nothing foul or dirty come out of your mouth. Say only what helps, each word a gift.

Proverbs 3:18 MSG

Rash language cuts and maims, but there is healing in the words of the wise.

Proverbs 18:21 MSG

Words kill, words give life; they're either poison or fruit—you choose.

Proverbs 25:11-12 MSG

The right word at the right time is like a custom-made piece of jewelry, And a wise friend's timely reprimand is like a gold ring slipped on your finger.

Ephesians 4:14-15 MSG

14 Then we will no longer be immature like children. We won't be tossed and blown about by every wind of new teaching. We will not be influenced when people try to trick us with lies so clever they sound like the truth. 15 Instead, we will speak the truth in love, growing in every way more and more like Christ, who is the head of his body, the church.

Colossians 4:5-6 MSG

5-6 Use your heads as you live and work among outsiders. Don't miss a trick. Make the most of every opportunity. Be gracious in your speech. The goal is to bring out the best in others in a conversation, not put them down, not cut them out.

Proverbs 20:16-24 MSG

It pays to take life seriously; things work out when you trust in GOD. *A wise person gets known for insight; gracious words add to one's reputation. True intelligence is a spring of fresh water, while fools sweat it out the hard way. They make a lot of sense, these wise folks; whenever they speak, their reputation increases. Gracious speech is like clover honey— good taste to the soul, quick energy for the body.*

Recovery Plan #2: Trigger plan

The Trigger Plan is the second part of the three-part Communication Plan. Communicating when someone has been triggered requires not only great communication skills, but some forethought as well. Triggers and reminders are a normal part of the recovery process. A frustrating and painful part of recovery-but a normal part, nonetheless. They are simply a part of dealing with trauma. Studies have shown that partners dealing with betrayal trauma are coping with a great number of triggers per day in the weeks and months following disclosure. We have had wounded partners tell us that, especially early on in recovery, they deal with 75+ triggers per day. If the wounding partner's disclosure was "dribbled" out over time, each instance of new information causes a separate trauma for the wounded partner, which makes dealing with triggers much more complex. This is why we recommend being 100% upfront and honest during the disclosure process.

Triggers, reminders, flashbacks, and the like kick the wounded partner's sympathetic nervous system into high gear. This part of the system is responsible for survival. When triggered, the body undergoes multiple changes in preparation for a physical response to threat. These include:

- Increased breathing rate
- Increased heart rate
- Muscle tension
- Changes to facial coloring (increased redness or paleness)
- Sweating
- Shaking, especially of the hands
- Rise in body temperature

These changes take place because the autonomic nervous system (which the sympathetic nervous system is a part of) floods the body with stress hormones such as adrenaline and cortisol. Additionally, blood flow is redirected from the gut to the muscles, and especially the hands, in preparation for physical exertion in the form of fighting. The arousal caused by all of this is very intense and can take from several hours to a few days to fully recover from. During this slow cool-down period, a person has a higher-than-normal likelihood of being retriggered and/or responding intensely to even minor triggers. One can see how this could create a problem for the wounded partner who has been traumatized and is getting re-triggered frequently throughout the day. Due to these constant triggers and reminders, a betrayed partner can be thrown into a vicious cycle of anger. This is one of the main explanations of why wounded partners can get, and stay, so angry. Depending on the personality of the triggered person, they may go on the attack, physically leave, or emotionally check out.

It is important that the wounding partner understand that, when the wounded partner becomes triggered and floods with emotion, that it is not an attempt on their part to punish them or make them suffer. It is simply a normal bodily reaction to the presence of a threat—real or perceived. Triggers are also not a sign that the wounded partner does not forgive the wounding partner. This is especially important for people who hold to religions where forgiveness is fundamental. We get wounded partners in our office on a regular basis that have been told by well-meaning counselors and/or by their partners that they are being unforgiving and need to work on it. This is simply not the case. As we stated previously, triggers are a normal part of the recovery process when it comes to infidelity. The wounded partner does not have control over where and when triggers come up. Triggers and reminders are a normal consequence of the primary bond that has been severed between the wounding and wounded partners because of betrayal.

Many couples we work with think that, when triggers show up, they are having a setback. This is not true either. Instead, we would like to present the idea that the triggers present opportunities for repair and intimacy between partners. If the wounding partner will show up with love and empathy when the wounded partner is triggered, it presents a unique opportunity for the wounding partner to change how the wounded partner sees them and, therefore, help increase connection. Additionally, if the wounded partner will openly talk about their pain and emotions without name-calling, threatening, etc., the relationship can grow in intimacy.

For the wounded partner, it is important to start managing their triggers in a productive way early on. We recommend that a trigger journal be kept by the wounded partner that identifies the following about each trigger:

1. What was the trigger?
2. What was I doing when it happened?
3. Was the wounding partner present? If so, what were they doing?
4. What time of day did the trigger happen?
5. Why do I think it happened?

Once a trigger has been identified, the wounded partner can answer the following questions about it:

1. Is what I am reacting to a current situation? (examples: wounding partner is defending, wounding partner is hiding their phone, etc.)

2. Is what I am reacting to a past situation? (example: a memory or a reminder)

3. Am I reacting to holes in the wounding partner's story? (example: wounding partner gave an account of events, butsomething doesn't make sense)

4. Am I reacting to a loss of connection with my partner? (example: the wounding partner withdrew, and it felt like abandonment)

As the wounded partner keeps a journal, they might begin to see patterns emerging. If a pattern is identified, they can dig deeper in order to identify specifically what trigger is associated with what pattern. For example, the wounded partner may notice that they are triggered in a certain type of place. This knowledge will then help them investigate further to find out what the trigger is really about. Although many triggers are obvious and can be added to the "Identifying Triggers" exercise below right away, some triggers may be harder to identify. Keeping a trigger journal can help the wounded partner do that.

Having conversations around how to deal with triggers can be hard for many couples, but it is imperative that these conversations happen if the couple hopes to successfully work through them. Oftentimes, the wounding partner wants to do something to help the wounded partner but doesn't know where to begin, and the wounded partner feels just as helpless. A trigger plan is extremely helpful for both partners to know what to do when a trigger arises. At a calm time, establish a plan for when triggers come. It is important not to do this in the heat of the moment. This can be somewhat counter-intuitive because, when things are going well, the subject of infidelity is not typically what either partner wants to be talking about. However, this exercise requires rational thought, which is impossible when the sympathetic nervous system is triggering either partner into "fight, flight, or freeze" mode.

While making the plan, the wounding partner should ask the wounded partner questions like:

1. What would help you feel safe when you are triggered?

2. What can I do?

3. Can you help me understand what's going on with you?

4. What do I do that makes you feel unsafe during thesetimes?

The answers to these and other questions will help develop your plan. Please note that the plan should be considered an official agreement between the wounded and wounding partners. It must be adhered to in order to work. Wounding partners: **going off script, defending, walling off, or leaving will only serve to escalate the situation and re-wound your partner.** Wounded partners: **threatening, shaming, yelling, and name-calling will short-circuit the process.** When developing a trigger plan, start with the "Identifying Triggers" exercise below.

Identifying Triggers

Specific Triggers	How does this apply to your situation?	Action plan
Seeing attractive people (with or without partner)		Hold your partner's hand if in public
Sex scenes in movies + TV		Change the channel Research programs before watching
Inconsistency/ unreliability of partner (e.g., being late)		Express concerns to partner gently
Times of day Days of the week (e.g., weekends, late nights)		Plan ahead to do something relaxing
Other:		
Other:		
Other:		

Notice that the "Identifying Triggers" table has a column entitled "Action Plan". Each trigger needs an action plan attached to it. This should be something that the wounded partner feels that the wounding partner can do to help the situation.

Next, fill out the "Trigger Coping Plan for Couples":

Trigger Coping Plan for Couples

The main triggers in our relationship are:	
Strategies for managing triggers:	
Time-out / alone time	
Making a request (e.g., for a hug, reassurance)	
Talking about it (using "I" statements)	
Behaviors to avoid:	

These tools have proven to be extremely effective for couples who are dealing with triggers. However, we acknowledge that there are times when an unexpected trigger arises that there was no plan for. In this case, the couple should adhere to the agreements made in the Communication Plan plus use the following guidelines:

1. Wounded Partner: Recognize the trigger and accept that it is happening.

2. Wounding Partner: If you notice that your partner is triggered and flooded with emotion, do not point it out to them. This never helps. Instead, ask them what they need from you in this moment. If they don't know, just let them know you are there for them.

3. Wounded Partner: Identify what you are reacting to. Is it something that is currently happening? Is it a reminder from the past? Is it a loss of connection with your partner?

4. Wounding Partner: Identify if you are also being triggered. If so, by what? Is it guilt and/or shame? Is it your partner's emotions?

5. Wounded Partner: Identify at least one thing that your partner can do in this moment to help you.

6. Wounding Partner: If possible, do whatever your partner is asking of you. Respond with humility, patience, and compassion.

7. Wounding Partner: Resist talking about how bad you feel and/or saying, "I'm sorry" immediately. Instead, use the Speaker/Listener technique from the Communication Plan to ensure that your partner feels heard.

8. Wounded and Wounding Partners: Avoid any of the "off-limits" behaviors outlined in your communication plan.

The word of God tells us to not react to triggers, but to control our tongue. Once something is said, it cannot be taken back!

James 1:19-27 NLT

Listening and Doing

19 Understand this, my dear brothers and sisters: You must all be quick to listen, slow to speak, and slow to get angry. 20 Human anger[g] does not produce the righteousness[h] God desires. 21 So get rid of all the filth and evil in your lives, and humbly accept the word God has planted in your hearts, for it has the power to save your souls.

22 But don't just listen to God's word. You must do what it says. Otherwise, you are only fooling yourselves. 23 For if you listen to the word and don't obey, it is like glancing at your face in a mirror. 24 You see yourself, walk away, and forget what you look like. 25 But if you look carefully into the perfect law that sets you free, and if you do what it says and don't forget what you heard, then God will bless you for doing it.

26 If you claim to be religious but don't control your tongue, you are fooling yourself, and your religion is worthless. 27 Pure and genuine religion in the sight of God the Father means caring for orphans and widows in their distress and refusing to let the world corrupt you.

Recovery Plan #3: Time Out Protocol

The Time Out Protocol is the final piece of the three-part Communication Plan. There will likely be occasions when one or both partners become overwhelmed with emotions to the point that they can't function in a way that will support the health of the relationship. When someone is flooded with emotion, they may say or do things that attack the other person—adding even more pain to an already painful situation.

As a countermeasure to overwhelming emotions, the couple should develop a code word or a non-verbal sign that is an indicator that one of them needs to stop talking before they do more damage than good. Once a code word is spoken or a non-verbal sign is shown, the couple will disengage and agree to come back later when things have calmed down. The couple should agree to the terms of time out ahead of time and consider the Time Out Plan to be a contract between the two parties like the other parts of the Communication Plan.

There are five main points to keep in mind when considering whether or not to call a time out:

1. USE THE CODE WORD or NON-VERBAL SIGN SPARINGLY. Time outs are considered an emergency option when all attempts at productive communication have failed. Understand that if either partner uses their codeword or non-verbal sign to get out of conversations that they just don't want to deal with, they are hurting their partner. Using the code word or non-verbal sign to stonewall is also an improper use of a time out.

2. The request for time out should be honored. One partner should not try to goad the other into reengaging. The conversation needs to stop when time out is called. No attempting to have the last word.

3. When a code word or non-verbal sign has been used, agree on a time to reengage. Otherwise, one or both partners could feel neglected and abandoned. Typically, 20-30 minutes is recommended for a time out.

4. When a time out is taken, it is recommended that each person practice self-care. This means that an activity should be done to take the mind OFF the present problem, as opposed to taking the time to stew about it and/or plan a rebuttal. Reading a book (not on the subject of the argument or betrayal), taking a shower/bath, or taking a walk are great activities to do. Time-outs do not work if either party uses the time to sit around and think about how angry they are or what they are going to say next in an effort to win the argument. The idea is to take your mind completely off the argument in order to give your flooded system a break.

5. When you come back from the time out, each partner needs to state at least one thing they appreciate about the other before resuming the conversation. When sharing feelings, use "I feel" statements as opposed to "you" statements. "You" statements come off as blaming. Blaming and/or criticizing will only make the problem worse. Focus on the solution as opposed to the problem(s) and be good listeners.

As with the Trigger Plan, the Time Out Plan should be developed at a calm moment.

Proverbs 10: 17, 19 MEV

He who keeps instruction is in the way of life, but he who refuses reproof errs…In the multitude of words sin is not lacking, but he who restrains his lips is wise.

Proverbs 15:1-4 MSG

A gentle response defuses anger, but a sharp tongue kindles a temper-fire. Knowledge flows like spring water from the wise; fools are leaky faucets, dripping nonsense. God doesn't miss a thing—he's alert to good and evil alike. Kind words heal and help; cutting words wound and maim.

Galatians 6:1-2 MSG

6 Live creatively, friends. If someone falls into sin, forgivingly restore him, saving your critical comments for yourself. You might need forgiveness before the day's out.

Prayer for the wounding and the wounded partner:

Father, give me the grace to give a gentle response so that anger is defused. I do not want to kindle a temper-fire with my tongue. I want knowledge to flow from my tongue. I want to speak words that heal and help, not words that wound and maim. Help me to forgive my partner and keep my critical comments to myself. In Jesus' name. Amen.

PART 19

Recovery Plan #4

Self-Care Plan

The term "self-care" encompasses the idea that human beings need to take care of themselves so that they can accomplish the tasks that they need to get done. Self-care is part of the answer to how we can effectively deal with stressors in our lives. When dealing with the aftermath of betrayal, both partners face a wide range of stressors that can seriously impede on the ability to maintain their health, do well at their jobs, maintain friendships, and care for their children or other people who depend on them.

Self-care means taking care of yourself in every area, not just physically. Good self-care includes the physical, spiritual, emotional/mental, social, and financial aspects of life. It also involves engaging in active recovery. Let's take a look at each one of the areas of self-care more closely:

Physical: This includes anything pertaining to our bodies. Examples of physical self-care include healthy eating, exercise, drinking plenty of water, good sleep hygiene, and even leisurely activities such as taking a bath or getting a massage. It can also include regularly going to the doctor for health checkups.

Romans 12: 1-2 MSG

12 1-2 So here's what I want you to do, God helping you: Take your everyday, ordinary life—your sleeping, eating, going-to-work, and walking-around life—and place it before God as an offering. Embracing what God does for you is the best thing you can do for him. Don't become so well-adjusted to your culture that you fit into it without even thinking. Instead, fix your attention on God. You'll be changed from the inside out. Readily recognize what he wants from you, and quickly respond to it. Unlike the culture around you, always dragging you down to its level of immaturity, God brings the best out of you, develops well-formed maturity in you.

1 Corinthians 6: 19-20 MSG

Or didn't you realize that your body is a sacred place, the place of the Holy Spirit? Don't you see that you can't live however you please, squandering what God paid such a high price for? The physical part of you is not some piece of property belonging to the spiritual part of you. God owns the whole works. So let people see God in and through your body.

Spiritual: It is important to take care of our spiritual side. Self-care in this area can include meditation, prayer, going to church, practicing mindfulness, connecting with God through nature, and reading spiritual literature.

2 Timothy 3:16 MSG

Stick with what you learned and believed, sure of the integrity of your teachers—why, you took in the sacred Scriptures with your mother's milk! There's nothing like the written Word of God for showing you the way to salvation through faith in Christ Jesus. Every part of Scripture is God-breathed and useful one way or another—showing us truth, exposing our rebellion, correcting our mistakes, training us to live God's way. Through the Word we are put together and shaped up for the tasks God has for us.

Matthew 4:4 MSG

4 Jesus answered by quoting Deuteronomy: "It takes more than bread to stay alive. It takes a steady stream of words from God's mouth."

Proverbs 20:27

27 The spirit of man is the candle of the Lord, searching all the inward parts of the belly.

Philippians 4:6-7 AMP

6 Do not be anxious or worried about anything, but in everything [every circumstance and situation] by prayer and petition with thanksgiving, continue to make your [specific] requests known to God. 7 And the peace of God [that peace which reassures the heart, that peace] which transcends all understanding, [that peace which] stands guard over your hearts and your minds in Christ Jesus [is yours].

Emotional/Mental: Our emotional and mental health is vital to our well-being. Self-care in this area could include listening to music, engaging in coaching or counseling, reading a good book, listening to helpful podcasts, and making a gratitude list (this one could also be counted as spiritual).

Luke 21:34 AMP

"But be on guard, so that your hearts are not weighed down and depressed with the giddiness of debauchery and the nausea of self-indulgence and the worldly worries of life.

Proverbs 17:22 MSG

A cheerful disposition is good for your health; gloom and doom leave you bone tired.

Matthew 6: 22-23 AMP 22

"The eye is the lamp of the body; so if your eye is clear [spiritually perceptive], your whole body will be full of light [benefiting from God's precepts]. 23 But if your eye is bad [spiritually blind], your whole body will be full of darkness [devoid of God's precepts]. So if the [very] light inside you [your inner self, your heart, your conscience] is darkness, how great and terrible is that darkness!

Social: It is important that partners don't isolate themselves when dealing with the challenges presented by betrayal. Self-care in this area could include scheduling regular phone calls with supportive friends and family, texting with friends and family, joining a support group and reaching out to other members, spending time with people you care about, attending social events, and going out on dates with your partner in order to provide time for much-needed reconnection.

Hebrews 10:24-25 TLB

24 In response to all he has done for us, let us outdo each other in being helpful and kind to each other and in doing good.

25 Let us not neglect our church meetings, as some people do, but encourage and warn each other, especially now that the day of his coming back again is drawing near.

Acts 2: 41-42 MSG

41-42 That day about three thousand took him at his word, were baptized and were signed up. They committed themselves to the teaching of the apostles, the life together, the common meal, and the prayers.

Matthew 18:18-20 MSG 18-20 "Take this most seriously: A yes on earth is yes in heaven; a no on earth is no in heaven. What you say to one another is eternal. I mean this. When two of you get together on anything at all on earth and make a prayer of it, my Father in heaven goes into action. And when two or three of you are together because of me, you can be sure that I'll be there."

Financial: A number of our clients claim they feel at a disadvantage because they have chosen to stay at home. For many, this creates an imbalance of power within the relationship which has an even greater impact after infidelity is discovered or disclosed. While staying at home and caring for the household is an extremely important job that doesn't get as much respect as it deserves, partners who stay at home often describe feelings of disempowerment and "stuckness" when it comes to their choice of whether or not to stay in the relationship because they are completely financially dependent on their partner. If this describes you, some ideas for self-care in this area could include gaining job skills, becoming more involved in the financial aspect of the relationship, or going back to work. Even if you don't feel stuck or disempowered in this area, going back to school, getting a job, or starting a new business can give you an added boost for your self-esteem.

Another financial area that often gets affected by betrayal is when the wounding partner spends money that belongs to both partners on their infidelity-related behavior. In this example, self-care could include ongoing accountability and transparency with finances moving forward.

Matthew 8:17-18 MSG

17-18 If you start thinking to yourselves, "I did all this. And all by myself. I'm rich. It's all mine!"—well, think again. Remember that God, your God, gave you the strength to produce all this wealth so as to confirm the covenant that he promised to your ancestors—as it is today.

1 Peter 5:2 NIV

Be shepherds of God's flock that is under your care, watching over them—not because you must, but because you are willing, as God wants you to be; not pursuing dishonest gain, but eager to serve; 3 not lording it over those entrusted to you, but being examples to the flock.

Proverbs 15:27 MGS

A greedy and grasping person destroys community; those who refuse to exploit live and let live.

Proverbs 27:23-24 TLB

Riches can disappear fast. And the king's crown doesn't stay in his family forever—so watch your business[b] interests closely. Know the state of your flocks and your herds; 25-27 then there will be lambs' wool enough for clothing and goats' milk enough for food for all your household after the hay is harvested, and the new crop appears, and the mountain grasses are gathered in.

Engaging in Active Recovery: When it comes to the damage done by betrayal, it is vitally important that both partners take charge of their own recovery. Reading this book is a sign that you are doing that already. Other ideas could include counseling or coaching, workgroups, reading self-help literature, and attending Becoming Well intensives, seminars, and conferences designed to support your healing.

Self-care is all about engaging in activities that benefit you. An important thing to realize about self-care is that it is not always about relaxing. In fact, it will often require you to expend energy on healthy activities or engage mentally with things that might feel uncomfortable. The purpose of self-care is to heal underlying issues and refuel so that you can deal with the challenges presented by betrayal. As important as it is to identify areas and ways that partners can take care of themselves, it is equally important to identify things that can detract from recovery. Here are some things that self-care is not:

- Being so busy with tasks or helping others that you becomedepleted
- Overindulging in food or spending
- Using addictive substances such as drugs and alcohol tocope with unwanted and/or unpleasant feelings

- Failing to control what you do and say in anger
- Neglecting your responsibilities

Although many of the activities listed here can seem appealing, they will not do anything to refuel you, and some can leave you stressed with feelings of guilt and shame.

Self-care is never as important as when a relationship is facing the aftermath of infidelity. The burden of the tsunami of intense feelings and emotional distress that accompany recovery can leave partners feeling seriously depleted. The danger for partners is expending all of their energy to fix the crisis the relationship is facing. For wounded partners in particular, the hypervigilance born out of betrayal can become all-consuming. It is important that a wounded partner take a step back, breathe, and understand that they can't immediately fix everything- as much as they might like to do so. Taking time to focus on self-care isn't selfish and will end up helping the relationship in the long run.

In our experience, there are several ways that partners engage in activities in the name of self-care that are actually self-care sabotage. The most common of these are:

- An overindulgence in self-soothing
- Unrestrained gratification of desires (self-indulgence)
- Laziness

Although these things are okay once in a while, an overindulgence in any of them typically sabotages recovery. The hard part is that self-care sabotage can actually feel like self- care in the moment. Self-care only works if a person uses it to grow- not if they use it to let themselves off the hook or avoid accountability. Here are some helpful questions that you can ask yourself in order to figure out if you are engaging in self-care or self-care sabotage:

- Will this activity support my overall well-being or the well-being of my relationship?
- Am I willing to let this challenge me, or am I avoiding being challenged?
- Am I isolating myself, or am I just resting up?
- Am I taking an active role in my recovery?
- Am I trying to escape or avoid something by choosing this activity?
- Does this activity connect me to myself and/or others, or do I feel disconnected?
- Am I going to feel better or worse after doing this activity?
- Am I indulging anger or self-pity by doing this activity?
- Will I be able to do the things I need to do better after doing this activity?

Another way that partners can sabotage self-care is by simply not setting aside time for it. Waiting for the schedule to "open up" so that you can care for yourself is not the best plan of action. Interruptions, unplanned events, distractions, and emotional and physical exhaustion can cause partners to constantly come in last when it comes to caring for themselves. If a person wants to succeed with self-care, it needs to be prioritized. Here are some ways you can make caring for yourself a priority:

- Set aside specific times and days for self-care activities
- Wake up a bit earlier
- Break up self-care time into small chunks
- Choose activities that you enjoy, especially when it comes to physical exercise
- Find an accountability partner
- Hire a babysitter if you have children
- Reduce time spent on social media, tv, or streaming services
- Use an alarm as a reminder
- Set specific goals
- Eliminate hurdles to self-care
- Communicate your goals to others
- Plan adequate time for activities (don't be a "time optimist")
- Create boundaries around self-care and be assertive with them
- Engage in short self-care activities often

Each partner should take the time to fill out the Self-Care Worksheet and the Self-Care Worksheet Schedule for themselves. At a calm time, you should discuss your individual plans with each other so that you can be on the same page and can support each other in your self-care efforts.

Self-Care Worksheet

Activities that support my physical well-being

Answer:	

Activities that support my spiritual well-being

Answer:

Activities that support my emotional/mental well-being

Answer:

Activities that support my social well-being

Answer:

Activities that support my financial well-being

Answer:

Activities that support my active recovery

Answer:

Self-Care Worksheet Schedule

Activity	Day	Time

Prayer for the wounding and the wounded partner:

Father, unless You build the house, they labor in vain who build it. We must take care of our physical bodies, because our bodies are the Temple of the Holy Spirit. We will take our everyday, ordinary life—our sleeping, eating, going-to-work, and walking-around life—and place it before God as an offering. We dedicate our spirit to You. Every part of Scripture is God-breathed and useful one way or another—showing us truth, exposing our rebellion, correcting our mistakes, and training us to live God's way. Through the Word, we are put together and shaped up for the tasks God has for us. We take care of our emotional and mental wellbeing. Our emotional and mental eye is the lamp of the body; so if your eye is clear, our whole body will be full of light benefiting from God's precepts. We dedicate our social lives to You. Help us to remember all that God has done for us and let us outdo each other in being helpful and kind to each other and in doing good. Financially, we will remember that God gave us the strength to produce wealth. We will discipline ourselves to be diligent in following our self-care plans. We will watch carefully over the state of our responsibilities and businesses. All we do, we do for God's glory. In Jesus' name, Amen.

PART 20

Recovery Plan #5

Individual Recovery Plans

Individual recovery plans for both the wounded and wounding partners are just that—individual. As such, it would take us pages upon pages to list all of the possibilities that might go into a person's recovery plan. Instead, we would like to highlight some of the areas commonly addressed. First, we will cover what typically goes into the wounding partner's recovery plan.

For the wounding partner, a recovery plan typically includes a relapse prevention plan as well. Here are the topics most commonly addressed:

- Pornography and/or sexually stimulating images
- Grooming behaviors
- Accountability phone calls
- Groups
- Coaching or counselling
- Recovery material such as books and workbooks
- Intimacy avoidant behavior
- Sexually anorexic behavior
- Accountability partners
- Gratitude
- Connection exercises with partner such as daily affirmations and weekly dates
- Entitlement
- Defensiveness, blame, playing the victim
- Lying
- Self-care
- Relapse research
- Replacements

- 24-hour tell policy
- Polygraph schedule
- Pornography blockers
- Location trackers
- Sex establishments
- Media boundaries (computer, phone, etc.)
- Contact with affair partner

As you can see, the list of things included in a wounding partner's recovery and relapse prevention plan is long. This is because we see clients with intimacy avoidance, sexual and emotional infidelity, and infidelity through pornography. Due to the wide range of issues, there are a number of things that have to be addressed depending on the specific issues with each individual. While most of these items don't need much explanation in terms of why being accountable for them is applicable to ongoing recovery, we would like to go more in-depth into the subjects of grooming behaviors, intimacy avoidant behavior, sexually anorexic behavior, gratitude, relapse research, replacements, and contact with an affair partner.

Proverbs 15:22 MSG

22 Refuse good advice and watch your plans fail; take good counsel and watch them succeed.

Proverbs 24:27 NLT

27 Develop your business first before building your house.

Luke 14: 28-35 TLB

25-27 One day when large groups of people were walking along with him, Jesus turned and told them, "Anyone who comes to me but refuses to let go of father, mother, spouse, children, brothers, sisters—yes, even one's own self! —can't be my disciple. Anyone who won't shoulder his own cross and follow behind me can't be my disciple.

28-30 "Is there anyone here who, planning to build a new house, doesn't first sit down and figure the cost so you'll know if you can complete it? If you only get the foundation laid and then run out of money, you're going to look pretty foolish. Everyone passing by will poke fun at you: 'He started something he couldn't finish.'

31-32 "Or can you imagine a king going into battle against another king without first deciding whether it is possible with his ten thousand troops to face the twenty thousand troops of the other? And if he decides he can't, won't he send an emissary and work out a truce?

33 "Simply put, if you're not willing to take what is dearest to you, whether plans or people, and kiss it good-bye, you can't be my disciple.

34-35 "Salt is excellent. But if the salt goes flat, it's useless, good for nothing.

"Are you listening to this? Really listening?"

Proverbs 16:3 MSG

Put God in charge of your work, then what you've planned will take place.

Grooming behavior: Grooming is a form of manipulation in which the person doing the grooming builds an emotional connection or rapport with another person that appears to be genuine. The motives underlying grooming behavior can be numerous, but typically involve control and/or sex. Grooming is marked by the groomer's desire to have a particular need met, despite what it may cost themselves, their partner, or the other person.

Grooming behavior is most associated with people who have a sexual addiction. We most often see this type of behavior in wounding partners who have engaged in multiple affairs and one- night stands. It is important to note that not all sexual addicts groom. However, when they do, it typically includes flirting, touching and/or hugging, revealing personal details about themselves, rescuing someone out of their circumstances, offering emotional support and/or encouragement, and complimenting.

Proverbs 29:5-6 MSG

A flattering neighbor is up to no good; he's probably planning to take advantage of you. Evil people fall into their own traps; good people run the other way, glad to escape.

Romans 16:17-18 MSG

17-18 One final word of counsel, friends. Keep a sharp eye out for those who take bits and pieces of the teaching that you learned and then use them to make trouble. Give these people a wide berth. They have no intention of living for our Master Christ. They're only in this for what they can get out of it and aren't above using pious sweet talk to dupe unsuspecting innocents.

Psalm 5:8-9 TLB

8 Lord, lead me as you promised me you would; otherwise, my enemies will conquer me. Tell me clearly what to do, which way to turn. 9 For they cannot speak one truthful word. Their hearts are filled to the brim with wickedness. Their suggestions are full of the stench of sin and death. Their tongues are filled with flatteries to gain their wicked ends. 10 O God, hold them responsible. Catch them in their own traps; let them fall beneath the weight of their own transgressions, for they rebel against you.

Psalm 12:1-8 MSG

1-2 Quick, God, I need your helping hand! The last decent person just went down, All the friends I depended on are gone. Everyone talks in lie language; Lies slide off their oily lips. They double talk with forked tongues. Slice their lips off their faces! Pull the braggart tongues from their mouths! I'm tired of hearing, "We can talk anyone into anything! Our lips manage the world." Into the hovels of the poor, into the dark streets where the homeless groan, God speaks: "I've had enough; I'm on my way to heal the ache in the heart of the wretched." God's words are pure words, Pure silver words refined seven times In the fires of his word-kiln, Pure on earth as well as in heaven. God, keep us safe from their lies, From the wicked who stalk us with lies, from the wicked who collect honors For their wonderful lies.

Intimacy avoidant behavior: The term intimacy avoidance refers to a situation in which one partner is withholding themselves in multiple ways from the other partner. Intimacy avoidance often goes unnoticed by the person withholding themselves yet can have lasting and devastating effects on their loved ones. Intimacy anorexic behaviors are intentional and include the withholding of emotional, physical, sexual, and/or spiritual connection from a partner for the purpose of creating distance and/or maintaining power and control. The difference between the two is intent.

Intimacy avoidant and intimacy anorexic behaviors can include ongoing criticism of the partner (often unwarranted), playing the victim when called on bad behavior, refraining from showing love in the way their partner wants to be loved, being too busy to spend time with the partner and/or being emotionally unavailable, offering little to no praise to their partner, and an unwillingness or inability to express emotions—especially to partner.

Ephesians 5:21-33 MSG

21 Out of respect for Christ, be courteously reverent to one another.

22-24 Wives, understand and support your husbands in ways that show your support for Christ. The husband provides leadership to his wife the way Christ does to his church, not by domineering but by cherishing. So just as the church submits to Christ as he exercises such leadership, wives should likewise submit to their husbands.

25-28 Husbands, go all out in your love for your wives, exactly as Christ did for the church—a love marked by giving, not getting. Christ's love makes the church whole. His words evoke her beauty. Everything he does and says is designed to bring the best out of her, dressing her in dazzling white silk, radiant with holiness. And that is how husbands ought to love their wives. They're really doing themselves a favor—since they're already "one" in marriage.

29-33 No one abuses his own body, does he? No, he feeds and pampers it. That's how Christ treats us, the church, since we are part of his body. And this is why a man leaves father and mother and cherishes his wife. No longer two, they become "one flesh." This is a huge mystery, and I don't pretend to understand it all. What is clearest to me is the way Christ treats the church. And this provides a good picture of how each husband is to treat his wife, loving himself in loving her, and how each wife is to honor her husband.

Sexually anorexic behavior: Sexual anorexia is a condition marked by the fear, dread, or avoidance of sexual activity. Although it can be marked by impotence or other physical problems, the cause is typically psychological.

Although we have seen some sexual anorexics who avoid sex in any setting, sexual anorexia is most commonly seen in connection to the anorexic's partner. This is because the root of the problem is typically a fear of intimacy. We often see sexual anorexia in conjunction with sexual and/or pornography addiction, intimacy avoidance, and intimacy anorexia. It is not uncommon for sexual anorexics to engage in sex outside of their primary relationship yet withhold sex from their primary partner. It is also extremely common for sexual anorexics to engage in pornography and masturbation.

If the wounding partner displays signs of sexual anorexia, a sexual schedule is typically included in the individual recovery plan—provided that the wounded partner feels ready to engage in sex.

Hebrews 13:1-4 MSG

13 1-4 Stay on good terms with each other, held together by love. Be ready with a meal or a bed when it's needed. Why, some have extended hospitality to angels without ever knowing it! Regard prisoners as if you were in prison with them. Look at victims of abuse as if what happened to them had happened to you. Honor marriage and guard the sacredness of sexual intimacy between wife and husband. God draws a firm line against casual and illicit sex.

Mark 7: 14-23 MSG

14-15 Jesus called the crowd together again and said, "Listen now, all of you—take this to heart. It's not what you swallow that pollutes your life; it's what you vomit—that's the real pollution."

17 When he was back home after being with the crowd, his disciples said, "We don't get it. Put it in plain language."

18-19 Jesus said, "Are you being willfully stupid? Don't you see that what you swallow can't contaminate you? It doesn't enter your heart but your stomach, works its way through the intestines, and is finally flushed." (That took care of dietary quibbling; Jesus was saying that all foods are fit to eat.)

20-23 He went on: "It's what comes out of a person that pollutes: obscenities, lusts, thefts, murders, adulteries, greed, depravity, deceptive dealings, carousing, mean looks, slander, arrogance, foolishness—all these are vomit from the heart. There is the source of your pollution."

Gratitude: Many of the clients we work with engage in negative thinking about their partner and/or their life in general. Keeping a running gratitude list is one of the ways to help combat this.

1 Thessalonians 1:2-3 MSG

Every time we think of you, we thank God for you. Day and night you're in our prayers as we call to mind your work of faith, your labor of love, and your patience of hope in following our Master, Jesus Christ...

Philippians 1:3 MSG

2-5 Every time we think of you, we thank God for you. Day and night you're in our prayers as we call to mind your work of faith, your labor of love, and your patience of hope in following our Master, Jesus Christ...

Relapse research: Relapse is unfortunate, but it does happen sometimes in early recovery. When our clients relapse, we want them to take stock of what happened and work with us and their accountability partners to try to figure out how it can be avoided in the future. The following relapse research questions were adapted from the book *101 Freedom Exercises* by Douglas Weiss, Ph.D.:

- What were my feelings prior to acting out?
- What red flags did I pass up?
- What recovery tools did I choose not to use?
- How many days have I been thinking about/planning this event?
- What was the cost associated with my acting out?
- What did I learn about myself from this relapse?
- What do I need to do differently?
- Do I need to change any boundaries to avoid this in the future?
- Who am I going to share this information with to help me stay accountable?

1 John 1:8-10 MSG

8-10 If we claim that we're free of sin, we're only fooling ourselves. A claim like that is errant nonsense. On the other hand, if we admit our sins—simply come clean about them—he won't let us down; he'll be true to himself. He'll forgive our sins and purge us of all wrongdoing. If we claim that we've never sinned, we out-and-out contradict God—make a liar out of him. A claim like that only shows off our ignorance of God.

Replacements: It is important to note that the wounding partner should look to replace undesired and/or unacceptable behaviors with new, productive ones. An example of this would be replacing pornography and masturbation with stress-relieving exercise such as running or biking. These activities can boost mood, train the body on how to deal with anxiety, and lead to a sense of accomplishment that can boost well-being. (Weir, 2011) It is important to replace unwanted habits, especially in the case of addiction, with healthy ones. Otherwise, a person is likely to be pulled back toward the undesirable behavior because of the rewards associated with it.

For the wounded partner, an individual recovery plan could include the following:

- Trigger journal (covered previously)
- Off-limits behavior list
- Replacements
- Accountability
- Support group
- Self-care
- Classes
- Recovery material such as books or workbooks
- Coaching or counseling
- Safe friends

Many of these items don't need much explanation in terms of why they would be included in the wounded partner's plan for ongoing recovery. However, we would like to go more in-depth into the subjects of the off-limits behaviors list, replacements, accountability, and classes.

Off-limits behaviors list: We want to preface this by stating that we are in no way implying that the wounded partner should take any of the blame for the wounding partner's behavior. However, as we mentioned previously, there are some behaviors that wounded partners engage in once betrayal has been discovered or disclosed that are not conducive to the recovery of the relationship. Behaviors such as yelling, threatening, name-calling, and/or shaming on an ongoing basis will tear at the fabric of an already-fragile relationship to the point that safety cannot be established. These types of behaviors are what should be included on the off-limits behaviors list and the wounded partner should work diligently in overcoming the need to engage in them.

Replacements: The wounded partner should replace undesirable behaviors with new, desirable ones. Acting out in anger can have its own addictive quality to it because it involves adrenaline and often feels empowering. If the wounded partner does not find healthy ways to nurture themselves when they are hurt and angry, chances are that they might fall back into engaging in angry outbursts.

Colossians 3:3-8 MSG

3-4 Your old life is dead. Your new life, which is your real life—even though invisible to spectators—is with Christ in God. He is your life. When Christ (your real life, remember) shows up again on this earth, you'll show up, too—the real you, the glorious you. Meanwhile, be content with obscurity, like Christ.

5-8 And that means killing off everything connected with that way of death: sexual promiscuity, impurity, lust, doing whatever you feel like whenever you feel like it, and grabbing whatever attracts your fancy. That's a life shaped by things and feelings instead of by God. It's because of this kind of thing that God is about to explode in anger. It wasn't long ago that you were doing all that stuff and not knowing any better. But you know better now, so make sure it's all gone for good: bad temper, irritability, meanness, profanity, dirty talk.

Accountability: It is important that wounded partners do not attempt to do recovery alone. There are several areas where accountability could be necessary for a wounded partner. Some of the most common include acting out in anger, isolating, and not enforcing boundaries with the wounding partner.

Romans 14:12 AMP

12 So then, each of us will give an account of himself to God.

James 5:16 AMP

16 Therefore, confess your sins to one another [your false steps, your offenses], and pray for one another, that you may be healed and restored. The heartfelt and persistent prayer of a righteous man (believer) can accomplish much [when put into action and made effective by God—it is dynamic and can have tremendous power].

Classes: At Becoming Well, we offer classes specifically designed for wounded partners who want to heal after the disclosure or discovery of betrayal. Visit our website at www.mybecomingwell.com to learn more.

Prayer for the wounding partner:

Father, I will take my recovery seriously and not refuse good advice and watch my plans fail. I will take good counsel and watch my plans succeed and the quality of my life improve. As I improve the quality of my life, I will improve the quality of my partner's life. I will not flatter anyone and use my tongue to gain a wicked end. I will be reverent towards my partner and support them. We will submit to each other and watch each other's backs. I will honor marriage and guard the sacredness of sexual intimacy between myself and my partner. God draws a firm line against casual and illicit sex. I will not pollute myself with obscenities, lusts, thefts, murders, adulteries, greed, depravity, deceptive dealings, carousing, mean looks, slander, arrogance, foolishness—all these are vomit from the heart. I will thank

God for my partner. Day and night, my partner will be in my prayers as I call to mind their work of faith, their labor of love and their patience of hope they have in me because they are following the example of our Lord Jesus Christ. I will kill off everything connected with the way of death; sexual promiscuity, impurity, lust, doing whatever I feel like whenever I feel like it, and grabbing whatever attracts my fancy. I will be accountable to God, to my partner and to my counselor. In Jesus' name, Amen.

Prayer for wounded partner:

Father, help me to continue with myself care and recovery plan. When I am flooded with emotion and pain, and should I give in to anger, I will confess my sins

and my offenses to my wounding partner. We will pray for one another and be healed and restored. Because I am righteous, my heartfelt and persistent prayer will accomplish much because God is effectively at work in answering our prayers. Our prayers will be dynamic and have tremendous power in changing our lives for the better. I thank God for this in Jesus' name, Amen.

PART 21

Recovery Plan #6

Plan for cutting off contact with an affair partner

As we stated previously, the wounding partner's failure to end infidelity-related behavior is the number one reason we see relationships fail to recover after infidelity has been discovered or disclosed. This is especially true for couples dealing with betrayal through emotional and/or sexual affairs. When the wounding partner fails to cut off contact with an affair partner it creates a lack of safety for the wounded partner which will interfere with recovery.

If you are a wounded partner reading this and your partner has not completely cut off contact with their affair partner, it is important that you put a boundary in place to keep yourself safe. It is also important that you understand that the wounding partner cannot be forced into making the decision to cut ties with an affair partner. As painful as it can be for you to wait for the wounding partner to act, cutting off contact takes a willingness and a commitment on their part that cannot be forced. This is especially true in the case of limerent affairs because the pull is so strong that much effort is required to maintain distance from the affair partner.

Does this mean that you simply have to put up with your partner's behavior? Certainly not. However, it is more effective for you as a wounded partner to distance themselves from your partner and give them a time limit to end the affair than it is to plead with or threaten them. We understand that this information might be extremely upsetting to you. While we certainly understand why it would be, we feel obligated to tell you that we have seen many cases where pleading and threatening on the wounded partner's part actually pushes the wounding partner closer to their affair partner. Additionally, we would advise that you not offer more sex to your partner in hopes of luring them back. In our experience, this leads the wounding partner to indulge in a situation where they can have their cake and eat it too. When the wounding partner engages in infidelity-related behavior and the wounded partner gives them more sex, they are actually rewarding the bad behavior. As a result, the wounding partner has little incentive to change their ways.

If you are a wounding partner reading this and are still in contact with an affair partner, we urge you to adopt a no-contact rule. Your relationship will not be able to recover in any meaningful way until you do this because you are creating an unsafe situation for your partner. This is going to require a sincere commitment on your part. We recommend that you take the following steps to end the contact:

- You need to firmly decide that you are going to end things for the good of your relationship. This is different from wishing that you could end things. If you do not make a firm decision to end contact, you are likely to be pulled back at some point.
- Write a letter to remind yourself why you are choosing to end contact with the affair partner. Read it often.
- Take responsibility for ending the contact and firmly state that you are the one deciding to end things. Do not put it off onto the wounded partner to end things for you.
- Don't say things to your affair partner like, "I'll always miss you, but I have to do this" or, "I wish I could still be with you, but…". This leaves ambiguity in the situation. Instead, firmly state that you are ending contact and leave it there.
- Don't tell your affair partner that you can still be friends. This leaves too much wiggle room for you to contact them and/or them to contact you. Over means over.
- Remember that the affair partner might get upset, but your loyalty belongs to your partner—not to them.
- Decide ahead of time what you will do if they reach out to you. State this clearly when you are ending things.
- Do not cut off contact by engaging in a face-to-face meeting with the affair partner. Email or phone call will suffice.
- Clearly state to the affair partner that this decision is what you want.
- Involve the wounded partner in drafting the email to the affair partner. If you call them, make sure your partner is there with you.
- If the affair partner contacts you, do not answer. It may be wise for you to change your phone number and/or email address. Additionally, you will need to block them on all social media.

Once you have ended things, it is important that you understand your vulnerability and put guardrails in place in the form of accountability immediately. Although not an excuse, relapse is a part of change. Be aware of this and be vigilant to protect your relationship and your boundaries.

We advise that the wounding partner find motivation for ending contact with an affair partner outside of wanting to save the relationship. When it comes to recovery from betrayal, wishing to save the relationship is not a strong enough reason. As we stated previously, the process takes most couples approximately two years, during which time there will be many obstacles and much turmoil. Because the process is not easy or quick, it is common for one or both partners to want to throw in the towel at some point. This is why the motivation for following through with the commitment to each other needs to come from a deeper place. For some, this is a commitment to God. For others, it is a commitment to integrity and/or morals. Whatever the personal motivation, the wounding partner should place a reminder for themselves somewhere that they can read often.

When it comes to holding to the commitment of no-contact, accountability is key. Ensuring that the wounding partner has people around them that will tell them the truth is of vital importance. This is why we include groups and accountability partners in the individual recovery plan. We have worked with many wounding partners who have the best of intentions but, at one point or another, fall into the trap of self-deception when it comes to what they can and can't manage. Putting people in place who will speak the truth will help the wounding partner gain clarity and perspective that can keep them from making decisions that will damage their partner. Additionally, it is important that the wounding partner engage with accountability and recovery partners because it provides a safe space for them to work out thoughts and feelings that might otherwise drag them toward making poor choices.

How does God want you to deal with this issue? Let's look at this incident in John, chapter 8.

John 8: 1-11 MSG

8 1-2 Jesus went across to Mount Olives, but he was soon back in the Temple again. Swarms of people came to him. He sat down and taught them.

3-6 The religion scholars and Pharisees led in a woman who had been caught in an act of adultery. They stood her in plain sight of everyone and said, "Teacher, this woman was caught red-handed in the act of adultery. Moses, in the Law, gives orders to stone such persons. What do you say?" They were trying to trap him into saying something incriminating so they could bring charges against him.

6-8 Jesus bent down and wrote with his finger in the dirt. They kept at him, badgering him. He straightened up and said, "The sinless one among you, go first: Throw the stone." Bending down again, he wrote some more in the dirt.

9-10 Hearing that, they walked away, one after another, beginning with the oldest. The woman was left alone. Jesus stood up and spoke to her. "Woman, where are they? Does no one condemn you?"

11 "No one, Master."

"Neither do I," said Jesus. "Go on your way. From now on, don't sin."

The Pharisees knew who this woman was having an adulterous affair with. When Jesus said, don't sin, it means cutting off the affair partner. Don't sin means NO MORE CONTACT!

If you continue contact, this is what Jesus says about not following His ways.

John 8 31-47 MSG

If the Son Sets You Free

31-32 Then Jesus turned to the Jews who had claimed to believe in him. "If you stick with this, living out what I tell you, you are my disciples for sure. Then you will experience for yourselves the truth, and the truth will free you."

33 Surprised, they said, "But we're descendants of Abraham. We've never been slaves to anyone. How can you say, 'The truth will free you'?"

34-38 Jesus said, "I tell you most solemnly that anyone who chooses a life of sin is trapped in a dead-end life and is, in fact, a slave. A slave can't come and go at will. The Son, though, has an established position, the run of the house. So if the Son sets you free, you are free through and through. I know you are Abraham's descendants. But I also know that you are trying to kill me because my message hasn't yet penetrated your thick skulls. I'm talking about things I have seen while keeping company with the Father, and you just go on doing what you have heard from your father."

39-41 They were indignant. "Our father is Abraham!"

Jesus said, "If you were Abraham's children, you would have been doing the things Abraham did. And yet here you are trying to kill me, a man who has spoken to you the truth he got straight from God! Abraham never did that sort of thing. You persist in repeating the works of your father."

They said, "We're not bastards. We have a legitimate father: the one and only God."

42-47 "If God were your father," said Jesus, "you would love me, for I came from God and arrived here. I didn't come on my own. He sent me. Why can't you understand one word I say? Here's why: You can't handle it. You're from your father, the Devil, and all you want to do is please him. He was a killer from the very start. He couldn't stand the truth because there wasn't a shred of truth in him. When the Liar speaks, he makes it up out of his lying nature and fills the world with lies. I arrive on the scene, tell you the plain truth, and you refuse to have a thing to do with me. Can any one of you convict me of a single misleading word, a single sinful act? But if I'm telling the truth, why don't you believe me? Anyone on God's side listens to God's words. This is why you're not listening—because you're not on God's side."

The choice to stop seeing the affair partner and to stop sinning is on the wounding partner. This is God's view of someone who continues in infidelity related behavior. In God's eyes, you are a SLAVE to SIN. It is the same view the wounded partner will have towards you as well.

Prayer for the wounding partner::

Father, Your word is clear about what it says for me to do. You do NOT want me to sin. I belong to You and to my wounded partner. I BELONG TO NO ONE AND NOTHING ELSE. There is no other option. Like the woman caught in adultery, You want me to go my way and not sin anymore. If I believe that You are my God, then I must follow Your precepts and not engage in any infidelity behaviors. I am Your child. Your truth sets me free and I am free indeed. I will no longer choose to keep any part of my sin and remain trapped in a dead end life. I will no longer be a slave to sin in any capacity. I choose to love You, Your word, and Your precepts. I hate the devil and I refuse to act like he is my father. I refuse to please him in any way, shape or form. The devil and his ways always guarantee my destruction and the destruction of all those connected to me. The devil is a liar, and I will not follow him and give him the freedom to annihilate my world. I choose to be on God's side, free from sin. I choose to live my life God's way and allow God the freedom to bless me. God's way is for me to stop sinning. PERIOD. All sin must go out of my life so I can start living the abundant life for God, for myself and for my wounded partner. In Jesus' name, Amen.

PART 22

Rebuilding Trust Pyramid Layer #3
Consistency

When betrayal is discovered or disclosed, it creates an enormous amount of uncertainty for the wounded partner. For them, the past, present, and future of the relationship are often all called into question. We work with many wounded partners that tell us they don't feel like they know their partner anymore and are suddenly experiencing doubt as to whether or not they ever really knew them at all. The trauma they experience from this break in attachment is intense and difficult to overcome. This is why consistency on the wounding partner's part is crucial to the rebuilding trust process. When the wounded partner sees consistency in the wounding partner, it builds trust because it begins to remove some of their uncertainty. Consistency will begin to show the wounded partner that the wounding partner is clear on what they want and are taking steps to reach their goals. It shows that they are committed to the relationship and understand the gravity of what they have done.

In the definitions section of this book we defined trust as "the ability to feel that one's partner is a source of security, support, safety, and dependability". We believe that the words "security", "support", "safety", and "dependability" are all related to the idea of consistency. What a person chooses to do consistently is a reflection of their true values and standards. This can show up as character strengths or character defects. For example, if a person consistently gaslights, minimizes, or defends, they are telling their partner that they value their own need to be right over that person's well-being. If a person consistently follows through on commitments, apologizes when wrong, and seeks to truly listen to what the other person is saying, it shows that they value that person and the relationship.

We read an article in *Forbes* a while back which outlined five areas as being associated with consistent, predictable, and reliable people. The author referred to these areas as "The Consistency Index" and, while he was referring to behavior in a professional environment, we feel that they apply to relationships in which infidelity has been an issue. The five areas are:

- Being a role model/setting a good example

Here is an example of a young man whose congregation was under persecution, being told by the Apostle Paul to be an example to his congregation. Imagine how much more Paul would expect of a believer who has the freedom to practice their religion and who are not young.

Titus 2:2-8 NLT

2 But as for you, speak up for the right living that goes along with true Christianity. 2 Teach the older men to be serious and unruffled; they must be sensible, knowing and believing the truth and doing everything with love and patience.

3 Teach the older women to be quiet and respectful in everything they do. They must not go around speaking evil of others and must not be heavy drinkers, but they should be teachers of goodness. 4 These older women must train the younger women to live quietly, to love their husbands and their children, 5 and to be sensible and clean minded, spending their time in their own homes, being kind and obedient to their husbands so that the Christian faith can't be spoken against by those who know them.

6 In the same way, urge the young men to behave carefully, taking life seriously. 7 And here you yourself must be an example to them of good deeds of every kind. Let everything you do reflect your love of the truth and the fact that you are in dead earnest about it. 8 Your conversation should be so sensible and logical that anyone who wants to argue will be ashamed of himself because there won't be anything to criticize in anything you say!

- Avoiding saying one thing and doing another

Proverbs 21: 2-5 TLB

2 We can justify our every deed, but God looks at our motives.

3 God is more pleased when we are just and fair than when we give him gifts.

4 Pride, lust, and evil actions are all sin.

5 Steady plodding brings prosperity; hasty speculation brings poverty.

- Honoring commitments and keeping promises

Numbers 30: 1 & 2 TLB

30 1-2 Now Moses summoned the leaders of the tribes and told them, "The Lord has commanded that when anyone makes a promise to the Lord, either to do something or to quit doing something, that vow must not be broken: the person making the vow must do exactly as he has promised.

- Following through on commitments

Psalm 106: 1-3 MSG

1-3 Hallelujah! Thank God! And why? Because he's good, because his love lasts. But who on earth can do it—declaim God's mighty acts, broadcast all his praises? You're one happy man when you do what's right, one happy woman when you form the habit of justice.

- Showing a willingness to go above and beyond when necessary (Folkman, 2019)

Jesus is our example, and He certainly showed a willingness to go above and beyond what was necessary. Should we do any less? God wants us to be all that we can be.

Romans 5:1-11 MSG

5 1-2 By entering through faith into what God has always wanted to do for us—set us right with him, make us fit for him—we have it all together with God because of our Master Jesus. And that's not all: We throw open our doors to God and discover at the same moment that he has already thrown open his door to us. We find ourselves standing where we always hoped we might stand—out in the wide open spaces of God's grace and glory, standing tall and shouting our praise.

3-5 There's more to come: We continue to shout our praise even when we're hemmed in with troubles, because we know how troubles can develop passionate patience in us, and how that patience in turn forges the tempered steel of virtue, keeping us alert for whatever God will do next. In alert expectancy such as this, we're never left feeling shortchanged. Quite the contrary—we can't round up enough containers to hold everything God generously pours into our lives through the Holy Spirit!

6-8 Christ arrives right on time to make this happen. He didn't, and doesn't, wait for us to get ready. He presented himself for this sacrificial death when we were far too weak and rebellious to do anything to get ourselves ready. And even if we hadn't been so weak, we wouldn't have known what to do anyway. We can understand someone dying for a person worth dying for, and we can understand how someone good and noble could inspire us to selfless sacrifice. But God put his love on the line for us by offering his Son in sacrificial death while we were of no use whatever to him.

9-11 Now that we are set right with God by means of this sacrificial death, the consummate blood sacrifice, there is no longer a question of being at odds with God in any way. If, when we were at our worst, we were put on friendly terms with God by the sacrificial death of his Son, now that we're at our best, just think of how our lives will expand and deepen by means of his resurrection life! Now that we have actually received this amazing friendship with God, we are no longer content to simply say it in plodding prose. We sing and shout our praises to God through Jesus, the Messiah!

As you move forward in your recovery, keeping these five areas in mind while evaluating your progress will go a long way in creating the consistency you need in order to rebuild trust

Consistency in behavior can lead the wounded partner to start to believe that the wounding partner is dependable, and this can eventually lead to trust.

Consistent and reliable behavior on the part of the wounding partner is comforting to the wounded partner because reliability is an indication that the wounding partner is focused on the relationship instead of solely on themselves.

This is crucial because self-focused behavior was what led to the infidelity-related behavior in the first place. If the wounded partner sees a continuation of this type of behavior, they will be unlikely to extend trust any time soon, if ever, to the wounding partner. Words will do little to soothe the pain of a wounded partner; consistent action over time is what is needed for trust to be rebuilt.

We feel a need to mention that it is not only important that the wounding partner show consistency in recovery, but it is important for the wounded partner to show consistency in their own recovery as well. As we have stated numerous times throughout this book, we are not implying that the wounded partner should take on any of the blame for the wounding partner's decision to engage in infidelity-related behavior. However, if the wounded partner consistently engages in angry outbursts, stonewalling or withdrawal, shaming, and threatening it will eventually end up damaging the relationship in a completely new and unfortunate way. We have worked with numerous couples that have come to us after years of trying to heal from betrayal on their own and are struggling to stay together. Aside from the wounding partner's infidelity-related behavior, we often see evidence that the wounded partner's behavior has made the rebuilding trust process far more difficult than it would have otherwise been. It is essential that **both** partners consistently adhere to communication ground rules, trigger plans, and time out protocols if the relationship is to recover.

While there are a few points in this chapter that address consistency on the part of the couple and/or the wounded partner, the majority of it will be dedicated to the wounding partner. Their consistency in individual recovery as well as in their focus on the relationship instead of on themselves is what will make the most difference—especially in the beginning phases of rebuilding trust. However, the lack of focus on the wounded partner does not imply that their own consistency in areas that they are responsible for is somehow less important.

Wounding Partner Consistency

Item #1: Keep the door shut (no-contact)

This one is specifically for wounding partners who have had sexual and/or emotional affairs. Although we highlighted steps that can be taken to go no-contact with an affair partner, we want to stress the importance of keeping the door shut to them. Trust during the recovery process is hard-earned, and nothing will break it down faster than if the wounding partner has contact with an affair partner. Even if the contact is mildly friendly with no sexual overtones, the wounded partner is likely to see any contact with an affair partner as another betrayal.

Although we previously covered accountability as a key component of holding fast to the no-contact rule, we also want to emphasize that it is important that the wounding partner have an overall plan in place. This plan should include several "how am I going to handle it…" scenarios. Some examples are:

- How am I going to handle it if my affair partner emails me?
- How am I going to handle it if my affair partner shows up at my work?
- How am I going to handle it if I am mad at my partner and miss my affair partner?
- How am I going to handle it if I start to romanticize the relationship with my affair partner again?
- How am I going to handle it if my affair partner texts or calls me from someone else's phone?

The list of possible scenarios is long, but hopefully you get the idea. It is important the wounding partner decide how they are going to handle these types of scenarios ahead of time. We advise that this plan is put into writing and that the wounding partner share it with the wounded partner along with at least one accountability partner. This plan is especially important for the wounding partner to develop immediately after betrayal because this is likely when they feel the most regretful about what has happened. If you are a wounding partner reading this, developing this plan early on and sharing it with people who can keep you accountable will help you stick to it when you are experiencing the prolonged turmoil that follows betrayal.

If the infidelity was pornography-related, we suggest that the wounding partner put monitoring software on all devices. Additionally, planning ahead is a must. Much like the "how am I going to handle it" scenarios listed above for stopping contact with an affair partner, the wounding partner with a pornography issue should make a list of possible scenarios where they might be tempted to look at pornography and make a plan for what they will do should that situation arise. These scenarios should not only include physical situations, but times when the wounding partner is likely to feel angry, lonely, tired, afraid, or any number of intense feelings that will tempt them to self-soothe with pornography and masturbation.

Stay away from all contact with the affair partner and/or pornography. God's word states that all those who practice sin are not His children.

1 John 3:4-17 MSG

4-6 All who indulge in a sinful life are dangerously lawless, for sin is a major disruption of God's order. Surely you know that Christ showed up in order to get rid of sin. There is no sin in him, and sin is not part of his program. No one who lives deeply in Christ makes a practice of sin. None of those who do practice sin have taken a good look at Christ. They've got him all backward.

7-8 So, my dear children, don't let anyone divert you from the truth. It's the person who acts right who is right, just as we see it lived out in our righteous Messiah. Those who make a practice of sin are straight from the Devil, the pioneer in the practice of sin. The Son of God entered the scene to abolish the Devil's ways.

9-10 People conceived and brought into life by God don't make a practice of sin. How could they? God's seed is deep within them, making them who they are. It's not in the nature of the God-born to practice and parade sin. Here's how you tell the difference between God's children and the Devil's children: The one who won't practice righteous ways isn't from God, nor is the one who won't love brother or sister. A simple test.

11 For this is the original message we heard: We should love each other.

12-13 We must not be like Cain, who joined the Evil One and then killed his brother. And why did he kill him? Because he was deep in the practice of evil, while the acts of his brother were righteous. So don't be surprised, friends, when the world hates you. This has been going on a long time.

14-15 The way we know we've been transferred from death to life is that we love our brothers and sisters. Anyone who doesn't love is as good as dead. Anyone who hates a brother or sister is a murderer, and you know very well that eternal life and murder don't go together.

16-17 This is how we've come to understand and experience love: Christ sacrificed his life for us. This is why we ought to live sacrificially for our fellow believers, and not just be out for ourselves. If you see some brother or sister in need and have the means to do something about it but turn a cold shoulder and do nothing, what happens to God's love? It disappears. And you made it disappear.

Item #2: Polygraph schedule

As described in the previous section on trust-building behaviors, the polygraph is a powerful instrument that can help pave the way to rebuilding trust in a relationship. It can provide a couple with a baseline of truth when there has been deception involved. Unfortunately, the word of the wounding partner often isn't enough for the wounded partner to feel safe and trusting. Due to the lies and deception typically involved, the wounding partner's assurances often mean little to nothing to the wounded partner. Consistent action is what they need to see. We often work with wounding partners who are frustrated with the fact that the wounded partner won't believe them when they say that they are sorry and promise to never do it again. If you are a wounding partner and this describes your situation, we would remind you that you likely made promises prior to your betrayal that you didn't uphold. It is unreasonable for you to expect that your words should be enough to fix things now.

For many couples, especially when sexual or pornography addiction is an issue, ongoing polygraphs are often an important component of rebuilding trust. A willingness on the wounding partner's part to take ongoing polygraphs can be an excellent way for them to show that they are being consistent with their recovery and have nothing to hide. When the wounding partner passes multiple polygraphs over a period of time, this aids in the wounded partner's feelings of overall safety in the relationship. If you are a wounding partner and are balking at the idea of taking multiple polygraphs, we would encourage you to see it as a gift you can give your partner that will help them. Additionally, especially if addiction to sex or pornography is an issue for you, it is a gift that you can give yourself because the ongoing accountability polygraphs provide will aid you in your recovery.

For those of you who wish to include a polygraph schedule as a component of the rebuilding trust process, we recommend that the wounding partner take a polygraph examination every 3-6 months for the first year, every 6 months for the second year, and once per year thereafter.

Truthfulness is vital in rebuilding trust. There is no other substitute for it.

Proverbs 12:17-22 MSG

Truthful witness by a good person clears the air, but liars lay down a smoke screen of deceit. Rash language cuts and maims, but there is healing in the words of the wise. Truth lasts; lies are here today, gone tomorrow. Evil scheming distorts the schemer; peace-planning brings joy to the planner. No evil can overwhelm a good person, but the wicked have their hands full of it. God can't stomach liars; He loves the company of those who keep their word.

Item #3: Weekly check-ins

For wounding partners dealing with addiction and/or intimacy avoidance, activities such as meetings, accountability phone calls, workbooks, etc. are an integral part of the individual recovery plan. When we work with couples, we often hear from the wounded partner that they feel left out of this portion the recovery process. While the following check-in sheet is what we use for members of our group meetings, the sheet can also be used to report out to the wounded partner and keep them up to date on the wounding partner's progress:

I'm recovering from_____(Sexual Addiction; Intimacy Anorexia, Emotional/Sexual Infidelity, being the Partner of an IA)

I'm also recovering from _____ trauma that I experienced when I was _____ by _____.

My SA Sobriety date is_____; I'm_____% responsible for the devastation and _____% responsible for my recovery from it

(No masturbation, touching self to arousal, intentionally viewing images for sexual arousal, fantasizing, for arousal during being sexual with spouse)

_____

My Infidelity Sobriety date is_____; I'm_____% responsible for the devastation and _____% responsible for my recovery from it.

_____

My IA Sobriety date is_____; I'm_____% responsible for the devastation and _____% responsible for my recovery from it.

(Sobriety for IA: Within 24hrs-acknowledge your IA behavior- repair- move towards partner not distancing)

I'm also recovering from other addiction(s): _____
_____

My sobriety date from intentionally lying or omitting the truth to my partner is:
_____

In the last 7 days, I_____(did/didn't) break any sobriety boundaries. If I did, they were _____ and the consequences I did are _____

I_____do/don't have a 24 tell policy and I _____did/didn't have to use it this week

_____is the day each week I do my Couples Accountability meeting and_____I did/didn't do it in the last 7 days

The last Workgroup meeting I attended was:_____I attended_____other 12 step sexual addiction meeting(s) in the last 7 days.

I did my Morning RECOVERY prayers _____ out of 7 days and I did my Evening RECOVERY prayers _____ out of 7 days

_____
_____
_____
_____

I made Calls _____ out of the last 7 days; I talked to someone _____ times in the last 7 days and did _____ pushups for days I didn't call

I'm on step _____ in my *SA* Steps workbook; I completed _____ pages in the last 7 days and I'm on page _____; Last worked on it _____

_____
_____

I'm on step _____ in my *IA* or *MA* Steps workbook; I completed _____ pages in the last 7 days and I'm on page _____; Last worked on it _____

_____
_____

My workgroup step partner is _____ and I've scheduled with him to share my next step on _____ (date)

_____
_____

In the last 7 days, In my 101 Freedom Exercises workbook, I did exercises _____; In my IA exercise work book, I did exercises _____

IF IA

- I did the 3-Dailies _____ out of the last 7 days
- I did connection exercises with my partner _____ out of the last 7 days
- The day each week I do my date with my partner is _____ and I _____ did/didn't do it in the last 7 days

> • I _____ do/don't have a Sexual agreement plan with my partner and I _____ did/didn't follow it in the last 7 days
>
> • I _____ did/didn't have to do consequences in the last 7 days. If I did, those were _____

I did/didn't play the victim towards my partner in the last 7 days If I did, I did it by:

_____

I did/didn't *half measure* it in my recovery in the last 7 days If I did, I did it by:

_____

I'm going to strengthen my recovery in the next 7 days by:

_____

We have been told by many couples that this check-in sheet is useful while they are trying to establish consistency within recovery. For the wounding partner, it serves as a reminder of the items they should be paying attention to. For the wounded partner, it gives them a picture of some of the many things the wounding partner is working on. We recommend that a weekly day and time be set aside for the wounding partner to go through the items on their check-in sheet with the wounded partner. We also recommend that the wounding partner ask the wounded partner to give them feedback on areas of recovery that could use improvement.

Weekly check-ins are an excellent tool for accountability.

Romans 15: 1-13 MSG

1-2 Those of us who are strong and able in the faith need to step in and lend a hand to those who falter, and not just do what is most convenient for us. Strength is for service, not status. Each one of us needs to look after the good of the people around us, asking ourselves, "How can I help?"

3-6 That's exactly what Jesus did. He didn't make it easy for himself by avoiding people's troubles but waded right in and helped out. "I took on the troubles of the troubled," is the way Scripture puts it. Even if it was written in Scripture long ago, you can be sure it's written for us. God wants the combination of his steady, constant calling and warm, personal counsel in Scripture to come to characterize us, keeping us alert for whatever he will do next. May our dependably steady and warmly personal God develop maturity in you so that you get along with each other as well as Jesus gets along with us all.

Then we'll be a choir—not our voices only, but our very lives singing in harmony in a stunning anthem to the God and Father of our Master Jesus!

7-13 So reach out and welcome one another to God's glory. Jesus did it; now you do it!

Proverbs 27:5-6 MSG

A spoken reprimand is better than approval that's never expressed. The wounds from a lover are worth it; kisses from an enemy do you in.

Proverbs 27:12 MSG

A prudent person sees trouble coming and ducks; a simpleton walks in blindly and is clobbered.

Proverbs 27:17 MSG

You use steel to sharpen steel, and one friend sharpens another.

Item #4: 24-hour tell policy

To build trust, we recommend that the wounding partner agree to a 24-hour tell policy. By this, we mean that the wounding partner will notify the wounded partner of any sexually acting out behavior, gaslighting, manipulating, or lying within 24 hours of that failure. Additionally, the wounding partner needs to inform the wounded partner what consequence(s) they did in conjunction with the failure. If the wounding partner has not yet done a consequence, they should inform the wounded partner what the consequence will be and when they are going to do it within the next 24 hours.

We most often recommend the 24-hour tell policy for those who are struggling with sexual or pornography addiction and intimacy avoidance. If you are a wounding partner reading this, we understand that you might be apprehensive about telling your partner about your failures when it comes to your recovery plan. However, in our experience, your partner is much more likely to have an issue with your deception around your behavior than they are about the behavior itself. (Of course, the caveat here is that that the behavior wasn't associated with a dealbreaker such as having another sexual affair). Time and time again, wounded partners tell us that the lies told by to them by the wounding partner are even harder to get over than the behavior itself. Adherence to the 24-hour tell policy will help with the issue of deception.

James 5:16 MSG

16-18 Make this your common practice: Confess your sins to each other and pray for each other so that you can live together whole and healed. The prayer of a person living right with God is something powerful to be reckoned with.

Item #5: Recovery deep dive

While it is important that the wounding partner regret their behavior, tell the wounded partner they are sorry, and promise to never do it again, it is rarely enough to create true safety and consistency in the relationship. This is because the wounding partner's decision to engage in infidelity-related behavior is often tied to past trauma and core beliefs. These thing must be dealt with on a deep level if the wounding partner is to overcome the need to engage in infidelity-related behavior in the future. If you are a wounding partner reading this, we would encourage you to engage in counseling or coaching to discover the attitudes and beliefs that led up to your infidelity-related behavior.

Recovery Deep Dive is, in fact, a biblical concept.

James 5:19-20 MSG

19-20 My dear friends, if you know people who have wandered off from God's truth, don't write them off. Go after them. Get them back and you will have rescued precious lives from destruction and prevented an epidemic of wandering away from God.

Proverbs 15:5-7 MSG

Moral dropouts won't listen to their elders; welcoming correction is a mark of good sense. The lives of God-loyal people flourish; a misspent life is soon bankrupt. Perceptive words spread knowledge; fools are hollow—there's nothing to them.

Proverbs 15:12 MSG

Know-it-alls don't like being told what to do; they avoid the company of wise men and women.

Proverbs 15: 14-16 MSG

An intelligent person is always eager to take in more truth; fools feed on fast-food fads and fancies. A miserable heart means a miserable life; a cheerful heart fills the day with song. A simple life in the Fear-of-God is better than a rich life with a ton of headaches.

Item #6: Trust-building with micro-trusts

Trust building, of course, applies to the larger issue of infidelity-related behaviors and related recovery plans that entail meetings, counseling, etc. However, the term "micro-trusts" applies to the seemingly small or unrelated things that wounding partners do every day. Wounded partners tell us time and time again that they consistently watch their partner's behavior to see if they are exhibiting any areas where they can't be trusted. This can include things that are seemingly unrelated to infidelity such as taking the garbage out as promised and without a bad attitude, helping with the kids, paying the bills on time, and being where the wounding partner said they were going to be. We refer to these areas of trust as micro-trusts. The reason these areas of micro-trust are such a big deal to wounded partners is that they are looking for evidence of a commitment to change on the wounding partner's part.

If you are a wounding partner, don't tell yourself that inconsistencies, however small, won't matter to your wounded partner. They will. We need you to understand that your partner will likely be examining your everyday behavior for signs that you are not to be trusted. If you can at all help it, we would encourage you not to give them a reason to feel that you are continuing to lie to them. Although some of your behavior may seem inconsequential to you, inconsistencies between your words and behavior will likely trigger your partner. Some examples of this could be telling them that you are going to be at a certain location for a meeting and not notifying them if the venue changes, telling them you are going out with a certain group of people and not letting them know that people have been added to your party, or telling them you are going to a particular restaurant and then going to another without letting them know. These could all be construed as an inability on your part to take the breach of trust you have created in the relationship seriously. Although the scenarios we have listed are relatively obvious as to why they could worry a wounded partner, we would like to point out that there will likely be other seemingly unrelated areas where not showing consistency could bother your partner as well. Some common ones include helping with the household without complaint, following through on agreements regarding childcare/ child rearing, and doing the bare minimum instead of the effort required to do something well.

Micro-trusts build character. When you have practice making small, numerous right decisions, you will be ready when the time to make a big, RIGHT decision comes along.

Proverbs 3:5-12 MSG
Trust God from the bottom of your heart; don't try to figure out everything on your own. Listen for God's voice in everything you do, everywhere you go; he's the one who will keep you on track. Don't assume that you know it all. Run to God! Run from evil! Your body will glow with health, your very bones will vibrate with life! Honor God with everything you own; give him the first and the best. Your barns will burst, your wine vats will brim over. But don't, dear friend, resent God's discipline; don't sulk under his loving correction. It's the child he loves that God corrects; a father's delight is behind all this.

Prayer for the wounding partner:

Father, I will no longer indulge in a sinful lifestyle, not in micro or macro form! I will not let anyone divert me from the truth, especially not an affair partner or pornographic image who I have allowed to take the place of my wounded partner. All sin is a major disruption of Your order. I cannot live in Christ and practice sin. I will partner with God and do what is right in His sight and humbly restore myself back to my wounded partner, where I belong. I will never practice or parade sin again. I have been transferred from the kingdom of darkness into the Kingdom of Light. I love God and I love my wounded partner. I want to be like Christ and sacrifice my life for my wounded partner, whom God entrusted to me. In Jesus' name, Amen.

PART 23

Relationship Consistency

Now that we have covered the important areas where wounding partners need to be consistent, we would like to cover two areas in which both parties need to be consistent if the rebuilding of trust is to become a possibility.

Item #1: Engaging in recovery-focused activities

Recovery from betrayal is often an isolating process since many couples struggling with issues common to it don't feel comfortable sharing their struggles with friends and family. This is why it is imperative that both the wounding and wounded partners engage in recovery-focused activities such as attending groups, classes, intensives, seminars, and individual coaching or counseling. We would especially like to emphasize the importance of group activities—both as a couple and as individuals. At Becoming Well, we offer work groups, seminars, and individual or group intensives as a way of supporting our clients through the process. We are told on a regular basis that group recovery activities help them feel less isolated, maintain a sense of hopefulness, and learn strategies from others that help them manage their own situations. For wounded partners in particular, group recovery activities help ease their emotional burdens by having a place to vent where they will be understood. They also have reported making important connections with other individuals that help them feel supported outside of group activities. For wounding partners, group recovery can provide much-needed accountability, a non-judgmental place to work on issues, as well as insight as to what has worked for others struggling with similar issues.

Hebrews 10: 23-25 AMP

Let us seize and hold tightly the confession of our hope without wavering, for He who promised is reliable and trustworthy and faithful [to His word]; 24 and let us consider [thoughtfully] how we may encourage one another to love and to do good deeds, 25 not forsaking our meeting together [as believers for worship and instruction], as is the habit of some, but encouraging one another; and all the more [faithfully] as you see the day [of Christ's return] approaching.

Item #2: Adherence to the communication plan

If you will remember, we discussed a 3-part communication plan in the safety section of this book. The three parts consist of general ground-rules for communication, the trigger plan, and the time-out protocol. Since we previously covered these thoroughly, we will not take the time here to cover the details again. Instead, we would like to stress how important it is that both the wounding and the wounded partner adhere to all three parts of the communication plan consistently. Betrayal creates stress and pressure in a relationship unlike anything else. As a result, communication around infidelity-related issues can cause severe communication break downs that often result in one or both partners throwing in the towel.

Although we often work with couples that were experiencing major breakdowns in communication prior to the discovery or disclosure of infidelity, we also work with a fair percentage of them that claim to have had very few communication issues prior. Whatever the case, betrayal can, in and of itself, create a situation in which communication breakdowns happen frequently, especially in the beginning. As previously mentioned, some of the most common culprits we see in our office of communication stall-outs are:

- Name-calling or other insults
- Character assassination
- Defending or blame-shifting
- Threatening
- Stonewalling
- Non-verbal signs of disrespect such as eye-rolling or heavy sighing
- Mind-reading
- "Always" and "never" statements

When it comes to rebuilding trust in order to save a relationship, it is important for both parties to remember that the other is not the enemy. Instead, it is imperative that both the wounded and wounding partners give up the idea of winning an argument. When individuals in a relationship communicate in order to win, the relationship loses. This is especially hard for the wounded partner to remember since the wounding partner seems exactly like an enemy in their own camp. However, if you hope to save your relationship, you must communicate in a respectful way. Although it can be tempting to take shots at your partner for hurting or humiliating you, a failure by either party to adhere to the communication plan is like being out in the middle of the ocean and shooting holes in your own boat. The relationship has a high likelihood of eventually sinking beyond retrieval. This is not to say that anger and other strong emotions cannot be expressed. They can and should. However, it is important that they are expressed in a way that nurtures the relationship instead of destroying it. Adhering to the 3-part communication plan will help you accomplish this.

Ephesians 4:17-32 MSG

17-19 And so I insist—and God backs me up on this—that there be no going along with the crowd, the empty-headed, mindless crowd. They've refused for so long to deal with God that they've lost touch not only with God but with reality itself. They can't think straight anymore. Feeling no pain, they let themselves go into sexual obsession, addicted to every sort of perversion.

20-24 But that's no life for you. You learned Christ! My assumption is that you have paid careful attention to him, been well instructed in the truth precisely as we have it in Jesus. Since, then, we do not have the excuse of ignorance, everything—and I do mean everything—connected with that old way of life has to go. It's rotten through and through. Get rid of it! And then take on an entirely new way of life—a God-fashioned life, a life renewed from the inside and working itself into your conduct as God accurately reproduces his character in you.

25 What this adds up to, then, is this: no more lies, no more pretense. Tell your neighbor the truth. In Christ's body we're all connected to each other, after all. When you lie to others, you end up lying to yourself.

26-27 Go ahead and be angry. You do well to be angry—but don't use your anger as fuel for revenge. And don't stay angry. Don't go to bed angry. Don't give the Devil that kind of foothold in your life.

28 Did you use to make ends meet by stealing? Well, no more! Get an honest job so that you can help others who can't work.

29 Watch the way you talk. Let nothing foul or dirty come out of your mouth. Say only what helps, each word a gift.

30 Don't grieve God. Don't break his heart. His Holy Spirit, moving and breathing in you, is the most intimate part of your life, making you fit for himself. Don't take such a gift for granted.

31-32 Make a clean break with all cutting, backbiting, profane talk. Be gentle with one another, sensitive. Forgive one another as quickly and thoroughly as God in Christ forgave you.

Wounded Partner Consistency

Aside from adhering to the communication plan, the area that we most commonly see the wounded partner lack consistency in is requiring the wounding partner to be ongoingly accountable for their behavior. This is not to say that the wounded partner should micromanage the wounding partner's recovery. However, we find in a number of couples that the wounded partner is so eager to move on from the pain caused by the betrayal that they move away from requiring ongoing accountability from the wounding partner because doing so reminds them of that pain. Although we can certainly understand why this would be the case, we almost always see this backfire. Although there is certainly a time when couples decided not to talk about the infidelity on a regular basis, dropping the requirement for the wounding partner to be ongoingly accountable early on in recovery is typically a decision made from an unhealthy place of wishing to stay in denial about the reality of the situation.

Although a requirement for ongoing accountability in a relationship should never be used to punish a wounding partner, it is a fundamental part of any romantic relationship. While each partner should be accountable to the other, it is especially important to the rebuilding trust process that the wounding partner is ongoingly accountable. Infidelity shows a profound lack of self-awareness as well as a lack of empathy and awareness of how the wounding partner's behavior affects their partner. A commitment to ongoing accountability will help the wounding partner build self-awareness, build empathy, and collaborate with the wounded partner on how they can help ensure the success of the relationship moving forward by doing the things that show commitment.

Colossians 3:5-17 CEV

5 Don't be controlled by your body. Kill every desire for the wrong kind of sex. Don't be immoral or indecent or have evil thoughts. Don't be greedy, which is the same as worshiping idols. 6 God is angry with people who disobey him by doing these things. 7 And this is exactly what you did, when you lived among people who behaved in this way. 8 But now you must stop doing such things. You must quit being angry, hateful, and evil. You must no longer say insulting or cruel things about others. 9 And stop lying to each other. You have given up your old way of life with its habits.

10 Each of you is now a new person. You are becoming more and more like your Creator, and you will understand him better. 11 It doesn't matter if you are a Greek or a Jew, or if you are circumcised or not. You may even be a barbarian or a Scythian, and you may be a slave or a free person. Yet Christ is all that matters, and he lives in all of us.

12 God loves you and has chosen you as his own special people. So be gentle, kind, humble, meek, and patient. 13 Put up with each other, and forgive anyone who does you wrong, just as Christ has forgiven you. 14 Love is more important than anything else. It is what ties everything completely together.

15 Each one of you is part of the body of Christ, and you were chosen to live together in peace. So let the peace that comes from Christ control your thoughts. And be grateful. 16 Let the message about Christ completely fill your lives, while you use all your wisdom to teach and instruct each other. With thankful hearts, sing psalms, hymns, and spiritual songs to God. 17 Whatever you say or do should be done in the name of the Lord Jesus, as you give thanks to God the Father because of him.

Patience is Key

When it comes to rebuilding trust, patience is key. This is especially true for the wounding partner. Every day in our offices, we hear wounding partners make comments such as, "when are they going to get over this?" and "I've done all I can do to say I'm sorry, I don't understand why they can't let this go." Rebuilding trust takes a long time, and so does forgiveness. Asking a wounded partner to "get over it" before they are ready conveys disrespect for their feelings and demanding they forgive within a timeframe specified by the wounding partner conveys selfishness on the wounding partner's part.

One of the areas that seems to be the hardest for wounding partners to have patience is in the questioning phase of recovery. It is not uncommon for the wounded partner to ask multiple questions (and even the same question repeatedly) daily for the first 3-6 months following the discovery or disclosure of any type of betrayal. This holds especially true for sexual and emotional infidelity. **We want to stress that this is a completely normal phase of recovery**. If you are a wounding partner reading this, we would encourage you to accept this as a part of recovery and commit to answering your partner's questions as thoroughly and as patiently as possible. **If you answer begrudgingly, get defensive, refuse to answer, or complain that they are repeatedly asking you to answer what seems like the same question over and over, you will, at best, prolong the process and, at worst, put your relationship in further jeopardy.**

Another area where patience is often required is within the communication plan. This is especially true if a couple has had a hard time with communication prior to the betrayal. When this is case, healthy communication often takes time and patience to establish. It is unfortunate that good communication must be established under the stressful circumstances that betrayal creates, but such is the reality of the situation. Even if a couple's communication seemed relatively healthy prior to the betrayal, the intense pain and stress that follows is enough to send a couple's communication way off course.

In his book *The Seven Principles of Making Marriage Work*, authors John Gottman and Nan Silver describe what they term as the "Four Horseman of the Apocalypse". These "four horsemen" are:

- Criticism
- Contempt
- Defensiveness
- Stonewalling

The reason the authors call these the Four Horseman of the Apocalypse is that, when they are present for an extended period of time, they tend to predict the death of a relationship. The first Horseman, criticism, is different than presenting a complaint. Bringing a specific issue to your partner's attention is acceptable. However, if it is accompanied by an attack on your partner's character, it is considered to be criticism and will often result in your partner becoming defensive. The second Horseman, contempt, happens when one partner takes a position of superiority over the other. Contempt is typically conveyed through things like sarcasm, ridiculing with words or mimicry, eye rolling or other disrespectful body language, and name calling. The third Horseman, defensiveness, is typically a response to criticism or perceived criticism. We very commonly see defensiveness in IA relationships. Defensiveness is often displayed through playing the victim, reversing accusations (I know

I did "x", but you did it too), blame (I wouldn't have done "x" if you didn't do "y"), and excuse-making. The fourth Horseman, stonewalling, can also be a response to criticism but it also a common response to contempt. It is also present in many IA relationships when the IA refuses to admit to wrongdoing because they want to retain power and control. It can also come out when either partner becomes flooded with emotion. Stonewalling often looks like giving up, saying comments such as, "never mind" or "fine" and following those comments with silence. Stonewalling can also look like the silent treatment or prolonged periods of no talking.

When we work with couples, it is not uncommon for us to see most, if not all, of the Four Horseman show up. Early on in recovery, helping couples eradicate them often becomes top priority. It is important for you to understand that the presence of the Four Horseman of the Apocalypse does not spell certain doom for your relationship and is even a normal occurrence after betrayal. However, prolonged use of any of these tactics will result in damage separate from that done by betrayal that could lead to the relationship's end. Luckily, John Gottman's research has proven that there are antidotes to each of the Horseman. These are:

- Gentle Start Up
- Building a Culture of Appreciation
- Taking Responsibility
- Psychological Self-Soothing

Antidote number one, the gentle start up, should be used to counteract criticism. This looks like honestly expressing feelings using "I" statements. The Speaker-Listener technique we mentioned previously is great for this. Antidote number two, building a culture of appreciation, should be used to counteract contempt. Building a culture of appreciation looks like reminding yourself of your partner's positive attributes and expressing gratitude for the good things they have done. If you refer back to Step 5 of the time-out protocol, you will notice that we ask each partner to state at least one thing that they appreciate about the other. This, along with other tools you will find in the final section on intimacy, will begin building a culture of appreciation in your relationship. The third antidote, taking responsibility, should be used to counteract defensiveness. Taking responsibility includes apologizing for wrongdoing and validating where your partner is coming from, even if you don't agree. We have discussed taking responsibility multiple times throughout these chapters. The fourth antidote, psychological self-soothing, should be used to counteract stonewalling. Instead of stonewalling your partner when you become emotionally overwhelmed, or yelling at them, use the Time-Out Protocol described earlier in this book to calm your emotions down. It is important to note that each partner should give the other a set time when they plan on coming back to the conversation in order to avoid abandoning their partner in the midst of their pain.

We are all human. As such, it is expected that failures in communication, and even the Four Horseman, will come up. When these inevitable failures do occur, it is important that each partner take immediate responsibility for their own actions. Although a failure to remain consistent with any part of the plan is not ideal, most (if not all) people understand that humans make mistakes and are willing to accept an apology in order to move on. When either partner admits to having failed with some part of the recovery plan, this will also build trust. If either one makes a mistake or refuses to admit it, even when called to account for it, it will break down trust in the relationship even further. The same holds true for a situation in which either partner defends themselves regarding their failure. Remember, defensiveness is one of the Four Horseman of the Apocalypse.

Galatians 6:1-10 MSG

6 1-3 Live creatively, friends. If someone falls into sin, forgivingly restore him, saving your critical comments for yourself. You might be needing forgiveness before the day's out. Stoop down and reach out to those who are oppressed. Share their burdens, and so complete Christ's law. If you think you are too good for that, you are badly deceived.

4-5 Make a careful exploration of who you are and the work you have been given, and then sink yourself into that. Don't be impressed with yourself. Don't compare yourself with others. Each of you must take responsibility for doing the creative best you can with your own life.

6 Be very sure now, you who have been trained to a self-sufficient maturity, that you enter into a generous common life with those who have trained you, sharing all the good things that you have and experience.

7-8 Don't be misled: No one makes a fool of God. What a person plants, he will harvest. The person who plants selfishness, ignoring the needs of others—ignoring God! — harvests a crop of weeds. All he'll have to show for his life is weeds! But the one who plants in response to God, letting God's Spirit do the growth work in him, harvests a crop of real life, eternal life.

9-10 So let's not allow ourselves to get fatigued doing good. At the right time we will harvest a good crop if we don't give up or quit. Right now, therefore, every time we get the chance, let us work for the benefit of all, starting with the people closest to us in the community of faith.

Prayer for the wounding and the wounded partner:

Father:

Give us the grace to forgive and restore each other when we fall into sin and to do it without critical comments. Give us the grace to stoop down and reach out to each other and share each other's burdens. Give us the grace to sink ourselves into this work of rebuilding trust in each other. Give us the grace to be generous with each other, communicate well, create good experiences and make each other the best we can be. Give us the grace to plant good seeds into this relationship, produce excellent fruit and reap a good and grand harvest.

Give us the energy to do only good deeds, one to another. Give us the grace to use every opportunity to bless and benefit each other and make this relationship all that You intended for it to be. In Jesus' name. Amen.

PART 24

Rebuilding Trust Pyramid Layer #4

Intimacy

Intimacy is something that we all crave, and yet so many of us avoid it. To have true intimacy in our primary relationship, we must be willing to expose our innermost selves to one another. This is something many people refuse to do. This is especially true in intimacy avoidant relationships, where intimacy is avoided by the IA at all costs. To be truly intimate with our partner, we must be willing to share every aspect of ourselves. We must be willing to let the other person see us—flaws and all. Intimacy involves consistently sharing our true selves with our partner in an unconstrained way without fear of rejection.

When people talk about intimacy, they most commonly refer to sex. While sex can be an expression of intimacy, it is not true intimacy in and of itself. A large percentage of our clients who have engaged in infidelity-related behavior are actually searching for intimacy and, instead, using sex as a replacement for it. Sex, in and of itself, often requires no true intimacy at all. Aside from the risk of possibly being rejected for actually getting to have sex, the act of sex takes very little risk on our part. This is why sex outside of the primary relationship, empty sex within the primary relationship (checking out emotionally), pornography, and even emotional affairs become enticing temporary substitutes for real intimacy to someone who struggles to share their true self with their partner. In the case of addiction, these temporary substitutes are clear examples of ways in which a person struggling to participate in true intimacy begins to fill the void in destructive ways.

Proverbs 5 MSG

1 Dear friend, pay close attention to this, my wisdom; listen very closely to the way I see it. 2 Then you'll acquire a taste for good sense; what I tell you will keep you out of trouble. 3 The lips of a seductive woman are oh so sweet, her soft words are oh so smooth. 4 But it won't be long before she's gravel in your mouth, a pain in your gut, a wound in your heart. 5 She's dancing down the primrose path to Death; she's headed straight for Hell and taking you with her. 6 She hasn't a clue about Real Life, about who she is or where she's going. 7 So, my friend, listen closely; don't treat my words casually. 8 Keep your distance from such a woman; absolutely stay out of her neighborhood. 9 You don't want to squander your wonderful life, to waste your precious life among the

hardhearted. 10 *Why should you allow strangers to take advantage of you? Why be exploited by those who care nothing for you?* 11 *You don't want to end your life full of regrets, nothing but sin and bones,* 12 *Saying, "Oh, why didn't I do what they told me? Why did I reject a disciplined life?* 13 *Why didn't I listen to my mentors, or take my teachers seriously?* 14 *My life is ruined! I haven't one blessed thing to show for my life!"*
Never Take Love for Granted

15 *Do you know the saying, "Drink from your own rain barrel, draw water from your own spring-fed well"?* 16 *It's true. Otherwise, you may one day come home and find your barrel empty and your well polluted.* 17 *Your spring water is for you and you only, not to be passed around among strangers.* 18 *Bless your fresh-flowing fountain! Enjoy the wife you married as a young man!* 19 *Lovely as an angel, beautiful as a rose - don't ever quit taking delight in her body. Never take her love for granted!* 20 *Why would you trade enduring intimacies for cheap thrills with a whore? for dalliance with a promiscuous stranger?* 21 *Mark well that God doesn't miss a move you make; he's aware of every step you take.* 22 *The shadow of your sin will overtake you; you'll find yourself stumbling all over yourself in the dark.* 23 *Death is the reward of an undisciplined life; your foolish decisions trap you in a dead end.*

Types of Intimacy

When it comes to intimacy, there are 5 different areas that we typically talk about. These are:

- Physical. This includes anything from small displays of affection such as placing a hand on someone's leg to large displays of affection such as sex.
- Emotional. This means feeling emotionally connected with your partner through the safe sharing of emotions and thoughts.
- Spiritual. This involves being able to share your spirituality with your partner without fear of judgement.
- Intellectual. This involves being able to share your thoughts and opinions with each other in a safe environment. It also involves stimulating each other's minds.
- Experiential. This type of intimacy describes the bonding that can happen through shared activity.

People experience intimacy in these areas at different levels, depending on who they are interacting with. Regarding healthy committed, romantic relationships, healthy intimacy should be shared at several levels. This includes being able to share your thoughts and opinions, hopes and dreams, feelings, vulnerabilities, and needs.

When betrayal happens in a relationship, it undermines all areas of intimacy—not just physical. This is because there is a lack of safety in the relationship, especially for the wounded partner. For them, the feeling of safety they may have had that rested on the sense that they were working toward something with a partner that was equally committed to the health of the relationship has been completely undermined. If you are a wounding partner reading this, we would stress the importance of understanding this truth.

When it comes to intimacy after betrayal, aside from the wounding partner ending their infidelity-related behavior, the expression of remorse, empathy, and compassion are the most important components of rekindling closeness. If the wounding partner cannot express remorse for what they have done, and show empathy and compassion toward their partner, intimacy is unlikely to develop, and recovery will stall out. When we think about real love, we tend to think about emotions and behaviors that are characterized by commitment and self-sacrifice. In committed relationships, this means laying down personal plans and agendas that conflict with the good of the relationship. Infidelity is the antithesis of love because it involves self-focus to the detriment of the relationship and the wounded partner. If intimacy is to be restored, love must be shown by the wounding partner's actions and attitudes. These actions and attitudes must support the good of the relationship and must show that the wounding partner is no longer putting their wishes and desires above those of the wounded partner. This includes defending, blaming, minimization, stonewalling, and any other attitude or action that puts the wounding partner's need to be right or protected from shame above the good of the wounded partner and the relationship.

Conversely, if intimacy is to be restored, the wounded partner will need to find a way to work through the resentments caused by the wounding partner's betrayal. Additionally, strict adherence to the communication plan will show a commitment on the wounded partner's part to the good of the relationship. Yelling, shaming, name-calling, although typical after a betrayal of trust, will hinder intimacy because the wounded partner is focused on their own need to vent rather than on the good of the relationship. When we make this statement to wounded partners, they often counter with the fact that they should not have to worry about the good of the relationship when the wounding partner obviously didn't care about it. While we certainly understand this sentiment, we must point out that two wrongs do not make a right. Each person in the relationship must take responsibility for their own actions, regardless of what the other person has done in the past or is still doing.

Luke 6: 43-49 MSG

A Tree Is Known by Its Fruit

43 *"You don't get wormy apples off a healthy tree, nor good apples off a diseased tree.* 44 *The health of the apple tells the health of the tree. You must begin with your own life-giving lives.* 45 *It's who you are, not what you say and do, that counts. Your true being brims over into true words and deeds*

The House Built on a Rock

46 *"Why are you so polite with me, always saying 'Yes, sir,' and 'That's right, sir,' but never doing a thing I tell you?* 47 *These words I speak to you are not mere additions to your life, homeowner improvements to your standard of living. They are foundation words, words to build a life on.* 48 *"If you work the words into your life, you are like a*

smart carpenter who dug deep and laid the foundation of his house on bedrock. When the river burst its banks and crashed against the house, nothing could shake it; it was built to last. 49 *But if you just use my words in Bible studies and don't work them into your life, you are like a dumb carpenter who built a house but skipped the foundation. When the swollen river came crashing in, it collapsed like a house of cards. It was a total loss."*

Resuming Sex After Betrayal

Probably the most common questions we get from couples we work with surround resuming sex after betrayal. First, we would like to state that when to resume sex after betrayal is a personal decision that must be made by the individuals in the relationship. That being said, we usually recommend a hiatus from sex within the first 60-90 days after disclosure of sexual infidelity because sex after infidelity is complicated and the first 2-3 months are typically fraught with indecisiveness and emotional volatility. Resuming sex too soon can cause confusion, not to mention that sex, when used incorrectly, can cover up a multitude of issues related to intimacy that need to be focused on.

Although most of the couples we work with have trouble resuming sex after infidelity, we felt it important to mention that a significant percentage of them actually report sex being more frequent and better than ever. This is not uncommon and is usually fueled by the insecurity created by the betrayal—which then creates an intense need to reconnect. It can also be fueled by the wounded partner's need to be desirable to the wounding partner. Although we want to stress that this is a completely normal response to the pain caused by betrayal, we want to also mention that it is not likely to last—and that is okay. This can be confusing for both partners, especially for the wounding partner, but it does not mean that the relationship is over or that it was wrong. There is no script for resuming sexual intimacy after infidelity. Additionally, if you want to continue to have sex on a regular basis, that is okay too. However, we would caution you not to use sex as your only form of intimacy. It is imperative that you both work on strengthening your bond in the other areas of intimacy as well. Otherwise, your relationship will likely fail to thrive in the long term.

If you are a wounded partner who has had trouble with sexual intimacy and is considering resuming sex after betrayal, we advise that you honor your mind and body while making your decision. This means paying close attention to the signs that you are experiencing any sort of trauma response. These can include feeling pressured to resume sex, tension around the subject, disassociation, intrusive thoughts, extreme anger, aggressiveness, overwhelming shame, or hyperarousal before, during, and after sex. The presence of these things are completely normal after experiencing the trauma of betrayal. However, they are signs that you may need to slow things down. Additionally, if your relationship has suffered from your partner's sexual infidelity, we always recommend STI/STD testing prior to resuming sex. You may find it helpful to work with a qualified coach or counselor on this subject, as going through this process can often produce intense emotions.

When it comes to resuming sex after betrayal, especially after sexual infidelity, communication and patience on the part of both partners are key. Resuming sexual intimacy can be a tricky business. The presence of flashbacks, intrusive thoughts, and resentments along with the erosion of trust make it difficult. Truly intimate sex requires vulnerability, and vulnerability is hard to come by when trust has been betrayed. This is why it is imperative that both partners stick to their recovery plans whenever possible. If defending, minimization, blaming, stonewalling, and unbridled emotional expression are taking place on a regular basis, sex will often feel unsafe. We feel it important to point out that resuming sexual intimacy after betrayal, especially after sexual infidelity, is usually slow going. Both partners will need to have patience with themselves as well as with the other. Making accommodations for your sex life in the light of betrayal is paramount. Unfortunately, the expectation that you can just pick up where you left off is unrealistic. If you do not realize this and make accommodations for it, you risk hurting yourself and your partner. There is no deadline for when things should be "back to normal". The truth is that your sexual intimacy may never be the same as it was prior to the betrayal. However, this does not mean that things can't ever be good again. Give yourselves time and patience while you reestablish your sexual relationship.

It is important that the wounded partner build up their vocabulary when it comes to expressing their needs around safety regarding sex. This includes not only expressing when they do and do not wish to engage in sexual intimacy, but also communication about how their sexuality has been affected by their partner's betrayal. Additionally, it is important that the couple be in regular communication regarding sex. This can be difficult to do in the face of trauma, particularly if the couple's sex life was a point of contention prior to the betrayal. We recommend that couples do not try to go this communication alone but enlist the help of a trained coach or counselor to help facilitate the process. We cannot stress enough that whoever you hire to help you should be trained and experienced in the area of recovery, as your situation will present unique obstacles and challenges that are unlike other intimacy issues found in relationships that have not been affected by betrayal.

Regarding intrusive thoughts and flashbacks, we want to stress that this is a normal part of the trauma response to betrayal. The frequency we see this in our practice can vary from person to person. However, in the case of sexual infidelity, we see at least some form of this in 100% of our clients. It is important that the couple communicate about this on a regular basis and that the wounding partner show empathy and concern for the wounded partner's experience. It is also important to understand that when the wounded partner has a traumatic response, both partners should stop the sexual activity to talk through the issue prior to resuming. We have never seen good results from wounded partners "powering through" traumatic responses. Nor have we seen benefit to the relationship or the wounded partner when the wounding partner pressures them to keep going or acts inconvenienced or annoyed that they had to stop.

If you are a wounding partner reading this, we would like to impress upon you that your partner's trauma response is involuntary and is not something they are doing to punish or shame you. Your partner's traumatic responses are a result of your infidelity-related behavior. We do not say this to shame you in any way. However, it is imperative that you understand the consequences of your behavior and show your partner compassion and empathy when they are working through their reactions.

One final thing we would like to add here is that much of the work to be done regarding triggers, intrusive thoughts, and flashbacks falls to the wounded partner. Although this may seem unfair, there is no way around it. Unfortunately, the wounding partner can only do so much to help the wounded partner heal. Working through resentments, developing productive communication skills, and finding ways to self-soothe when triggered are all important to the process of rebuilding sexual intimacy. Additionally, the wounded partner may also benefit significantly from EMDR therapy. Eye Movement Desensitization and Reprocessing (EMDR) therapy is a therapy that has been proven to be effective when it comes symptoms of trauma such as PTSD and has helped many betrayed partners heal. This type of therapy uses bilateral stimulation to help the brain work through the fears, thoughts, beliefs, and pain often associated with betrayal trauma.

2 Corinthians 10:3-6 MSG

3 The world is unprincipled. It's dog-eat-dog out there! The world doesn't fight fair. But we don't live or fight our battles that way - never have and never will. 4 The tools of our trade aren't for marketing or manipulation, but they are for demolishing that entire massively corrupt culture. 5 We use our powerful God-tools for smashing warped philosophies, tearing down barriers erected against the truth of God, fitting every loose thought and emotion and impulse into the structure of life shaped by Christ. 6 Our tools are ready at hand for clearing the ground of every obstruction and building lives of obedience into maturity.

Romans 12: 6-21 MSG

If you preach, just preach God's Message, nothing else; 7 if you help, just help, don't take over; if you teach, stick to your teaching; 8 if you give encouraging guidance, be careful that you don't get bossy; if you're put in charge, don't manipulate; if you're called to give aid to people in distress, keep your eyes open and be quick to respond; if you work with the disadvantaged, don't let yourself get irritated with them or depressed by them. Keep a smile on your face. 9 Love from the center of who you are; don't fake it. Run for dear life from evil; hold on for dear life to good. 10 Be good friends who love deeply; practice playing second fiddle. 11 Don't burn out; keep yourselves fueled and aflame. Be alert servants of the Master, 12 cheerfully expectant. Don't quit in hard times; pray all the harder. 13 Help needy Christians; be inventive in hospitality. 14 Bless your enemies; no cursing under your breath. 15 Laugh with your happy friends when they're happy; share tears when they're down. 16 Get along with each other; don't be stuck-up. Make friends with nobodies; don't be the great somebody. 17 Don't hit back; discover beauty in everyone. 18 If you've got it in you, get along with everybody. 19 Don't insist on getting even; that's not for you to do. "I'll do the judging," says God. "I'll take care of it." 20

Our Scriptures tell us that if you see your enemy hungry, go buy that person lunch, or if he's thirsty, get him a drink. Your generosity will surprise him with goodness. 21 *Don't let evil get the best of you; get the best of evil by doing good.*

Prayer for the wounded and the wounding partner:

Father,

Give us the grace to demolish warped philosophies and tear down barriers that erect themselves against the truth of God's word. Give us the grace to take every loose and destructive thought, emotion and impulse and restructure our mind, will and emotions to live a life shaped by Christ. Give us the grace to love ourselves and our partner from our core. Give us the grace not to quit in hard times and pray all the harder. Cause us to discover the beauty in ourselves and in each other. We love You and submit our lives to You. In Jesus' name. Amen.

PART 25

The Importance of Cultivating Good Intimacy Habits

As we alluded to previously, it is important that your approach to intimacy after betrayal be a balanced one. This means cultivating intimacy in all areas. When it comes to physical intimacy, it is important to note that non-sexual touch is extremely important in creating safety in the relationship. This is especially true if addiction has been a factor. If you are a wounding partner and have an addiction to sex or pornography, it will be important that you learn to express your desire for your partner in other ways besides asking for sex. Many times wounded partners in relationships with addicts report feeling used. When a wounding partner only expresses their need for intimacy in a sexual manner or only seems interested in their partner when they know that sex is on the table, this compounds the problem. It is also important to note that an addictive mindset can put undue pressure on the wounded partner to resume sex before they are truly ready. If you are a wounding partner reading this and addiction is an issue for you, you will need to pay close attention to how much pressure you are putting on the wounded partner to fill your sexual needs. Badgering, demanding sex from them as "proof" that they love you, reacting negatively with hurt, anger, sadness or resentment, or threatening negative consequences to the relationship (either overtly or subtly) is coercive. Although this may get you what you want in the short term, it will eventually backfire.

When it comes to the cultivation and development of healthy intimacy habits, it is important to realize that the process is similar to building any healthy habit. When developing habits that support an intimate relationship, here are some things to keep in mind:

- Focus on creating one habit at a time (in the case of recovery, this could be several related habits)
- Commit to a set amount of time for each habit (usually between 30 and 90 days)
- Anchor the new habit in something you already do regularly. (An example would be doing an intimacy-building exercise prior to engaging in your morning routine of getting ready for work.)

- Do the intimacy-building activity every day without fail
- Plan for challenges or obstacles by using if/then scenarios. (An example of this would be if you can't do the activity before work, then you will take time to do it in the middle of your day.)
- Put accountability in place around your new habit

Once a couple gets through the discovery/disclosure phase, it will be important that intimacy-building routines be established. The idea here is to give each partner a chance to connect to the other while giving the relationship room to breathe away from discussions around the betrayal. This often includes the following:

- Regular dates
- Meditation, gratitude and/or prayer
- Daily expression of appreciation
- Daily sharing of feelings
- Shared activities
- Discussion about the betrayal or related issues
- Sex

Let's take a closer look at each one:

Intimacy-Builder #1: Regular Dates

For couples looking to rebuild intimacy, regular time set aside to spend together is key. We recommend that dates be done on a weekly basis. One caveat here is that the time set aside for the date should not be used to discuss the betrayal. The purpose of a weekly date is to allow the couple time to reconnect outside of what has taken place. Discussions after betrayal are often all-consuming. Early on, it is not unusual for conversations around what happened to take up several hours per day. If you are to reconnect with each other in any meaningful way, it will be important to protect your weekly date by committing to each other that discussion of infidelity-related issues is off limits.

Weekly dates are particularly important for relationships in which intimacy avoidance is a complicating factor. Since these relationships are typically devoid of true intimacy, time set aside to focus on one another is part of recovery. When we work with intimacy avoidants during intensives, we always include the weekly date as part of the recovery plan. It is important to note that the IA should plan the date each week as a part of their commitment to ongoing recovery. The IA should plan the date for a set period of time. Once recovery in this area is established, each partner can trade off planning the date. For couples where intimacy avoidance is not an issue, partners can take turns in the planning.

In order to facilitate connection, we recommend that you commit to asking each other questions in order to get to know each other better and to discover what each of you appreciates about the other. John and Julie Gottman, co-authors of the book *Eight Dates: Essential Conversations for a Lifetime of Love*, have developed whole card decks with many open-ended questions that couples can ask each other in order to help facilitate connection. Generally speaking, questions should not be ones that can be answered with a simple yes or no, but ones that require thought. Here are some examples:

- If you could be one age forever, which age would you choose and why?
- What in your life makes you feel the most grateful? Why?
- What is the best gift you have ever received? Why?
- If you could live in any era, what would it be and why?
- What have you done that you feel the proudest of? Why?
- What is the funniest thing you have ever had happen to you?

Intimacy-Builder #2: Meditation, Gratitude, or Prayer

For those couples who pray, prayer is a time when partners can feel spiritually connected. It gives each partner insight into what is important to the other, which can bring a couple closer. If you are not a couple who prays, meditation is also a powerful way to spiritually connect. Additionally, making a gratitude list is not only a great practice, but it can also help partners feel closer when each one learns what the other is grateful for.

Intimacy-Builder #3: Daily Expression of Appreciation

Let's face it, few things can put a negative spin on a relationship quite like infidelity can. If you refer back to the time-out protocol in the section on safety, you will see that we ask partners to state at least one positive attribute about each other prior to resuming a tough conversation. This is because it creates a culture of appreciation in the relationship. Much in the same vein, we recommend that each partner state at least 2 things they appreciate or admire about the other one at the start of each day and at least 1 thing prior to going to bed each night. If you are not able to be together in person, consider texting or emailing each other. Please note that this does not cancel out the legitimate pain caused by the wounding partner's betrayal in any way. However, when expressing appreciation is made a priority, it can help combat the negativity that inherently comes from the discovery or disclosure of betrayal.

Intimacy-Builder #4: Daily Sharing of Feelings

Many couples have trouble sharing emotions with each other. This is particularly true of relationships characterized by intimacy avoidance. When we work with couples, we always ask them to share two feelings with each other at the same time each day. One caveat here is that the feelings shared should not be related to those caused by the betrayal. Much like weekly dates, this time should be protected from the turmoil caused by the wounding partner's behavior. We recommend that two feelings be shared at the same time as daily expression of appreciation.

Intimacy-Builder #5: Shared Activities

Shared activities are important building blocks of intimacy and friendship. These shared activities should take place at a time when you can both agree to put discussion of the betrayal aside in order to give your relationship some breathing room. Some simple ideas for shared activities include:

- Exercise together
- Reading the same book and discussing it
- Cooking a meal together
- Eating together
- Volunteering together

Intimacy-Builder #6:

Discussion About the Betrayal and Related Issues

For couples dealing with the aftermath of betrayal, it is important that time is set aside to discuss the betrayal, feelings surrounding what has happened, and any other related issues. It is especially important to note that the wounding partner should make themselves available to the wounded partner as a way of showing them that they care about what has happened. When the wounding partner avoids conversations, or shuts them down with defensiveness, indifference, annoyance, or stonewalling, they send a message to the wounded partner that they don't care about how their actions have affected them. We understand that conversations around betrayal are likely uncomfortable for the wounding partner and often bring on feelings of guilt and even shame. However, some of the most powerful examples we have seen of couples who have healed from betrayal are those where the wounding partner made it a point of being available for these tough conversations by asking the wounded partner what questions they could answer or if they needed to express their feelings regarding what they had done.

Intimacy-Builder #7: Sex

As we previously explained, sex after betrayal (particularly sexual infidelity) can be tricky. (See previous section on resuming sex after betrayal.) We want to reiterate that patience, compassion, and empathy are crucial to this process. We also want to point out that it is imperative that sex be resumed when the wounded partner is ready and that it should not be driven by the wounding partner's needs to be satisfied. Many couples we work with find it helpful to schedule a time to be sexually intimate with each other. We realize that scheduling sex may seem counter-intuitive when it comes to intimacy. However, in our experience, the subject of sex is often avoided by couples—especially after betrayal. Scheduling a regular time to be sexually intimate can provide opportunities for a couple to work through the many issues that inevitably arise from betrayal.

2 Peter 1:3-11 MSG

3 Everything that goes into a life of pleasing God has been miraculously given to us by getting to know, personally and intimately, the One who invited us to God. The best invitation we ever received! 4 We were also given absolutely terrific promises to pass on to you - your tickets to participation in the life of God after you turned your back on a world corrupted by lust.

5 So don't lose a minute in building on what you've been given, complementing your basic faith with good character, spiritual understanding, 6 alert discipline, passionate patience, reverent wonder, 7 warm friendliness, and generous love, each dimension fitting into and developing the others. 8 With these qualities active and growing in your lives, no grass will grow under your feet, no day will pass without its reward as you mature in your experience of our Master Jesus. 9 Without these qualities you can't see what's right before you, oblivious that your old sinful life has been wiped off the books. 10 So, friends, confirm God's invitation to you, his choice of you. Don't put it off; do it now. Do this, and you'll have your life on a firm footing, 11 the streets paved and the way wide open into the eternal kingdom of our Master and Savior, Jesus Christ.

Romans 8:37-39 NLT

No, despite all these things, overwhelming victory is ours through Christ, who loved us. 38 And I am convinced that nothing can ever separate us from God's love. Neither death nor life, neither angels nor demons, neither our fears for today nor our worries about tomorrow-not even the powers of hell can separate us from God's love. 39 No power in the sky above or in the earth below-indeed, nothing in all creation will ever be able to separate us from the love of God that is revealed in Christ Jesus our Lord.

Prayer for the wounding and the wounded partner:

Father, we are convinced that despite all that we have been through, overwhelming victory is ours through Christ who loved us. Nothing can separate us from Christ's love. And we will mimic Christ and not allow the powers of hell to separate us. We will not lose a minute on rebuilding our lives on the information we've been given, complementing our basic faith with good character, spiritual understanding, alert discipline, passionate patience, reverent wonder, warm friendliness, and generous love for each other. We will learn to grow in each dimension, fitting into each other's lives and developing each other. We will live in the light of God's word and be transformed into the image of Christ. In Jesus' name. Amen

Part 26

What is Forgiveness?

We want to start off by saying that these chapters on forgiveness are not going to be as applicable to you as other chapters of this book if you are still in the discovery/disclosure phase of infidelity. This is not to say that the words and ideas contained in these chapters won't be worth reading. However, wounded partner, if you don't have a clear idea of what has transpired, it is best to hold off on trying to forgive until you have the full picture because you can't forgive what you are not aware of. This section on forgiveness is most applicable to couples who have been out of the discovery/disclosure phase for at least 6 months and are trying to find a way to move forward.

The term "forgiveness" describes a person's conscious decision to let go of feelings of resentment and/or the need for revenge toward a person or people who have harmed them. Forgiveness is a personal decision that can happen whether or not the person or people being forgiven actually deserve it and/or are sorry for their behavior. Forgiveness is entirely different from reconciliation, which we will discuss in more detail later.

Jesus gives us an example of how we can forgive people regardless of whether they are sorry for what they have done to us.

Luke 23:24 ESV

"Jesus said, 'Father, forgive them, for they do not know what they are doing.' And they divided up His clothes by casting lots."

Jesus asked the Father to forgive those who were killing him while they were actively sinning against Him and gambling for His clothing. If Jesus had been focused on injustice, He would not have been focused on His Father. Instead, He would have been in bondage to their sins against Him. He couldn't have been comforted by the presence of His Father in the midst of His suffering if He had focused on the wrongs being done to Him.

We know that none of us is Jesus and so forgiving those who do us wrong often seems like an impossible task. However, Jesus was our example of what a life submitted to the Father looks like, and we are to try and follow His example.

Ephesians 5:1-2 ESV

Therefore be imitators of God, as beloved children. And walk in love, as Christ loved us and gave Himself up for us, a fragrant offering and sacrifice to God.

When we talk to our clients about forgiveness, we like to use the analogy of debt. Let's say that a person who borrowed money from you owes you $500, but it becomes apparent for one reason or another that they will never be able to repay you. You could waste precious time and energy on trying to get them to repay you, but the fact of the matter is that the debt can't be repaid. You could decide, for your own sake, to forgive the debt because you don't want to spend any more time on it. The person may or may not be sorry that they can't repay you, but that is irrelevant. You decide for your own sake to let it go because you determine that spending time and energy on something that can't be repaid is a poor use of your resources. That is forgiveness in a nutshell.

This scenario is similar to the debt owed to wounded partners when they learn of the wounding partner's infidelity. As sad as it is, infidelity creates a debt that can never be repaid. This is not to say that accountability isn't important, but that has more to do with reconciliation than it does with forgiveness. At some point, a wounded partner has to make a personal decision about whether they are going to try to make their partner "pay" for what they have done, or if they are going to give up the right to seek restitution and retribution for their partner's unfaithful actions. Based on our experience with working with hundreds of wounded partners, we will tell you that trying to make someone pay for their misdeeds and/or be sorry for their actions is a waste of time and energy. Time and time again, we have seen that it produces nothing but anger, pain, and frustration.

Exodus 14:14 ESV

The Lord will fight for you, and you have only to be silent.

Wounded partner, if you are facing a situation in which your partner is not repentant for the wrongs they have done to you, we are truly sorry for your pain. Instead of wasting your time and energy trying to make them sorry, set it in your mind that God will do the fighting for you. As you decide to be silent, know that God will be working on this in His own way. It may not make sense to you, or you may not be able to see it, but it IS happening. Your silence will allow God to fight. You are stepping aside and giving it to Him. Being quiet is an act of faith. Pray that God will step into the situation for you because, otherwise, your anger will destroy you and He does not want that.

Wounded partner, the act of forgiveness is an internal matter. It is not done for someone else, and it is not done because someone is sorry (although hopefully they are). It is done for your own sake. The act of forgiveness allows you the opportunity to live in peace of mind and heart. It can give you the ability to put your partner's bad actions behind you and move forward, however you choose to do that, without the weight of those actions around your neck. It can also help you stay out of a powerless "victim" mentality, because forgiveness is a decision you use your internal power to make in order to move on from the actions of others. As such, it means that what someone did to you does not have to rule your life forever. *Forgiveness is the antidote to the corrosiveness of anger, resentment, and the need for vengeance.*

James 1:20 ESV

For the anger of man does not produce the righteousness of God.

Sometimes we hold onto our anger, hurt, and resentment because it makes us feel powerful in a powerless situation. We can also hold onto it because we think that the person who hurt us will get off the hook if we let it go. While anger can be a useful catalyst for confrontation when someone's actions need correcting, holding onto it won't produce long-term change in that person. Only God can change their heart. We need to understand that our anger cannot make someone else do right by us, nor can it substitute for someone else's conscience. Anger can eventually become an idol that harms our relationship with God. Our power is in Him, not in our anger and resentment.

A Word About "Instant" Forgiveness

True forgiveness is difficult to achieve. It is a process, not a one-time event. True forgiveness isn't something that can be manufactured, and it is not something that can, or should, be decided upon quickly.

When she was young, Laura's family occasionally went camping. She remembers watching her dad put out the campfire. She noticed that he took several steps to accomplish that. First, he stopped adding the fuel that was keeping the fire going.

Psalm 37:8 ESV

Refrain from anger and forsake wrath; do not fret, it leads only to evil.

> *Fixating on our circumstances is the fuel that keeps the fire of anger going. If we fix our eyes on God instead, it will allow for the flames of our rage to burn out.*

Next, he let the fire burn down so that the flames were much smaller. After that, he poured water on it. Then, he stirred the ashes of the fire to mix the water through.

Isaiah 12:3-4 ESV

With joy you will draw water from the wells of salvation, and you will say on that day: "give thanks to the Lord, call upon His name. Make known His deeds among the peoples, proclaim that His name is exalted."

> *The water we can pour onto the fire comes from the wells of salvation. To draw this water up, we need to praise God and call on His name instead of fretting. Remember what He has done for you and others. Proclaim that He is bigger than your issues. His is the name above all names. As you proclaim this, you will be proclaiming this both to God and to yourself, and as your spirit hears this, it will begin to be soothed.*

Finally, he came back and checked the fire to make sure that it was out. If it was still going, he would repeat some of those steps.

Proverbs 4:23, 25-26 ESV

Keep your heart with all vigilance. For from it flow the springs of life. Let your eyes look directly forward and your gaze be straight before you. Ponder the path of your feet, then all your ways will be sure.

> If we aren't vigilant enough to keep coming back to check on the fire, it can flare up in our hearts. We have to keep pouring the water on, because the fire is intense and large, and it will take a while to douse. This requires diligence.

Proverbs 21:5 ESV

The plans of the diligent lead surely to abundance, but everyone who is hasty comes only to poverty.

Be diligent in your recovery work.

Wounded partner, the pain of your partner's infidelity often creates a burning fire, and the process of forgiveness is like the steps Laura's dad took to put the fire out. *Forgiveness is not water that you can pour over the raging fire of infidelity in hopes that it will snuff out the pain caused by it, nor the present and future damage done by it.* If the proper steps aren't taken to put out the fire, it is highly likely to resurface.

Although forgiveness can be elusive and difficult for many of our clients, a handful of them seem to have the opposite issue. We have had a number of clients in our office that tell us that they have already forgiven their partner's infidelity-related behavior within months, weeks, days, and even a few hours of discovering it. This is not to say that you can't have a willingness to consider forgiveness now. However, we must warn you that forgiving too quickly will only set you up for heartache and frustration later on. We wish we had better news to tell you but, the truth is, there is simply no shortcut to forgiveness.

Our experiences have led us to conclude that our clients offer forgiveness too soon for the following reasons:

- They receive messages from friends, family, religious leaders, or coaches or counselors that they must forgive right away.
- They feel pressured by the wounding partner's need to be forgiven and/or the wounding partner is actively pressuring them to forgive.
- They are putting pressure on themselves to forgive.
- They are forgiving in an attempt to escape their pain.

Let's take a look at each one of these more closely:

1. **They receive messages from friends, family, coaches or counselors, or religious leaders that they must forgive right away.** Unfortunately, this is quite common. Well-meaning family, friends, religious leaders, and even coaches and counselors can send the message that if you would only forgive, everything would get better. This isn't accurate and, although they mean well, we would advise you to disregard their advice in this matter. Additionally, if someone tells you that nothing will get better until you forgive or that your pain is an indication of unforgiveness, we urge you to disregard this type of advice as well. Although most people who give this type of advice are well-meaning, there are also some who will shame you for not forgiving soon after the infidelity. What I would say to that is there's a difference between having an attitude of forgiveness and actually forgiving. An attitude of being open to forgiveness is something to strive for. Instantaneous forgiveness is unrealistic and damaging to everyone involved.

2. **They feel pressured by the wounding partner's need to be forgiven and/or the wounding partner is actively pressuring them to forgive.** Although it's certainly understandable that your partner may want to be forgiven, we advise you to hold off on saying that you forgive them until you are truly ready. The guilt felt by your partner for what they have done to you and the relationship is theirs to deal with, not yours. If your partner is pressuring you to "get over it" or "just forgive," this is actually a red flag. We have seen many wounding partners do this in an attempt to alleviate their own suffering. While we never advocate for wounded partners to hold forgiveness over the wounding partner's head as a way to make them pay, it's not appropriate for you to forgive them at the expense of your own wellbeing — which is what you would be doing. If you are dealing with either of these two scenarios, our advice would be to answer with, "I want to forgive you, and I am working toward it. However, I am not there yet." If your partner persists, you may need to enlist expert help in order to help them to understand why this isn't appropriate.

3. **They are putting pressure on themselves to forgive.** In our experience, some wounded partners put a large amount of pressure on themselves to forgive. This is typically because either, a) they want to adhere to the requirements of their religion, or b) they want to ensure that the relationship makes it. Although there may be other reasons as well, these are the two most common reasons that we see in my office. While we can appreciate the desire to adhere to religious requirements, Bible verses dealing with forgiveness are often misinterpreted. Although it is true that God forgives us instantaneously, we would ask you to remember that God has abilities that we as humans do not. While we can ask God to help us to eventually forgive, we can also rest assured that God understands our human struggles and limitations.

> When partners want to forgive so that the relationship makes it, it is usually because a) they fear how their anger and hurt might damage their relationship, or b) their partner is unrepentant and has threatened to withdraw or leave if they do not let it go. Although it is understandable that some of us fear how our pain might influence us to react, we

can assure you that instantaneous forgiveness does nothing to fix our feelings. If your partner is unrepentant or threatening physical and/or emotional abandonment, this is inappropriate and abusive. Unfortunately, this is not uncommon in relationships, especially if the wounding partner struggles with sexual or pornography addiction, intimacy avoidance, or intimacy anorexia®. If this describes your situation, please reach out to a coach or counselor who is trained in this area to help you remain strong in your boundaries. Help can also be found at www.coda.org for those of you who may be struggling with codependency.

4. **They are forgiving in an attempt to escape their pain.** Unfortunately, forgiveness is not a magic pill you can take to escape the pain our partner's actions have caused you. Just like in the analogy of the fire we used above; the fire caused by the pain of infidelity-related behavior needs to be carefully tended in order to ensure that it doesn't reignite later on. If you remain in denial about the ways in which your partner's actions have affected you, you will only delay and/or prolong your pain.

In our experience, wounded partners who forgive too quickly set themselves up for pitfalls later on. Wounded partner, here are some of the ways that forgiving too soon can affect you:

1. **You may stuff your emotions.** Stuffing emotions, especially the intense emotions resulting from infidelity, can cause a myriad of problems to your mental, spiritual, and physical health. Studies have linked repressed emotions to depression, anxiety, heart disease, digestive issues, and more.

2. **You set yourself up for unnecessary guilt later on.** Instantaneous forgiveness is not real forgiveness. When you say you forgive your partner and then realize you still have pain and anger, you can set yourself up for self-criticism and/or judgment. We have had numerous partners come to us because they felt guilty about not forgiving their partner's infidelity-related behavior. The issue with instant forgiveness is that you can only forgive what you are aware of at a particular moment in time. This is not possible in the case of infidelity because wounded partners experience new awareness of its effects for months and years beyond discovery/disclosure. This is a normal part of the recovery process.

3. **You might be sending confusing messages to our partner.** When you tell your partner that you forgive them and then struggle with your feelings later on, you risk sending confusing messages. It would be better to tell them that you will try to work toward forgiveness than that you have totally forgiven them. As we stated previously, it is a normal part of a wounded partner's recovery process to become newly aware of pain resulting from their partner's actions months and years after discovery/disclosure of the infidelity. Forgiveness will be an ongoing process as new realizations come to light and bring new pain with them.

4. **You deny yourself the ability to explore your pain.** You will likely feel the pain of betrayal for numerous reasons. Wounded partners can feel pain from the actual betrayal, the fact that your partner shared intimacy with someone other than you, being gaslit, being lied to, and more. Forgiving your partner too quickly will be detrimental to your healing in the long run. It will take time to dissect your partner's betrayal in order to identify and deal with each of the areas that the pain is coming from.

5. **You might be letting the wounding partner off the hook too easily.** Let us preface this by stating that we are not advocating for the wounded partner to hold forgiveness over the wounding partner's head in order to make them pay. However, letting your partner off the hook by telling them you forgive them too soon can backfire. Your partner needs to do their own recovery work and forgiving them too soon can send the message that they do not need to take what they did seriously.

Although we advocate for partners to forgive when they are ready, forgiveness is an item of high value and should never be handed out cheaply. A wounded partner's willingness to forgive the wounding partner's egregious behavior is an act of mercy. It is at the core of who we are as people. Once a wounded partner forgives, they are relinquishing their right to future retribution and/or restitution. This is important, and it costs them something. Although the idea that the wounded partner should make the wounding partner pay by refusing to forgive them is an erroneous one, it does not mean that their willingness to extend forgiveness to them is worthless or should be offered lightly.

Part 27

What Forgiveness Is Not

As important as it is to talk about what forgiveness is, it is equally as important to talk about what it is not. When we get pushback from our clients on the concept of forgiveness, it is almost always because they have misconceptions about what it means to forgive. Here is a list of some of the things forgiveness is not:

- A one-time event
- The same as forgetting about what happened
- An obligation to reconcile
- The same as extending trust
- Agreeing with, excusing, condoning, or denying a wounding partner's bad behavior
- A feeling
- The same as tolerating bad behavior

Let's look at each one of these in greater detail:

1. **Forgiveness is not a one-time event.** Forgiveness is more of a process than a one-time event. A wounded partner can decide to forgive someone but still have times when they remember the pain and are angry about it. Just because a wounded partner feels hurt, sad, and angry about what has happened does not mean that they are unforgiving. If you, as a wounded partner, are working toward forgiveness, reestablish your commitment to forgive each time you have painful memories so that bitterness, anger, and resentment don't take over.

2. **Forgiveness is not the same as forgetting about what happened.** Just as the ability to sense danger has helped the human race survive, so has the ability to remember traumatic events. Our brains are wired to remember painful and/or dangerous situations so that we can learn from them. As a wounded partner, you will always remember what has happened. However, the purpose of forgiveness is to allow you to remember without being taken over by the emotions that accompany your memories.

3. **Forgiveness is not an obligation to reconcile.** Although forgiveness is a key component of reconciliation, to forgive someone **does not** necessarily mean that a wounded partner is ready, willing, or able to reconcile with a wounding partner. Remember that forgiveness is for the wounded partner more than it is for the wounding one. When we forgive, we are freeing ourselves from the pain that resentment and bitterness can cause for us in the future. It does not mean that we need to stay with a person who was unfaithful to us if we do not want to or are not able to.

Matthew 18:15-17 ESV

If your brother sins against you, go and tell him his fault between you and him alone. If he listens to you, you have gained your brother. But if he does not listen, take one or two others along with you so that every charge may be established by the evidence of two or three witnesses. If he refuses to listen to them, tell the church. And if he refuses to listen even to the church, let him be to you as a gentile and tax collector.

These verses make it clear that it is not always possible to reconcile with your "brother," especially if he is unwilling to change his ways. The Greek word for *listen* here is **akouó**, which does mean "to listen." However, this is different from simply hearing. It means to heed — which implies that someone not only hears what is being said, but pays careful attention to it, acknowledges the validity of it, and takes action. The wounding partner must not only hear what is being said about the wrongness of their actions, but they must also accept it as valid and do something to change the attitudes that led to their infidelity-related behavior.

Proverbs 15:31-32 ESV

The ear that listens to life-giving reproof will dwell among the wise. Whoever ignores instruction despises himself, but he who listens to reproof gains intelligence.

If the wounding partner listens and heeds life-giving reproof, then reconciliation may be possible.

4. **Forgiveness is not the same as extending trust.** As we established earlier, forgiveness can be extended even when someone refuses to apologize or change their behavior. This does not hold true when extending trust. In order to trust the wounding partner again after they have proven to be unfaithful, a wounded partner needs to see tangible evidence of change on their part. We need to know that they are sorry for what they have done and understand how their actions have affected us. We also need to evaluate their actions over time in order to determine whether or not they are committed to doing whatever it takes to keep themselves from betraying us again. Confusing forgiveness and trust can put you as a wounded partner in a high-risk situation where you are likely to be hurt again.

5. **Forgiveness is not agreeing with, excusing, condoning, or denying the wounding partner's bad behavior.** In our experience, this is the number one reason that wounded partners have trouble with the concept of forgiveness. When we forgive, we are releasing the

right to restitution and/or revenge for our own mental health. However, for many of us, it is important to understand who or what we are releasing those rights to. We are releasing our rights to God. When we do this, it is often important for us to believe that it will be made right somehow in the end.

Romans 9:17-19 KJV

Repay no one evil for evil. Have regard for good things in the sight of all men. If it is possible, as much as depends on you, live peaceably with all men. Beloved, do not avenge yourselves, but rather give place to wrath; for it is written, "Vengeance is Mine, I will repay," says the Lord.

6. **Forgiveness is not a feeling.** As we stated earlier, forgiveness is a conscious choice to let go of feelings of resentment and/or the need for revenge. If we wait until we "feel" forgiving, that feeling may never come. Forgiveness is a personal choice, and, as such, must be made by each individual when the time is right. Wounded partner, if you are suffering from the effects of your anger and resentment, it is probably time to contemplate forgiveness for your own sake. Additionally, since it is a choice, you can choose more than once to forgive as bitter and painful memories come up for you over time. As we wrote previously, forgiveness is a process, not a one-time event.

7. **Forgiveness is not the same as tolerating bad behavior.** Wounded partner, deciding to forgive the wounding partner only means that you are relinquishing your rights to restitution and vengeance for their past actions, not excusing their ongoing bad behavior. It is important that you observe our partner's behavior in order to determine if you should stay with them or not. Excusing and tolerating continued infidelity-related behavior and/or abuse is never advisable. *Forgiveness is not a license for your partner to treat us with ongoing callousness and disrespect.*

Part 28

Reconciliation

We believe there has been quite an error made, especially in religious circles, when it comes to forgiveness and reconciliation. The message often given to wounded partners is that they are being unforgiving if they do not choose to or do not know if they want to reconcile with the wounding partner. This is simply not true. As we explained earlier, forgiveness can be extended to a wounding partner regardless of whether they are sorry for their actions because forgiveness is a personal choice based on the need or desire to let anger and resentment go. This is not true of reconciliation, which is completely dependent on actions. *The main difference between forgiveness and reconciliation is that forgiveness is something we can choose to do regardless of another person's attitudes and actions, while true reconciliation requires forgiveness plus action. Forgiveness is a component of reconciliation but does not guarantee it if both people are not willing to do what it takes in order to reconcile the relationship.* If a wounded partner chooses not to reconcile with a wounding partner, they likely have very good reasons for their choice. To say that a wounded partner who is unable to reconcile with an unfaithful partner is being unforgiving is incorrect at best and, at worst, unfair and cruel.

If you look up the word "reconcile" in the Merriam-Webster dictionary, you will see that it means "to restore to friendship or harmony." In order to do this, multiple things have to take place over an extended period of time. We would like to add here that merely "staying together" after infidelity does not qualify as reconciliation if the relationship is riddled with shaming, defensiveness, fighting, and distrust. The key to reconciliation is truly in its definition — a restoration of friendship and harmony.

As we wrote in the paragraph above, in order for reconciliation to truly take place, multiple things must happen over an extended period of time. In our experience, couples break up more often over how discussions about the infidelity are handled than around the infidelity itself. Here is a list of things that we believe are necessary if a relationship is to truly be reconciled:

- The infidelity-related behavior must stop
- The wounding partner must be willing to divulge all of the facts surrounding any infidelity-related behavior
- The wounding partner must show remorse for what they have done
- The wounding partner must not defend and must listen with empathy
- The wounded partner must be open to forgiveness
- The wounding partner must be accountable for their past, present, and future actions
- The wounded partner must get their anger under control
- Both parties must have patience with the process
- Both parties must be consistent
- The wounded partner must actively engage in their own recovery
- Both parties must learn how to effectively deal with triggers and reminders
- Both parties must agree to be vulnerable
- Both parties must learn how to talk about the infidelity in an open and productive manner
- Both parties should seek outside, infidelity-specific help

Let's take a closer look at each one of these points:

1. **The infidelity-related behavior must stop.** This seems like a no-brainer, but you would be surprised at how many couples come to us expecting to make progress when the unfaithful partner is unwilling or unable to decide whether or not they want to end an affair, quit looking at pornography, stop avoiding intimacy, etc. In our experience, it is impossible for a relationship to truly be reconciled when the wounding partner refuses to stop acting in ways that hurt their partner.

1 Corinthians 5:11 ESV

"Now I am writing to you not to associate with anyone who bears the name of 'brother' if he is guilty of sexual immorality or greed or is an idolator, reviler, drunkard, or swindler—not even to eat with such a one."

Paul is clear here that someone who continues in sexual sin is not to be associated with. If someone claims to be a Christian, yet continues to unrepentantly engage in sexual sin, we are to avoid them completely. Wounding partner: although you can certainly give the wounding partner time to come to their senses, the marriage may need to be reevaluated if they refuse to stop engaging in their sin.

2. The wounding partner must be willing to divulge all of the facts surrounding any infidelity-related behavior. Besides ending the infidelity-related behavior, a willingness on the wounding partner's part to "come clean" about their unfaithful actions is one of the biggest determining factors as to whether or not a relationship can be reconciled. Earlier in this book, we described how damaging "dribbling" disclosure and/or withholding information can be because, each time new information is received, it creates a new trauma for the one receiving it. Over time, this can become so damaging that the wounded partner's ability to reconcile or even to recover will likely be greatly diminished.

Proverbs 28:13 ESV

Whoever conceals their sins does not prosper, but the one who confesses and renounces them finds mercy.

The concealment of sin will cause the guilt and shame to continue. This can make it difficult for the wounding partner to move forward in their recovery. The term "finds mercy" pertains to our relationship with God. Concealing sin will derail not only a committed partner relationship, but also our relationship with God. While confessing does not guarantee the wounding partner reconciliation with you as the wounded partner, it does make it so they can be reconciled with God. This makes it possible for true and lasting change to happen, regardless of whether or not the relationship survives the infidelity.

3. The wounding partner must show remorse for what they have done. When it comes to reconciliation, this point is just as important as divulging all of the information regarding the infidelity-related behavior. If a wounding partner can't show remorse for what they have done *on a regular basis over an extended period of time*, hopes for reconciliation will be greatly reduced.

4. The wounding partner must not defend and must listen with empathy. The wounding partner's ability to listen with empathy and not defend themselves is another important factor when it comes to reconciliation. The process of recovery after infidelity is long and difficult. Defensiveness and a lack of empathy on the wounding partner's part will only cause the wounded partner to have doubts about whether or not their partner is truly remorseful.

Philippians 2:3 ESV

Do nothing out of selfish ambition or vain conceit. Rather, in humility, value others above yourselves.

When we work with wounding partners who continue to be defensive, it is often related to a lack of true humility. They fail to truly understand and accept how their actions have affected the wounded partner. When a wounding partner defends or minimizes their actions, they show the wounded partner that they are more worried about their own ego than about how their actions have hurt them. This self-serving attitude is the same one that led to infidelity in the first place.

The Bible says that sexual sin is a sin against our own body **(1 Corinthians 6:18)**. Since the Bible is clear about sexually immoral behavior being wrong, defending it in any way is absurd.

5. **The wounded partner must be open to forgiveness.** This is a tough one for many wounded partners to accept. However, wounded partner, if your relationship is to truly be restored to friendship and harmony, an attitude of unforgiveness will surely stand in the way of that. While forgiveness does not guarantee reconciliation, it is necessary if reconciliation is going to have a chance. As we wrote earlier, forgiveness does not mean excusing, condoning, or forgetting what has transpired. However, without forgiveness, you are likely to prevent yourself and your relationship from moving forward by harboring anger and resentment.

6. **The wounding partner must be accountable for their past, present, and future actions.** A lack of willingness on the wounding partner's part to be accountable for what they have done by admitting their actions, showing remorse, and attempting to understand how their actions have affected their partner will make it difficult for the relationship to be truly reconciled. Furthermore, a willingness to be held accountable for future actions is a must in order to reestablish trust.

If lasting recovery is to take place, it is imperative that the wounding partner become accountable for their actions not only to the wounded partner, but to others as well. We are not meant to do recovery alone.

Ecclesiastes 4:9-10 ESV

Two are better than one, because they have a good return for their work: if one falls down, his friend can help him up. But pity the man who falls and has no one to help him up.

James 5:19-20 ESV

"My brothers, if one of you should wander from the truth and someone should bring him back, remember this: whoever turns a sinner from the error of his way will save him from death and cover over a multitude of sins."

Proverbs 27:17 ESV

As iron sharpens iron, so one person sharpens another.

7. **The wounded partner must get their anger under control.** Unbridled anger in the form of yelling, cursing, shaming, threatening, etc. will be just as damaging to a relationship after infidelity has occurred as it would have been prior to it. Wounded partner, although anger and even rage are completely understandable reactions to your circumstances, you must commit to making a serious effort to communicate your intense emotions in appropriate ways.

8. **Both parties must have patience with the process.** Recovery from the effects of infidelity-related behavior is a long and trying process. On average, a couple recovering from an affair takes about 2 years to get to a point where reconciliation seems possible, and recovery is well underway. The process is full of ups and downs. A lot of it is repetitive, especially question-asking from the wounded partner about the infidelity. This can seem defeating at times. Patience with each other will be required as you travel the road to recovery.

9. **Both parties must be consistent.** When we talk to couples about rebuilding trust after infidelity-related behavior, we explain how consistency plays a vital role in reconciliation. This includes consistent efforts around communication, accountability, and any other recovery behavior that has been agreed upon such as attending meetings, working specific programs, etc.

10. **The wounded partner must actively engage in their own recovery.** As a wounded partner, you have sustained traumatic injuries from the discovery of your partner's infidelity-related behavior. As nice as it would be to let your partner fix what they broke, it simply does not work that way. When wounded partners ask us why they have to do recovery work even though they did nothing to cause the situation, we like to use the analogy of getting hit while crossing the road. If a car hits us, even if we are in the crosswalk and minding our own business, we will sustain injuries that may require surgery, physical therapy, etc. If we do not do what it takes to address those injuries, we may never regain full use of our bodies. In the same way, injuries sustained from traumatic events can affect us in every area of our lives. If these are not properly addressed, we will likely have problems functioning personally, relationally, emotionally, and spiritually.

11. **Both parties must learn how to effectively deal with triggers and reminders.** Unfortunately, triggers and reminders are a normal part of the process when it comes to infidelity recovery. It is not uncommon for wounded partners to experience 100 or more triggers per day in the weeks and months following discovery or disclosure of infidelity. If the wounding partner defends, blames, or acts without empathy, the wounded partner will be further injured, making reconciliation less likely. If the wounded partner doesn't learn to voice their anger, disappointment, hurt, and fear without inflicting damage, it will be hard for the relationship to recover.

12. **Both parties must agree to be vulnerable.** Let us qualify this statement by saying that we are not referring to a situation in which the wounded partner opens themselves back up to a wounding partner who has not proven themselves repentant. What we are saying is that wounded partners need to be honest and open about their true feelings without using anger as a smokescreen for more vulnerable emotions. Vulnerability on the wounding partner's part means no blaming, defending, or stonewalling when it comes to communication. Also, they must let down their pride and become willing to be accountable to their partner and to others.

13. **Both parties must learn to talk about the infidelity in an open and productive manner.** Most therapists and coaches agree that couples should openly talk about affairs and/or any other infidelity-related behavior. Research has even shown that couples who can talk about such things have higher success rates when it comes to staying together. That being said, it is imperative that communication around these matters be productive. If the conversations are fraught with defending, yelling, calling names, denial, stonewalling, and/or a lack of transparency, talking about it will likely do more harm than good.

Proverbs 15:1 ESV

A soft answer turns away wrath, but a harsh word stirs up anger. A gentle tongue is the tree of life, but perverseness in it breaks the spirit.

Good communication, although tricky at times, is extremely important after infidelity. While it is okay to express angry feelings, how these things are expressed can make or break a reconciliation. If the wounding partner defends or minimizes, it will stir up additional pain and anger because it will be seen as blaming. Blaming will break the wounded partner's spirit. Additionally, if the process is riddled with shaming, name calling, etc. by the wounded partner, it will be difficult for true reconciliation to happen.

14. **Both parties should seek outside, infidelity-related help.** While family counseling is good for many different situations, couples and individuals who are facing the aftermath of infidelity-related behavior are dealing with specific issues that many counselors and coaches are not adequately trained to deal with. Talking to someone that has experience and training specifically around infidelity, sex addiction, intimacy avoidance, and other related issues will be much more helpful to you on your path to reconciliation.

Proverbs 19:20 NIV

Listen to advice and accept instruction, and in the end you will be wise.

Proverbs 15:22 NIV

Plans fail for lack of counsel, but with many advisers they succeed.

Psalm 1:1-3 NIV

Blessed is the man who does not walk in the counsel of the wicked or stand in the way of sinners or sit in the seat of mockers. But his delight is in the law of the Lord, and on His law he meditates day and night. He is like a tree planted by streams of water, which yields its fruit in season and whose leaf does not wither. Whatever he does prospers.

For Wounded Partners: How do you know if you should pursue reconciliation?

When we work with wounded partners, this is one of the most common questions we are asked. We wish we had a better answer, but the truth is that we can't tell anyone exactly when they should stay and when it is time to leave. We can, however, give some advice based on our experience working with couples and individuals suffering from the negative impacts of infidelity-related behavior. We suggest that you consider the following pieces of advice when you are trying to understand whether or not reconciliation is truly possible:

1. **Give yourself time to decide.** Finding out that your partner has been engaged in infidelity-related behavior or is an intimacy avoidant creates intense pain. While it is normal to want to escape that pain, leaving the relationship soon after you discover your partner's infidelity may not be the best choice for you in the long run. When your mind is clouded with pain, anger, outrage, and humiliation it is impossible to make a rational decision. If a temporary separation is what you need to get your mind around what has happened, by all means do that. However, our best advice to you is to give yourself enough time to calm down in order to decide what it is you truly want.

2. **Consider the attitudes and actions of your partner.** The best relationship outcomes we have witnessed always start with the wounding partner displaying grief over what they have done. Anything less than a willingness to end the infidelity-related behavior and become accountable, honest, and transparent moving forward does not bode well for reconciliation. If your partner is not willing to end the affair or other infidelity-related behavior, listen to you with empathy, and become accountable to you and to others, our advice would be to give them a short window of time (6-12 months) to come to their senses. If they do not change their ways within that time frame, it may be best for you to consider moving on.

Here are some common warning signs that we see from wounding partners that ultimately make healing virtually impossible for the wounded partner:

- An unwillingness to apologize for the betrayal
- An unwillingness to participate in coaching or counseling
- An unwillingness to do recovery work
- Continued lying
- Refusal to take responsibility for their actions
- Blaming the partner or others for their behavior
- Meeting conversations around what happened with avoidance, denial, blame-shifting, and defensiveness

3. **Consider the history of your relationship.** This can be a challenge due to the fact that wounded partners tend to see the relationship in a negative light once infidelity is discovered. Once you have reached a calm state, we encourage you to make a pros and cons list for your relationship. Create a document and list all of the positive things about your relationship on one side and all of the negative things on the other. If you find that your relationship has quite a few positives, you may consider sticking around to see if reconciliation is possible. In my experience, the more positives a relationship had prior to the infidelity or still has, the more likely reconciliation will be. We will add that kids,

especially those under the age of 18, tend to play a major role in whether a wounded partner decides to stay or not.

4. **Understand your own baggage.** Let us preface this part by stating that infidelity is never the fault of the wounded partner. Your partner's choice to be unfaithful is 100% their responsibility. That being said, it will be helpful for reconciliation if you understand what your emotional baggage is and when you might be reacting out of it. For example, if you are someone who tends to personalize things, it is possible that you might believe that what your partner did says something about you. In our experience, wounded partners who attribute their partner's actions to perceived shortcomings or flaws on their part feel a higher level of pain than those who do not Another example would be that if you are a person who has power and control issues, your anger could be amplified by the fact that you perceive your partner's choices to have taken power away from you. In our experience, a need for power often creates grandiose behavior in which the wounded partner will try to punish or control their partner in order to regain control.

Part 29

Wounding Partner: What Are You Really Asking For?

As we outlined in Part 28, there are many things that you as a wounding partner must do in order to create an atmosphere in your relationship where reconciliation is possible. If you are doing that with all your heart, keep going! Although the reconciliation process takes place over a long period of time, if you continue to approach the situation with empathy and humility, this will make reconciliation possible (although it does not guarantee it).

Hebrews 12:11 NIV

No discipline seems pleasant at the time, but painful. Later on, however, it produces a harvest of righteousness and peace for those who have been trained by it.

However, if you are a wounding partner who is demanding forgiveness based on the fact that you feel your wounded partner owes it to you as a Christian, we must warn you that your attitude is incorrect and will not yield any good in the end.

In our practice, it is not uncommon for us to hear wounding partners say things like, "If my partner could just forgive me, we would be fine!" or, "We aren't moving forward as a couple because he/she won't forgive me!" One of the most damaging statements a wounding partner can make is a statement that indicates that forgiveness is owed to them by their wounded partner. An example of such a statement goes something like, "My partner is so unforgiving, yet God commands it. How can they expect that they can be forgiven if they won't forgive me?" For many Christians, this type of statement seems to stem from the following passage:

Matthew 6:14-15 NIV

For if you forgive other people when they sin against you, your Heavenly Father will also forgive you. But if you do not forgive others their sins, your father will not forgive your sins.

While we are commanded as Christians to forgive in the Bible, the issue here is not necessarily one of forgiveness at all. This type of statement seems to come from a place of lumping forgiveness, reconciliation, and trust together. As we have outlined in this book, those three things are very different from each other. This type of statement comes from someone who wants to be excused for their behavior because it intrudes on the world working for them in the way that they feel it should.

Let us be clear. Forgiveness is a gift that your partner can choose to give you. It should never be expected. It should never be demanded. Although it makes sense why you as a wounding partner may wish for it, demanding it from your wounded partner shows that you are struggling with entitlement and are being self-focused. Your primary concern does not seem to be for your partner, whom you have wounded terribly, but for yourself and your own comfort. An entitled statement that indicates that your partner owes you forgiveness may as well be followed up with the logical conclusion that you will not change until they give you what you want.

Biblical Perspective:

Husbands and Wives are Joint Heirs in Christ

We added this section not to imply that it is only husbands that need to treat their wives with respect. God expects both people in the relationship to love Him and love each other. However, we felt it was necessary to add this section for those in relationships where a husband is not respecting his wife and using the Bible to justify asking her to submit and forgive, regardless of his attitude. Unfortunately, we see this scenario on a regular basis when working with Christian clients.

1 Peter 3:7 KJV

Likewise, ye husbands, dwell with them according to knowledge, giving honor unto the wife, as unto the weaker vessel, and as being heirs together of the grace of life; that your prayers be not hindered.

"*Dwell with them*" (1) is only mentioned one time in the entire Bible, and it is here. It means a domestic association or intercourse between a husband and wife.

To dwell together speaks of the relationship between husband and wife living together, sharing domestic responsibilities, and sharing their bodies through sexual intercourse with each other. Period. They are exclusive.

They are dwelling together "*According to Knowledge*" (2).

Knowledge signifies general intelligence, understanding, and the general knowledge of Christian religion. It also refers to the deeper, more perfect, and enlarged knowledge of this religion, such as the kind that belongs to the more advanced, esp. of things lawful and unlawful for Christians and moral wisdom, such as is seen in righteous living.

True knowledge comes from God and in that knowledge the riches of life are found.

Romans 11:33 KJV

O the depth of the riches both of the wisdom and knowledge of God! how unsearchable are His judgments, and His ways past finding out!

Godly knowledge is the opposite of false science, which is profane in God's sight.

1 Timothy 6:20 KJV

Timothy, keep that which is committed to thy trust, avoiding profane and vain babblings, and oppositions of science falsely so called.

Of course, we understand that women are physically weaker than men. Contextually, at the time of this writing, women did not have financial independence or the societal rights of men. Paul was actually advocating for the protection of women from being abused morally (husbands having only one wife and living in a way that protects this relationship in every aspect of life) and legally (3).

Dwelling together according to knowledge is *"Giving honor unto the wife"* (4).

Honor is a value by which the price is fixed, or of the price itself, or of the price paid or received for a person or thing bought or sold. Honor which belongs or is shown to one. Honor which one has by reason of rank and state of office which he holds. Honor refers to deference or reverence.

What is the price that God fixed on women?

Romans 12:10 KJV

Be kindly affectioned one to another with brotherly love; in honor preferring one another

We are to honor each other, and it doesn't matter what sex you are!

1 Corinthians 12:24 KJV

For our comely parts have no need: but God hath tempered the body together, having given more abundant honor to that part which lacked

We are to honor our private body parts and our sexual identities.

Hebrews 2:7 KJV

Thou madest him a little lower than the angels; thou crownest him with glory and honor, and didst set him over the works of thy hands

Men and women have been created a little lower than the angels and crowned with honor!

Genesis 1:27 KJV

So God created man in His own image, in the image of God created him; male and female created them.

Men and women must honor each other, they are made in the likeness and image of God! That is the value God places on us!

Romans 13:7 KJV

Render therefore to all their dues: tribute to whom tribute is due; custom to whom custom; fear to whom fear; honor to whom honor.

We are to honor those who have authority over us.

Wives have rank! Paul is letting the husbands know that they must understand what honor is due toward the wife because of their exclusive covenant relationship.

To hold the wife in honor means to have deference towards her. According to the Merriam-Webster dictionary, to honor is the respect and <u>esteem</u> due to a superior or an elder (5).

What does that look like in the relationship? It means the partners make all decisions together. They consult one another. They are on the same page.

And that is why Paul says *"they are heirs together"* (6).

Heirs together or *joint heirs* are created when one obtains something assigned to himself alongside others, as a joint participant.

A husband cannot make a decision that doesn't affect his wife. All decisions, micro and macro, affect the quality and status of their relationship.

They are heirs together *"of the grace of life"* (7).

Grace of life is defined as that which affords joy, pleasure, delight, sweetness, charm, loveliness, grace of speech, goodwill, loving-kindness, and favor. It's the merciful kindness by which God, exerting His holy influence upon souls, turns them to Christ and keeps, strengthens, and increases them in Christian faith, knowledge, and affection, and kindles them to the exercise of the Christian virtues. One's spiritual condition is governed by the power of divine grace. The token or proof of grace is obvious through the benefits, gifts, bounty, services, favors, recompense, and rewards in one's life.

So, with the comprehension and knowledge of being joint heirs with his wife, the husband will experience the joy, pleasure, delight, sweetness, charm, loveliness, and grace of wholesome and wise speech that builds each other up and benefits both parties. God will extend his merciful kindness to both parties, keeping them holy, strong, productive; and increasing in faith, knowledge, and affection. This grace kindles them to a self-discipline that propels them to exercise Christian virtues. Together they abound with favor from God and man, and they are rewarded for their godliness with spiritual blessings and the bounty of the earth.

"*That your prayers* (8) *be not hindered*" (9).

Prayers can be hindered, which literally means to be cut off, as parts of a tree or an occasion are metaphorically cut off.

Paul warns that if a husband does not treat his wife with this high level of love and respect, God will not answer his prayers. The husband's rights to the graced life, which are entitled to him as a result of his marriage covenant, will be cut off. He will be like a tree that has been chopped at the roots, with the stump slowly decomposing and decaying with fungus and disease.

Lesson:

Don't place your wife in a position where she needs to forgive you for not treating her as your joint heir! Fear God and keep your covenant with your wife. Be the best husband you can be! If you are a woman reading this, be sure that you are treating your husband with respect and honor as well.

Prayer for the wounding and wounded partner:

Father,

Help me to be everything You created me to be. I will keep the covenant I made before You and my partner forever. I will never put my partner in a position where they must forgive me for not treating them as my joint heir. I will love and honor You and my partner all the days of my life. In Jesus' name,

Amen.

References:
1). Strong's Concordance G4924
2). Strong's Concordance G1108
3). https://jewsforjesus.org/learn/the-role-of-women-in-the-bible
4). Strong's Concordance G5092
5). https://www.merriam-webster.com/dictionary/deference
6). Strong's Concordance G4879
7). Strong's Concordance G5485
8). Strong's Concordance G4335
9). Strong's Concordance G1581

While you as a wounding partner can receive forgiveness from God, it is important for you to understand if you are truly asking for forgiveness or for something else.

Let's look at this passage on the woman caught in adultery:

John 8:1-11

But Jesus went to the Mount of Olives. ² At dawn he appeared again in the temple courts, where all the people gathered around him, and he sat down to teach them. ³ The teachers of the law and the Pharisees brought in a woman caught in adultery. They made her stand before the group ⁴ and said to Jesus, "Teacher, this woman was caught in the act of adultery. ⁵ In the Law Moses commanded us to stone such women. Now what do you say?" ⁶ They were using this question as a trap, in order to have a basis for accusing him.

But Jesus bent down and started to write on the ground with his finger. ⁷ When they kept on questioning him, he straightened up and said to them, "Let any one of you who is without sin be the first to throw a stone at her." ⁸ Again he stooped down and wrote on the ground.

⁹ At this, those who heard began to go away one at a time, the older ones first, until only Jesus was left, with the woman still standing there. ¹⁰ Jesus straightened up and asked her, "Woman, where are they? Has no one condemned you?"

¹¹ "No one, sir," she said.

"Then neither do I condemn you," Jesus declared. "Go now and leave your life of sin."

Clearly, God is willing to forgive those who engage in infidelity-related behavior. If you are a wounding partner, God is willing and able to forgive you. However, be sure not to overlook the last part of verse 11: *"Go now and leave your life of sin."*

If you are a wounding partner who is demanding forgiveness from your wounded partner, getting defensive, blame-shifting, or any other behavior that indicates you do not understand the magnitude of the damage your sin has caused, you need to ask yourself if you are truly sorry. Are you asking humbly for forgiveness, or are you asking to be excused? Have you done enough self-reflection to "go and sin no more"?

In his essay on forgiveness, C.S. Lewis wrote, "*Now it seems to me that we often make a mistake both about God's forgiveness of our sins and about the forgiveness we are told to offer to other people's sins. Take it first about God's forgiveness, I find that when I think I am asking God to forgive me I am often in reality (unless I watch myself very carefully) asking Him to do something quite different. I am asking him not to forgive me but to excuse me... If you had a perfect excuse, you would not need forgiveness; if the whole of your actions needs forgiveness, then there was no excuse for it. But the trouble is that what we call "asking God's forgiveness" very often really consists in asking God to accept our excuses. What leads us into this mistake is the fact that there usually is some amount of excuse, some "extenuating circumstances." We are so very anxious to point these things out to God (and to ourselves) that we are apt to forget the very important thing; that is, the bit left over, the bit which excuses don't cover, the bit which is inexcusable but not, thank God, unforgivable. And if we forget this, we shall go away imagining that we have repented and been forgiven when all that has really happened is that we have satisfied ourselves with our own excuses.*"

If you are a wounding partner who is claiming the forgiveness of God over your infidelity-related behavior and demanding that your wounded partner forgive you because "God most certainly has," you may actually be asking to be excused for your own comfort. This is especially true if your demeanor is not one of self-reflection, gratitude, and humility.

Luke 7:40-47

Jesus said to him, "Simon, I have something to tell you."

"Oh? Tell me."

[41-42] "Two men were in debt to a banker. One owed five hundred silver pieces, the other fifty. Neither of them could pay up, and so the banker canceled both debts. Which of the two would be more grateful?"

[43-47] Simon answered, "I suppose the one who was forgiven the most."

"That's right," said Jesus. Then turning to the woman, but speaking to Simon, he said, "Do you see this woman? I came to your home; you provided no water for my feet, but she rained tears on my feet and dried them with her hair. You gave me no greeting, but from the time I arrived she hasn't quit kissing my feet. You provided nothing for freshening up, but she has soothed my feet with perfume. Impressive, isn't it? She was forgiven many, many sins, and so she is very, very grateful. If the forgiveness is minimal, the gratitude is minimal."

The point of this story is to show that people who understand the nature of true forgiveness are deeply changed by it. Being excused does not bring about the changes necessary to help ensure that you will not repeat your infidelity-related behavior. Nor will it bring about reconciliation. Changed behavior does that. And you can't change if you keep making excuses for your actions.

In the same essay referenced earlier, C.S. Lewis wrote, *"Real forgiveness means looking steadily at the sin, the sin that is left over without any excuse, after all allowances have been made, and seeing it in all its horror, dirt, meanness, and malice, and nevertheless being wholly reconciled to the man who has done it."*

If you are demanding forgiveness from God and/or your wounded partner, it is highly likely that you have not taken the time to truly reflect on what you have actually done. And this is going to make it even harder for your wounded partner to forgive you and make it impossible for them to be reconciled to you. You need to take a long, hard look at what your actions have done to them and express true remorse for the pain you have put them in. Only then will your relationship have the chance to move forward.

Part 30

Self-Pity, Shame, and True Repentance

2 Corinthians 7:8-13a NIV
"Even if I caused you sorrow by my letter, I do not regret it. Though I did regret it—I see that my letter hurt you, but only for a little while— [9] yet now I am happy, not because you were made sorry, but because your sorrow led you to repentance. For you became sorrowful as God intended and so were not harmed in any way by us. [10] Godly sorrow brings repentance that leads to salvation and leaves no regret, but worldly sorrow brings death. [11] See what this godly sorrow has produced in you: what earnestness, what eagerness to clear yourselves, what indignation, what alarm, what longing, what concern, what readiness to see justice done. At every point you have proved yourselves to be innocent in this matter. [12] So even though I wrote to you, it was neither on account of the one who did the wrong nor on account of the injured party, but rather that before God you could see for yourselves how devoted to us you are. [13] By all this we are encouraged."

When we work with clients, we often hear "But I *am* sorry! Can't you see how bad I feel?" in response to our comments that a wounding partner is not helping their wounded partner and is, instead, making it all about them. We would like to take the time to point out that there is a big difference between feeling guilty (which often leads to shame and self-pity) and feeling Godly grief that leads to true repentance.

In Corinthians 7, Paul is writing to the church in Corinth and is referring to a difficult visit he had had earlier with them from which he found it necessary to write a severe letter of rebuke. In this passage, Paul is rejoicing over the fact that the church in Corinth, after initially feeling hurt over the letter, approached Paul's rebuke with humility. This, in turn, led to Godly grief over what they had done, and they set out to make the situation right. As a result of their true repentance, the relationship between the church and Paul was able to be restored.

Godly grief over something we have done, which leads to true repentance, is different from guilt and shame, which often lead to self-pity. Too often, our clients are simply sorry they got caught. They lament over having to live with the consequences of their behaviors and are more worried about being taken down a few notches in other peoples' eyes than they are about the pain they have caused to their partner.

As Christians, we all understand how sinful pride is. The Bible talks about it constantly. In fact, pride is such an important subject, that there are over 100 verses throughout the Bible warning against it. Take this passage, for example:

Proverbs 16:18-20 (NIV)

Pride goes before destruction, a haughty spirit before a fall. [19] ***Better to be lowly in spirit along with the oppressed than to share plunder with the proud.*** [20] ***Whoever gives heed to instruction prospers, and blessed is the one who trusts in the Lord.***

It is clear throughout the Bible that God hates pride (see Proverbs 8:13), but more interesting than the fact that He hates it is *why* He hates it. Proverbs 16:20 (above) says that when we trust in the Lord and listen to Him, we will prosper. But why does this verse follow the ones about pride? We think it is to highlight the fact that pride keeps us from listening to God. When you are puffed up with pride, you are not listening to anyone other than yourself. And that self-centeredness will bring you to ruin because your focus is no longer on God and what He wants for your life. As a result, you will stop listening to Him and destruction follows.

In his book *Mere Christianity*, author C.S. Lewis has a great deal to say about pride. In Chapter 8 of Book III titled "The Great Sin," he writes, "*If anyone would like to acquire humility, I can, I think, tell him the first step. The first step is to realise that one is proud. And a biggish step, too. At least, nothing whatever can be done before it. If you think you are not conceited, it means you are very conceited indeed*" (Lewis, C.S., 1957, Book III, p. 128).

And this brings us to the subject of shame.

On the surface, someone in the middle of feeling shame often appears remorseful. However, we would like to point out that someone in shame is pointed in the opposite direction of Godly grief that leads to true repentance. We say this because, if you look and pride and shame, they have one major thing in common. And that thing is self-centeredness. Pride and shame are two sides of the same coin. One says, "look at me, I'm so great" and the other says, "look at me, I'm so sorry." But the operative phrase here is *look at me*.

The last sentence of the C.S. Lewis quote above says, "*If you think you are not conceited, it means you are very conceited indeed.*" We believe this applies most of all to shame because someone rooted in shame often believes that they are being repentant and just can't understand why everyone is picking on them. Therein lies the self-deception that keeps them from looking to God.

There are two ways a person can go with this type of grief. One way leads to Godly repentance and, therefore, to God. The other leads to feeling bad, feeling shame, and becoming self-centered. Many people think that, because they feel grief over what they have done, that they have repented. However, if they can't seem to see beyond their own feelings, then they have not truly repented at all. Instead, they ruminate on their mistakes and wallow in self-pity. Godly grief turns people toward God and leads them to the actions He would have them take to change themselves and make things right. Worldly grief keeps people stuck within themselves and they become stagnant.

Wounding partner, if you find that the grief over what you have done is leading you toward God and making the changes He would have you make, we encourage you to keep going. When you involve God and let Him speak into your life, He will never waste the opportunity to teach you valuable lessons and transform you into someone who resembles Him.

However, if you find yourself wallowing in self-pity and shame, we ask you to acknowledge that. Turn away from yourself, become humble before God, and ask Him what He would have you do. Ask others who know more than you to help you if you find yourself stuck. Then, once you have a clear idea about what God wants you to do, how He wants you to act, and what attitudes He wants you to embody, pray. Ask Him every day — every minute of the day — for the strength to move forward in true repentance.

The Path to Forgiveness

Repentance:

The wounding partner must be truly repentant

First, we must repent. According to Strong's Concordance, **repent** means to change one's mind, i.e. to repent, to change one's mind for better, **heartily to amend with abhorrence of one's past sins** (emphasis ours) (1).

Matthew 3: 1-12 NIV

In those days John the Baptist came, preaching in the wilderness of Judea and saying, "Repent, for the kingdom of heaven has come near." This is He who was spoken of through the prophet Isaiah:

"A voice of one calling in the wilderness,

'Prepare the way for the Lord,

make straight paths for him.'"

John's clothes were made of camel's hair, and he had a leather belt around his waist. His food was locusts and wild honey. People went out to him from Jerusalem and all Judea and the whole region of the Jordan. Confessing their sins, they were baptized by him in the Jordan River.

But when he saw many of the Pharisees and Sadducees coming to where he was baptizing, he said to them: "You brood of vipers! Who warned you to flee from the coming wrath? Produce fruit in keeping with repentance. And do not think you can say to yourselves, 'We have Abraham as our father.' I tell you that out of these stones God can raise up children for Abraham. The ax is already at the root of the trees, and every tree that does not produce good fruit will be cut down and thrown into the fire.

"I baptize you with water for repentance. But after me comes one who is more powerful than I, whose sandals I am not worthy to carry. He will baptize you with the Holy Spirit and fire. His winnowing fork is in his hand, and he will clear his threshing floor, gathering his wheat into the barn and burning up the chaff with unquenchable fire."

Biblical Insight:

Counterfeit Salvation

John was a seer. He could see into the spirit realm and determine if someone was honest with him. What he saw in the spirit realm were broods of vipers. Vipers come from the Latin word *viviparity*, meaning to give live birth (2). The meaning behind his vision is that the Pharisees and Sadducees were live offspring of the snake in the Garden of Eden who deceived Adam and Eve. John discerned their insincerity and erroneous belief system. The Pharisees' pride in being biological descendants of Abraham was the foundation for their belief that they were children of God. John accurately judges them by the fruit of their character. Without true repentance, God cannot forgive the abhorrent acts of sin. Repentance is obvious because it bears good fruit.

And that is always the foundation of counterfeit salvation: overwhelming pride based on a false premise, insincerity and imitating the sheep.

True Repentance:

What entails true repentance?

Luke 15: 11-24 AMP

And He said, There was a certain man who had two sons; And the younger of them said to his father, Father, give me the part of the property that falls [to me]. And he divided the estate between them. And not many days after that, the younger son gathered up all that he had and journeyed into a distant country, and there he wasted his fortune in reckless and loose [from restraint] living. And when he had spent all he had, a mighty famine came upon that country, and he began to fall behind and be in want. So he went and forced (glued) himself upon one of the citizens of that country, who sent him into his fields to feed hogs. And he would gladly have fed on and filled his belly with the carob pods that the hogs were eating, but [they could not satisfy his hunger and] nobody gave him anything [better].

Then when he came to himself, he said, How many hired servants of my father have enough food, and [even food] to spare, but I am perishing (dying) here of hunger! I will get up and go to my father, and I will say to him, Father, I have sinned against heaven and in your sight. I am no longer worthy to be called your son; [just] make me like one of your hired servants. So he got up and came to his [own] father. But while he was still a long way off, his father saw him and was moved with pity and tenderness [for him]; and he ran and embraced him and kissed him [fervently]. And the son said to him, Father, I have sinned against heaven and in your sight; I am no longer worthy to be called your son [I no longer deserve to be recognized as a son of yours]!

But the father said to his bond servants, Bring quickly the best robe (the festive robe of honor) and put it on him; and give him a ring for his hand and sandals for his feet. And bring out that [wheat-]fattened calf and kill it; and let us revel and feast and be happy and make merry, Because this my son was dead and is alive again; he was lost and is found! And they began to revel and feast and make merry.

The youngest son acted shamefully, proud, and greedy. He dishonored his father, lived a dangerous life, and blew his money on mayhem and foolishness. But then he "came to himself." The prodigal son's eyes were opened, and the overwhelming pride based on the false premise of "live today for tomorrow we die" was unveiled.

"Dad's servants have enough food and I don't. They have more than enough food and I am starving!"

The prodigal's pretentious and insincere attitude fell off of him. He became honest with himself and assessed his situation with clarity and truth.

"I will HUMBLE myself before my father and give up the status of 'son.' I will BEG him to hire me as one of his hired servants, possibly, a servant without pay."

The prodigal became one of the sheep in his father's household. He intended to submit to his father's regulations in order to remain on the property and work for him. Based on an attitude of humility, the fruit of repentance, a person can become honest with themselves and their situation. They submit to God and His standards by making themselves one of His sheep. That is true repentance!

Judge them by their fruit
Luke 3:7-10 TLB
Here is a sample of John's preaching to the crowds that came for baptism:
"You brood of snakes! You are trying to escape hell without truly turning to God! That is why you want to be baptized! First go and prove by the way you live that you really have

repented. And don't think you are safe because you are descendants of Abraham. That isn't enough. God can produce children of Abraham from these desert stones! The ax of his judgment is poised over you, ready to sever your roots and cut you down. <u>Yes, every tree that does not produce good fruit will be chopped down and thrown into the fire."</u>

<u>The crowd replied, "What do you want us to do?"</u> (emphasis ours).

The Fruit of Repentance

Luke 3:11-14 TLB

"If you have two coats," he replied, "give one to the poor. If you have extra food, give it away to those who are hungry."

Even tax collectors—notorious for their corruption—came to be baptized and asked, "How shall we prove to you that we have abandoned our sins?"

"By your honesty," he replied. "Make sure you collect no more taxes than the Roman government requires you to."

"And us," asked some soldiers, "what about us?"

John replied, "Don't extort money by threats and violence; don't accuse anyone of what you know he didn't do; and be content with your pay!"

The Fruit of Repentance includes giving, sharing, honesty, peacefulness, and contentment.

Galatians 5:13-25 TLB

LOVE of God and your fellow man is the SEED of the Good Fruit of REPENTANCE:

For, dear brothers, you have been given freedom: not freedom to do wrong, but freedom to love and serve each other. For the whole Law can be summed up in this one command: "Love others as you love yourself." But if instead of showing love among yourselves you are always critical and catty, watch out! Beware of ruining each other.

I advise you to obey only the Holy Spirit's instructions. He will tell you where to go and what to do, and then you won't always be doing the wrong things your evil nature wants you to. For we naturally love to do evil things that are just the opposite from the things that the Holy Spirit tells us to do; and the good things we want to do when the Spirit has his way with us are just the opposite of our natural desires. These two forces within us are constantly fighting each other to win control over us, and our wishes are never free from their pressures. When you are guided by the Holy Spirit, you need no longer force yourself to obey Jewish laws.

The Bad Fruit of UNREPENTANCE:

But when you follow your own wrong inclinations, your lives will produce these evil results: impure thoughts, eagerness for lustful pleasure, idolatry, spiritism (that is, encouraging the activity of demons), hatred and fighting, jealousy and anger, constant effort to get the best for yourself, complaints and criticisms, the feeling that everyone else is wrong except those in your own little group—and there will be wrong doctrine, envy, murder, drunkenness, wild parties, and all that sort of thing. Let me tell you again, as I have before, that anyone living that sort of life will not inherit the Kingdom of God.

The Good Fruit of REPENTANCE:

But when the Holy Spirit controls our lives he will produce this kind of fruit in us: love, joy, peace, patience, kindness, goodness, faithfulness, gentleness and self-control; and here there is no conflict with Jewish laws.

Those who belong to Christ have nailed their natural evil desires to his cross and crucified them there. If we are living now by the Holy Spirit's power, let us follow the Holy Spirit's leading in every part of our lives. Then we won't need to look for honors and popularity, which lead to jealousy and hard feelings.

Reference:

1. Strong's Concordance G3340
2. (Wikipedia https://en.wikipedia.org › wiki › Viper)

Prayer for the wounding partner:

Father,

I desire to love You with all of my heart and mind and soul and strength. I desire to love my neighbor as myself. I desire for the Holy Spirit to control my life and bring forth the good fruit in everything I think, say, and do. In Jesus' name,

Amen.

Conclusion

As we stated in the introduction, our goal in writing this book was to give you a clear path to rebuilding trust after betrayal. We feel that the Rebuilding Trust Pyramid provides that clear path. Hopefully you do as well. The four layers of honesty, safety, consistency, and intimacy—along with the information contained here regarding the components of each of these— should provide you with what you need in order to begin your healing journey.

When it comes to the bottom layer, honesty, you discovered that honesty is the foundation of every relationship. This foundation has been severely damaged by the wounding partner's choices. As a result, it is imperative that honesty moving forward is given great emphasis, as it is pivotal to the rebuilding trust process. Until honesty is established, recovery will stall out. Next, you learned several ways in which you can begin to build safety back into your relationship. As we explained, betrayal violates the safety of the relationship and it is essential that each partner, especially the wounding partner, do their part to see that safety is restored. Next, you learned about how to create consistency as a part of cementing safety in your relationship. Although this layer of rebuilding trust can take the longest to establish, a couple is likely to continue to struggle to rebuild trust if much time and effort is not put toward strengthening this layer. Lastly, you learned how honesty, safety, and consistency are all ingredients to rebuilding intimacy in the relationship. Without these key ingredients, partners will fail to build true intimacy with each other. Additionally, we provided you with some ideas on how to begin to connect with each other in small but meaningful ways in order to help strengthen your bond.

At Becoming Well, we work with couples and individuals to help restore relationships after betrayal. We also work with couples whose relationships are suffering from the devastating effects of intimacy avoidance. If you are interested in our various workgroups, classes, sessions, and intensives, please visit us at www.mybecomingwell.com to learn more about what we offer.

Finally, we would like to thank you for taking the time to read this book. We know that you and your relationship will benefit greatly from following the advice contained here. As always, we wish you all the best in your journey to recovery.

Romans 8: 26-39 MSG

26 *Meanwhile, the moment we get tired in the waiting, God's Spirit is right alongside helping us along. If we don't know how or what to pray, it doesn't matter. He does our praying in and for us, making prayer out of our wordless sighs, our aching groans.* 27 *He knows us far better than we know ourselves, knows our pregnant condition, and keeps us present before God.*

28 *That's why we can be so sure that every detail in our lives of love for God is worked into something good.*

29 *God knew what he was doing from the very beginning. He decided from the outset to shape the lives of those who love him along the same lines as the life of his Son. The Son stands first in the line of humanity he restored. We see the original and intended shape of our lives there in him.* 30 *After God made that decision of what his children should be like, he followed it up by calling people by name. After he called them by name, he set them on a solid basis with himself. And then, after getting them established, he stayed with them to the end, gloriously completing what he had begun.*

31 *So, what do you think? With God on our side like this, how can we lose?* 32 *If God didn't hesitate to put everything on the line for us, embracing our condition and exposing himself to the worst by sending his own Son, is there anything else he wouldn't gladly and freely do for us?* 33 *And who would dare tangle with God by messing with one of God's chosen?* 34 *Who would dare even to point a finger? The One who died for us - who was raised to life for us! - is in the presence of God at this very moment sticking up for us.* 35 *Do you think anyone is going to be able to drive a wedge between us and Christ's love for us? There is no way! Not trouble, not hard times, not hatred, not hunger, not homelessness, not bullying threats, not backstabbing, not even the worst sins listed in Scripture:* 36 *They kill us in cold blood because they hate you. We're sitting ducks; they pick us off one by one.* 37 *None of this fazes us because Jesus loves us.* 38 *I'm absolutely convinced that nothing - nothing living or dead, angelic or demonic, today or tomorrow,* 39 *high or low, thinkable or unthinkable - absolutely nothing can get between us and God's love because of the way that Jesus our Master has embraced us.*

References

Bower, S., Bower, G. (2004) *Asserting Yourself: A Practical Guide for Positive Change*. Addison-Wesley Pub. Co. Reading, MA

Chapman, G., Thomas, J. (2022) *The 5 Apology Languages: The Secret to Healthy Relationships*. Northfield Publishing. Chicago, IL.

Cluff-Schade, L., Sandberg, J. (2012) Healing the Attachment Injury of Marital Infidelity Using Emotionally Focused Couples Therapy: A Case Illustration. The American Journal of Family Therapy. 40(5), p. 435

Contributors to the Converus Website, https://converus.com/

Dweck, C. (2014) "Developing a Growth Mindset with Carol Dweck", TED Talks, https://www.youtube.com/ watch?v=hiiEeMN7vbQ

Dweck, C. Ph. D. (2006) *Mindset: The New Psychology of Success*. Random House Publishing. New York City, NY

Folkman, J. (2019, 17 October) "Your Inconsistency is More Noticeable Than You Think", Forbes. https://www.forbes.com/ sites/joefolkman/2019/10/17/your-inconsistency-is-more- noticeable-than-you-think/?sh=558938e13d50

Gordon, K. C., & Baucom, D. H. (1999). A multitheoretical intervention for promoting recovery from extramarital affairs.

Clinical Psychology: Science and

Practice, 6(4), 382–399. https://doi.org/10.1093/clipsy.6.4.382

Gottman, J., Schwartz-Gottman, J. Abrams, D., Abrams, R. *Eight Dates: Essential Conversations for a Lifetime of Love*. Workman Publishing Company, Inc. New York City, NY

Gottman, J., Silver, N. (2000). *The Seven Principals for Making Marriage Work*. Orion Publishing Group. London, England.

Guha, A. (2021) "When it Might Not Be Gaslighting". Psychology Today. https://www.psychologytoday.com/us/blog/ prisons-and-pathos/202107/when-it-might-not-be-gaslighting

Harvard Health, (2020, 6 July), "Understanding the Stress Response", https://www.health.harvard.edu/staying- healthy/understanding-the-stress-response#:~:text=The%20sympathetic%20nervous%20system%20functions,system%20 acts%20like%20a%20brake.

Iacono WG, Ben-Shakhar G. Current status of forensic lie detection with the comparison question technique: An update of the 2003 National Academy of Sciences report on polygraph testing. Law Hum Behav. 2019 Feb;43(1):86-98. doi: 10.1037/ lhb0000307. Epub 2018 Oct 4. PMID: 30284848.

Johnson, S. M. (2004). Attachment Theory: A Guide for Healing Couple Relationships. In W. S. Rholes & J. A. Simpson (Eds.), Adult attachment: Theory, research, and clinical implications (pp. 367–387). Guilford Publications.

Marin, R., Christensen, A., Atkins, D., (2014), Infidelity and

Behavioral Couple Therapy: Relationship Outcomes Over 5 Years Following Therapy. American Psychological Association. Couple and Family Psychology Research and Practice. 3(1), 1-12

Perel, E. (2014) "Are We Asking Too Much of Our Spouses?", TED Radio Hour, https://www.npr.org/transcripts/301825600

Perry SL, Schleifer C. Till Porn Do Us Part? A Longitudinal Examination of Pornography Use and Divorce. J Sex Res. 2018 Mar- Apr;55(3):284-296. doi: 10.1080/00224499.2017.1317709. Epub 2017 May 12. PMID: 28497988.

Pittman, F. (1990) *Private Lies: Infidelity and the Betrayal of Intimacy*. Norton. New York

Real, T. (2008) *The New Rules of Marriage: What You Need to Know to Make Love Work*. Ballantine Books. New York City, NY

Savulescu, J., Sandberg, A. (2008), Neuroenhancement of Love and Marriage: The Chemicals Between Us. Neuroethics. 1: 31-44 Doi 10.1007/s12152-007-9002-4

Tennov, D. (1989), *Love and Limerence: The Experience of Being in Love*. Scarborough House. Chelsea, MI

University Of California - Los Angeles. (2003, October 10). Rejection Really Hurts, UCLA Psychologists Find. ScienceDaily. Retrieved from www.sciencedaily.com/releases/2003/10/031010074045.htm

Vaughn, P. (2010) *Help for Therapists (and Their Clients) in Dealing With Affairs*. p. 3, Dialog Press. San Diego, CA.

Voon V, Mole TB, Banca P, Porter L, Morris L, Mitchell S, et al. (2014) Neural Correlates of Sexual Cue Reactivity in Individuals with and without Compulsive Sexual Behaviours. PLoS ONE 9(7): e102419. https://doi.org/10.1371/journal.pone.0102419

Weaver, Jane (2017, April 16) "Many cheat for a thrill, more stay for true love". Health News. https://www.nbcnews.com/ health/health-news/many-cheat-thrill-more-stay-true-love- flna1c9446137

Weir, K. (2011) "The Exercise Effect", American Psychological Association, 42(11), p. 48, https://www.apa.org/ monitor/2011/12/exercise

Weiss, Douglas Ph.D., (2010) *Intimacy Anorexia: Healing the Hidden Addiction in Your Marriage*, Discovery Press. Colorado Springs, CO.

Whitcomb, L. (2021, 10 May) "Why Does 'Emotional Pain' Hurt?". LiveScience. https://www.livescience.com/why- emotional-pain-hurts.html

Truth About Deception (2022), The Cheating Spouse Quiz Results, https://www.truthaboutdeception.com/community- features/online-quizzes/cheating-spouse-results.html

Young L J. The Neural Basis of Pair Bonding in a Monogamous Species: A Model for Understanding the Biological Basis of Human Behavior. In: National Research Council (US) Panel for the Workshop on the Biodemography of Fertility and Family Behavior; Wachter KW, Bulatao RA, editors. Offspring: Human Fertility Behavior in Biodemographic Perspective. Washington (DC): National Academies Press (US); 2003. 4. Available from: https://www.ncbi.nlm.nih.gov/books/NBK97287/

Glossary

24-Hour Tell Policy: An agreement between partners that if either one engages in off-limits behaviors, they will tell the other partner within 24 hours. Typically done in conjunction with a self-imposed consequence.

Ambivalence: The state of having mixed feelings or contradictory ideas about someone or something. (Oxford Languages) Ambivalence after infidelity is common for both the wounded partner and the wounding partner.

Betrayal Trauma: A type of emotional trauma that happens when a person or people that someone depends on significantly violate that person's trust or well-being. Betrayal trauma also happens when there is a severe violation of attachment.

Circle of Safety: This term is used in conjunction with therapeutic disclosure. The wounded partner's circle of safety includes friends, family members, co-workers, and any property owned or regularly visited by the wounded partner such as homes, cars, vacation rentals, etc.

Disclosure: A process in which the wounding partner willingly admits to infidelity, hidden porn usage, or any other infidelity- related behavior. Disclosure is recommended and is the most conducive to the rebuilding of trust.

Discovery: The process in which the wounding partner's infidelity-related behavior is discovered by the wounded partner accidentally or against the will of the wounding partner. Not recommended and makes the process of rebuilding trust extremely difficult.

Dribbling Disclosure: A process in which the wounded partner is given a partial information regarding their partner's infidelity- related behavior. The wounding partner, for fear of consequences, purposely holds back important information but then "dribbles" it out over time. Not recommended. The results are similar to those of discovery.

Emotional Flooding: Becoming overwhelmed with emotion to the extent that a person shuts down, screams and yells, threatens, or cries uncontrollably. Emotional flooding is a sign that the sympathetic nervous system has been engaged.

Emotional Infidelity: Also referred to as an "emotional affair". Emotional Infidelity can be defined as a situation in which a person shares an intimate, emotional connection with someone other than their partner. It is different than a platonic friendship in that it usually involves some sort of romantic or sexual tension. It also involves focusing the emotional energy that should belong to a partner on someone else.

Fight or Flight Response: A physiological reaction associated with survival that prepares the body to stay and fight or run from a situation.

Gaslighting: This term describes a subtle or overt form of manipulation in which the person doing the gaslighting attempts to sow seeds of doubt in their partner's mind about the validity of their emotions and reality.

Grooming: A form of manipulation in which the person doing the grooming builds an emotional connection or rapport with another person that appears to be genuine. The motive underneath grooming behavior can be anything from control to sex but is marked by the groomer's desire to have a particular need met, despite what it may cost the other person.

HOVA: This acronym stands for "Hand, Oral, Vaginal, Anal", and is used to describe sex acts. It is most often used in disclosure and polygraph tests because the meaning of the word "sex" can vary from person to person.

Infatuation: An intense passion for someone that is typically short-lived.

Infidelity-Related Behavior: Behavior associated with a breach of trust, disloyalty, or wrongdoing. This includes even seemingly mild behavior such as ogling or "rubbernecking".

Infidelity through Pornography: (See description for pornography) Although defining pornography use as infidelity can be controversial, we at Becoming Well hold that it is. This holds especially true if the partner using the pornography lies about it or covers it up in any way.

Intimacy Anorexia®: This term, coined by Dr. Doug Weiss, is defined as "the active and intentional withholding of emotional, physical sexual, and/or spiritual connection from a partner for the purpose of creating distance."

Intimacy Avoidance: The term intimacy avoidance refers to a situation in which one partner is withholding themselves in multiple ways from their partner. Intimacy avoidance often goes unnoticed by the person withholding themselves yet can have lasting and devastating effects on their loved ones.

Limerence: A strong state of emotional infatuation, longing, and even obsession that lasts as little as 6 months and as long as 3 years. (In some cases, longer) It is characterized by a fixation on an object—usually a particular person and the idea of that person

Limerent Object: The subject of a romantic fixation or ideal. The wounding partner will tend to exaggerate the limerent object's positive traits while simultaneously minimizing their flaws.

Lust: A very strong sexual desire

Marathon Conversation: A conversation that should take 45 minutes or less to discuss but ends up turning into a conversation that lasts for hours, and even days.

Masturbation: The stimulation of one's own genitals for the purpose of sexual arousal, sexual pleasure, or orgasm.

Micro-Trust: Considered the "baby steps" of rebuilding trust. We define micro-trusts as small areas where trust can be earned. Sometimes seemingly small breaches of trust can add up to a large problem. This is especially true when infidelity has affected a relationship.

Narcissistic Behavior: Behavior that can be characterized as arrogant, abusive, entitled, manipulative, self-serving, or egocentric. People struggling with this issue will often have an exaggerated sense of self-importance, show a lack of empathy, be highly sensitive to criticism (real or perceived), and will often use gaslighting and blame shifting as a way to escape accountability for their actions.

Pink Clouding: A term used to describe a situation in early recovery, especially from addiction and/or intimacy avoidance, where the wounding partner feels extremely optimistic about the recovery process.

Pornography: Any type of printed or visual material, whether explicit or not, that is being used for the purpose of stimulating sexual or erotic feelings and/or is used for the purpose of sexual fantasy or masturbation.

Recovery: Regaining something that was lost or damaged by engaging in certain actions or processes.

Sexual Anorexia: A condition marked by the fear, dread, or avoidance of sexual activity. Although it can be marked by impotence or other physical problems, the cause is typically psychological.

Sexual Establishment: This term includes establishments that provide live visuals for the purpose of sexual stimulation such as strip clubs, adult bookstores, peep shows, and live sex shows. It can also include bikini baristas and "breastaurants" such as Hooters and Twin Peaks.

Sexual Infidelity: Commonly referred to as "cheating". This term is used to describe a situation in which someone engages in a sexual act (HOVA) with a person who is not their spouse or committed partner.

Sympathetic Nervous System: The network of nerves that are responsible for the "fight or flight" response.

Therapeutic Disclosure: A planned and professionally facilitated event in which the wounding partner discloses to the wounded partner all of the information regarding infidelity-related behavior and/or sexual/pornography addiction.

Trigger: Any situation, idea, or action that causes intense emotions and/or emotional discomfort. In the case of infidelity, triggers are associated with traumatic events, especially the discovery of betrayal. A trauma trigger can be described as anything that reminds a person of a past trauma.

Trust: As it pertains to relationships, we define trust as the ability to feel that one's partner is a source of security, support, safety, and dependability.

Wounded Partner: A party associated with a committed relationship who has been betrayed and hurt by their relationship partner.

Wounding Partner: A party associated with a committed relationship who has committed an act of betrayal, a breach of trust, an act of wrongdoing, or an act of disloyalty that emotionally, physically, financially, and/or spiritually affects their relationship partner.

About the Authors

Matt Burton

Matt Burton is a certified sexual addiction recovery coach (SRC), partners recovery coach (PRC), partner betrayal trauma coach (PBTC), intimacy anorexia® coach (IAC) through the American Association for Sexual Addiction Therapy (AASAT). He is also a nationally certified recovery coach (NCRC), nationally certified family recovery coach (NCFRC), life coach, certified clinical trauma specialist for both individuals and families (CCTSI) (CCTSF) and certified clinical trauma specialist for trauma and addiction (CCTSA).

Matt was part of starting Pure Desire (formerly known as For Men Only/For Women Only) for pornography and sexual addiction recovery. Since 1994, Matt has worked with couples impacted by sex and pornography addiction, physical and emotional infidelity, and intimacy avoidance to help them find healing, maintain sobriety, and heal and restore their relationships.

Additionally, for over two decades, Matt has worked with men that have experienced many forms of trauma and is the author of the groundbreaking book *The Unbound Man*. He has helped men and their partners heal from trauma.

Laura Burton

Laura Burton is a trained and certified partners recovery coach (PRC), partner betrayal trauma coach (PBTC), sexual addiction recovery coach (SRC), and intimacy anorexia® coach (IAC) through the American Association for Sexual Addiction Therapy (AASAT). She is also a nationally certified life coach (NCLC) through The Addictions Academy. What makes Laura such an amazing coach and guide for partners is her own personal journey as a partner through the impacts of pornography addiction, infidelity, and intimacy avoidance.

Partners are often overlooked. Laura's ability to walk through the healing process as a partner, find profound healing and health, learn to be a part of a healthy marriage, and then turn around and help others to do the same is invaluable. She understands how living with an addict can negatively impact partners in all areas of their lives. She has helped hundreds of partners of sex addicts, unfaithful partners, and intimacy avoidants become more balanced in mind, soul, and body.

Together, Matt and Laura are co-founders of Becoming Well, LLC. They have also been instrumental in starting Intimacy ICU; a non-profit offering conferences around the United States on the subjects of rebuilding trust and intimacy, sexual addiction, sexual anorexia, intimacy avoidance, and infidelity. Additionally, Intimacy ICU offers scholarships to help couples and individuals afford the care they need while struggling to recover.

www.ingramcontent.com/pod-product-compliance
Lightning Source LLC
LaVergne TN
LVHW081454060526
838201LV00051BA/1800